# The Comic Book Curriculum

## Other Recently Published Teacher Ideas Press Titles

Gateways to Westward Expansion: Using Literature and Primary Sources to Enhance Reading Instruction and Historical Understanding
*Ann Claunch and Linda L. Tripp*

More Readers Theatre for Middle School Boys: Adventures with Mythical Creatures
*Ann N. Black*

Multi-Grade Readers Theatre: Picture Book Authors and Illustrators
*Suzanne I. Barchers and Charla R. Pfeffinger*

Story Starters and Science Notebooking: Developing Student Thinking Through Literacy and Inquiry
*Sandy Buczynski and Kristin Fontichiaro*

Fun with Finance: Math + Literacy = Success
*Written and Illustrated by Carol Peterson*

Paper Action Figures of the Imagination: Clip, Color and Create
*Paula Montgomery*

Fairy Tales Readers Theatre
*Anthony D. Fredericks*

Shakespeare Kids: Performing his Plays, Speaking his Words
*Carole Cox*

Family Matters: Adoption and Foster Care in Children's Literature
*Ruth Lyn Meese*

Solving Word Problems for Life, Grades 6–8
*Melony A. Brown*

Abraham Lincoln and His Era: Using the American Memory Project to Teach with Primary Sources
*Bobbi Ireland*

Brushing Up on Grammar: An Acts of Teaching Approach
*Joyce Armstrong Carroll, EdD, HLD, and Edward E. Wilson*

# THE COMIC BOOK CURRICULUM

## Using Comics to Enhance Learning and Life

James Rourke

A Teacher Ideas Press Book

LIBRARIES UNLIMITED

AN IMPRINT OF ABC-CLIO, LLC
Santa Barbara, California • Denver, Colorado • Oxford, England

**Library of Congress Cataloging-in-Publication Data**

Rourke, James.
    The comic book curriculum : using comics to enhance learning and life
  / James Rourke.
      p. cm.
  Includes bibliographical references and index.
    ISBN 978-1-59884-396-5 (pbk : alk. paper)—ISBN 978-1-59884-397-2
(ebook)  1.  Comic books, strips, etc.—Study and teaching.  2.  Comic
strip characters—Study and teaching.  3.  Education—Curricula.  I.
Title.
PN6710.R598 2010
371.33—dc22        2010007468

ISBN: 978-1-59884-396-5
EISBN: 978-1-59884-397-2

14 13 12 11 10   1 2 3 4 5

This book is also available on the World Wide Web as an eBook.
Visit www.abc-clio.com for details.

Libraries Unlimited
An Imprint of ABC-CLIO, LLC

ABC-CLIO, LLC
130 Cremona Drive, P.O. Box 1911
Santa Barbara, California 93116-1911

This book is printed on acid-free paper ∞
Manufactured in the United States of America

*Dedicated to my Grandmother, Mary Malinowski,
who bought me my first comic book, and my Mother,
Virginia Rourke, who let me keep it.*

# Contents

# Section II
## Teachers' Tools

# Acknowledgments

This book, in some ways, started being written when I was six or seven years old and my grandmother bought me my first comic book. Three decades have passed since then, and it's about time I thanked her, even posthumously, for that simple gesture that helped spark a love of reading. As family lore has been passed on to me, my mother would occasionally read the comics to make sure they were worth having. I am glad they passed her test.

I would also like to thank my agent, Andy Whelchel, who helped organize my original idea so I could write this book and found ABC-CLIO to publish it. I am also very thankful to Sharon Coatney's enthusiasm when she first heard of the project, for it came as welcome validation as I struggled to form the initial chapters. I am also thankful to the other skilled professionals at ABC-CLIO who helped me through the publication process, specifically Rachel Neal, Deborah LaBoon, and Elizabeth Budd.

Lorraine Dooley offered invaluable help as the writing process unfolded. Lorraine, a self-identified "non-comic person," read each chapter to make sure I was not writing for comic fans only. Any clarity found in these pages owes its existence to Lorraine and her willingness to slog through rough draft after rough draft.

Phil Marchesault, Jesse Coule, Brian Burdick, Neal Curland, Chris Justie, and Karen Diaz all aided in the editing process. Phil was exceptionally helpful in giving the introduction a sharper focus and increasing the fluency of the first few chapters. Jesse was particularly helpful in shaping the chapter on Wolverine as he shared his reflections on *Hagakure* with me.

I owe a hearty thank you to John Sedgwick, owner of Arkham Asylum in Norwich, Connecticut. John ably filled my comic book orders and offered ideas for comics to review. Don Bastin of Arkham Asylum also suggested some titles and shared ideas on a number of characters. The conversations with John and Don helped form the bibliography of comics used in this book.

Special thanks must go out to my brother and fellow comic fan, Tim Rourke. Tim and I had many conversations about comic books and characters as I worked on this project. Some ideas made it into the final cut, and some conversations were just interesting to have.

My final words of appreciation are for my wife, Shannon Rourke. She knew the idea could become a book before I did and that I was capable of finishing it even when I doubted. Her support made this book possible.

# Introduction

In the introduction to *The Dark Knight Returns,* Frank Miller informs the reader that he "fell into comics" at a young age and never quite "climbed his way out." This is the perfect description for what schools should want for all children—for the magic of a well-woven tale to find a permanent home in their beings. This appreciation is not innate but fostered through the introduction of timeless themes, heroic quests, engaging characters, and stories that resonate with both personal and universal relevance.

There is, unfortunately, no denying the reality that many students do not possess or have not developed this trait. Reading is often no more than a task to perform. This mind-set has been found in students for generations and will continue to be an issue in the future. It is incumbent upon educators to find new methods to inspire these students to seek their own motivation to read, learn, and develop as students and people.

As I reflected on my own reading history, I realized I share a common trait with Frank Miller: comics never let go of me either. They were my gateway into reading. The themes found in their pages were recognized in other tales. The quest for engaging characters went from Marvel Comics to H. G. Wells. Was that Captain America looking back on his life with frustration or King Lear? The dreary society created in *1984* could well be the society created by Dr. Doom. The X-Men battled prejudice with all the resolve and vigor exhibited by Martin Luther King Jr.

The most important question, however, is, can comics be used in schools to inspire students to become more engaged readers? The answer is yes. Used correctly, students who previously showed limited interest in class will be aroused by the fascinating world found in the pages of comics. Comic books, with all their mythic elements, will serve our students well.

This book proposes the use of comic books to introduce such concepts as honor, hope, commitment, sacrifice, nobility, and loyalty and to high school students (Grades 9–12). The lessons and concepts can be brought to middle school (Grades 7–8) students as well, although teachers would likely need to make some modifications. Historic themes and concepts, such as the civil rights movement, the Holocaust, and the samurai Bushido code, are also found in the pages of comics. The philosophy of Plato, the wisdom of Buddha, and the psychology of Abraham Maslow can all be referenced in the struggles of heroes and villains. Current events from the struggle between privacy and security to the use, or misuse, of religion to justify despicable deeds can also be addressed using comics.

By using comics, a habitually unproductive student may be moved to complete his or her homework. Successful students will, in some cases, be introduced to a new form of literature and American culture. The reading of comics can be accompanied by a homework questionnaire, a class discussion the next day, an essay, or a quiz. These evaluation tools are common to teachers. It is the materials that may challenge the students and teachers alike.

Because comic books may not be something you and your students are used to and may be viewed as incompatible with academics, one goal of this book is to reveal the depth of meaning present in the works that, at first glance, may seem incapable of possessing such potential. For these alternative assignments to be effective, teachers must be willing to use materials with which they may not be familiar. This may cause them to feel slightly awkward when first introducing a "superhero lesson," but the slight discomfort will be well worth it if a student who routinely does nothing suddenly performs in class. If three or four such students suddenly read and submit an assignment, perhaps rapport could improve and future success could be built on this foundation. Spider-Man can never replace Shakespeare, but he could build a bridge for a student, spanning the gap from comics to classics.

This trip, like any taken in the classroom, will not be easy. Teachers need to familiarize themselves with the new materials before using them in class. The first section of this book, therefore, is dedicated to aiding the reader in becoming more familiar with various comic book heroes. Beyond introducing characters, the reader will also be introduced to various stories that can be used to illuminate any number of themes. The dual analysis of characters and stories will reveal the comic book hero to be far more complex than some may realize.

The second section of the book is dedicated to providing teachers with curriculum connections for their own lesson planning, along with premade lesson plans that are easily transferable to the classroom. These materials are designed to aid in the implementation of the ideas in the back and are merely a starting point, not the final word, on the potential uses of comics in the classroom.

The comic book world is teeming with valuable lessons and captivating stories. We extol the virtue of responsibility, and in the pages of Spider-Man and Thor are characters that provide ideals of responsibility. Other stories focus on the complexity of relationships—husband to wife or parent to child—which could open a discussion in your classroom. The concept of grieving, coping with loss, and overcoming obstacles and failure are recurring themes in comic books and important concepts for students to consider.

To reiterate, this book does not propose replacing classic works of literature with comic books. The goal is to provide teachers with a new item for their bag of motivational tricks, or perhaps to act as a foundation for a new course dedicated to incorporating comic books as a teaching tool. Perhaps a student will fall into comics as Frank Miller did and, in doing so, conclude that reading and learning is a lot more interesting than he or she suspected.

# Section I

---

## The Heroes

# Part I

Comic Icons and Heroic Quests

# CHAPTER 1

# Superman

Superman could well be the most recognized figure in the entire superhero universe. One does not need to be a dedicated comic fan to know some of the basic facts of Superman's story or recognize the iconic Superman emblem. Many know his powers of flight, super strength, invulnerability, and extraordinary vision. Others may be aware that he is an alien named Kal-El from the planet Krypton. He was sent to Earth as an infant, traveling across space in a rocket as his home planet exploded. Martha and Jonathan Kent in the Midwestern town of Smallville found him. His secret identity is that of reporter Clark Kent, made complete by fake eyeglasses. He was raised to have sturdy values and be a caring, if unique, individual. The fact that many people recognize some aspects of the character, however, does not mean Superman is truly known.

It is not the ability to fly or lift a train that makes Superman unique. As the comic-book world expanded, we find many heroes capable of flight. Others can bring buildings tumbling down with a single blow. We see beings that run so fast, they race across water. Others can breathe water and communicate with aquatic life. Many beings can emit laser beams from either their hands or eyes. Yet Superman remains exceptional in the midst of others who share his stage. In the end, there is something else besides the wondrous powers that make Kal-El "super." His desire to do good and his understanding of what it means to do good outdistances many of his superpowered peers.

The Greek philosopher Socrates is in many ways the father of Western philosophy, just as Superman is the father of the superhero. Socrates argued that if a person knows what is good, he would invariably do it.[1] Looking at the world around us, we may believe Socrates was incorrect in his assessment. Think about the microcosm of a school. How many students know what is right, can articulate it, and still engage in malicious gossip, mistreat friends and family, or place themselves in situations that can cause grave harm? How many administrators know what is right but choose that which is expedient? How many phone calls or after-school study sessions should we run, as teachers, but don't? If these questions prod us in ways we prefer they did not, they merely remind us why Socrates, the gadfly of Athens, faced animosity from those in power. They are also reminders that the good and the easy are often located on different roads.

Others may think "doing good" is merely an act of self-gratification, leaving others neglected or pained in their wake. They fulfill their needs without considering others, mistaking personal pleasure for the overriding good that Socrates sought.

We can also examine the word "know" and realize it means more than just being able to recall information from memory. To know, therefore, is to do more than memorize a list of appropriate behaviors and perform them robotically. It is to appreciate and eventually love that which is good. Loving something may still not be the final goal.

The Chinese philosopher Confucius taught that "To understand something is nothing like loving it. And to love something is nothing like delighting in it." The use of the phrase "nothing like" reveals that there is a great deal of distance between the three levels—understanding, loving, and delighting—Confucius pinpoints. Superman, in many ways, embraces goodness much more completely than others. In doing so, he embraces humanity much more fully than most humans.

He does good not merely because it is "the right thing" or because he has set his will to it. He does not do good because someone makes him or he fears punishment if he does something evil. Krypton's only son does good because he strives with great vigor to become goodness. He delights in doing good and understands how his actions have an impact on others. In many ways, due to his progress in this arena, Superman cannot fully comprehend why one would not choose to do good, for the lasting joy it brings far exceeds the momentary pleasures of crime and claiming power over another. When one steals, they live under the shadow of possibly being caught. When one claims power, in a friendship, a classroom, a marriage, or a political position, the individual, unless very mature, lives under the constant fear of losing power. This fear can cause him or her to succumb to the ego-driven need to protect this power through any means necessary, be they intimidation or manipulation.

When one delights in doing good, there is no limit to the joy that can be felt simply by doing more good. To achieve such a level of being, however, is very difficult. To be mature to this degree is rare indeed. Consider the calamities that break the heart of a child or even a teenager but that an adult considers trivial. Yet how many times have we all heard adult friends, colleagues, and (in moments of clarity) ourselves fret and worry over relatively trivial matters as well, making adults appear more like children.[2] There is a level of maturity that eludes many, and Superman seems to be a character who has progressed to a level of psychological maturity that few achieve.

Mark Waid, author of *Superman: Birthright,* evaluated this aspect of Superman's character as he prepared to pen his story. Waid found the key to understanding Superman is to remember that he is an alien, the last of his race, and probably more alone in this world than most of us will ever be. Yet we all, even Superman, have a psychological need to belong. Waid concludes:

> It's fair to presume, that, despite his extraterrestrial origins, Kal-El feels the same basic need for community that is shared by all human beings around him; if not, he most likely wouldn't bother being Clark Kent at all and would just as soon soar off to explore the greater solar system and galaxies beyond than work a nine-to-five in Metropolis.[3]

Working from that hypothesis, Waid then wrestled with the question of how Superman connected to the world around him. Waid's conclusion was that Superman embraced his Kryptonian heritage. By being all he can be, Kal-El is most alive. He feels completely integrated when living up to his full potential as Superman, not when hiding behind Clark Kent's persona. His most authentic interaction with the world around him is as Superman. By embracing who he is, he brings his gifts to others, helping them to feel joy, hope, and inspiration. Only by being completely Kryptonian on Earth can he be an exuberant Earthman, being good to himself while always mindful of his impact on others.[4] Is there any lesson we would want students to embrace more fully than discovering that which Superman has grasped so effortlessly?

Therefore, Waid concludes, Superman is a paradox; by fulfilling his need to belong, he exhibits the virtue of selflessness. The result is a perfect balancing of the needs of the community and his own psychological needs. He is altruistic while simultaneously acting to satisfy his own desire. There is no contradiction found with his selflessness serving both himself and the community. There is time and joy enough for both to be satisfied. By being the best he can be for himself, Kal-El is the best he can be for others.[5]

The concepts of selfishness and selflessness have almost no meaning in an evaluation of Superman's character. He merely serves the good of everyone—including himself. The dichotomies of life have melted into a non-dual reality in which his being transcends the everyday labels we would affix to it. If this sounds like philosophic double-talk, consider that such concepts are found in twentieth-century psychology and philosophy. As a psychologically mature individual "gets to be more purely and singly himself he is more able to fuse with the world…. That is, the greatest attainment of identity, autonomy, or self-hood is itself simultaneously a transcending of itself, a going beyond and above selfhood. The person can then become relatively egoless."[6]

It is this sense of balance that Superman's ally, Batman, never wholly grasped. Where Batman could never find the balance of relationships and mission, Superman couldn't imagine a world where they didn't fit together. Perhaps it is little wonder that Superman, the hero from another planet, finds time to marry, but Batman does not. This may well be the most outstanding aspect of Superman: he has found the contented life, despite being the last of his race and a foreigner to our world. Having found it for himself, he tirelessly strives to help others achieve it as well. Sometimes, as the next chapter reveals, such a struggle can cripple even the mightiest of men.

# CHAPTER 2

## Kingdom Come: The Heroic Quest of Superman and Everyman

The graphic novel *Kingdom Come* brings the reader to the not so distant future. The heroes of Superman's generation are in their fifties and sixties. Many have unwillingly retired from crime fighting. A new generation of heroes has emerged, one more aggressive and less responsible than its predecessor. The world embraces this new attitude, seeing it as more effective in dealing with superpowered criminals. The heroes of yesteryear have disappeared, leaving the world with great memories and lessons ignored.

One of the key characters in this drama is an elderly pastor named Norman McCay. Norman is a good man, but his faith is all but shattered by the world around him. It is through Norman that we are first introduced to the new generation of heroes. On an afternoon walk, Norman stumbles into a battle zone, as the heroes are battling each other. There are no super villains left to defeat, so the heroes, seeking entertainment rather than productivity, amuse themselves by fighting each other. The importance of not just reading the words in a comic but looking at and examining the artwork becomes apparent during this scene.

This fact is driven home by the presence of a small girl, standing in the middle of the heroes' joyous melee. A stray laser causes an explosion, and rubble falls at the girl. Norman runs to the girl, scoops her up, and takes her from harm's way. While doing so, his glasses fall off—shades of Clark Kent removing his glasses. Another combatant is slammed through a wall. He smiles and laughs as the battle continues. He and his peers are oblivious to the tears rolling down the little girl's cheeks. His joy brings her terror—and he couldn't care less. This is the world of Norman McCay, one where anyone can become the victim of their "protector's" recklessness. The new breed of heroes, in many ways, embraces a kind of moral relativism: if what you do feels good to you, then it is good, even if the world trembles in your wake. That would be the world's problem, not yours. The battle halts only because their attention is drawn to a newscast on a giant, outdoor television screen.

With the background established, Norman McCay begins his heroic quest. Joseph Campbell, in his book *The Hero with a Thousand Faces*, articulates that any heroic journey passes through three phases: the departure, the initiation, and the return. One aspect of the departure phase is when the hero receives a call or summons to act. Norman McCay receives a summons as he is sitting alone in his church. He is terrified at the prospect of the future when the immensely powerful, wraithlike hero the Spectre comes to him.

The Spectre senses a great evil about to unfold, and his duty is to judge who is responsible and punish them. He seeks a human point of view to more effectively judge the evil and decide just punishment. Norman has also been having random apocalyptic visions since the death of a friend who was haunted by the same glimpses of the future. These visions are of importance to the Spectre, and he would like Norman to join him and share his revelations. The pair will silently witness events unfold to the conclusion foreshadowed by Norman's visions. After a brief conversation, Norman, with understandable nervousness, agrees to join the Spectre and travels the world with him in an ethereal form.

The first place they visit is Superman's Fortress of Solitude. Here we find an embittered Man of Steel working as a farmer on a simulation of the Smallville farm where he grew up. The use of language is very important in this scene, as Wonder Woman arrives and attempts to initiate Superman's heroic quest. She greets her friend as "Clark," only to receive a cold glare. She quickly rewords her greeting, saying Kal instead. During their terse discussion, Kal will refer to his deceased parents and wife as "Earthlings," allowing the reader to start to understand just how removed Superman is from the world and from his humanity.

We also glimpse the first piece of the story that led to Superman's self-imposed exile. He responds to Wonder Woman's statement that the new heroes are out of control by stating, "I tried to tell them that ten years ago." His warnings obviously went unheeded. This event was crushing to Superman, for his words became irrelevant. He, despite his powers, became irrelevant. So he gave up the struggle for truth and justice for a life of solitude. Still, his sentence reeks of the immature phrase, "I told you so." Whatever level of maturity Superman had achieved (as discussed in the previous chapter), he has evidently regressed to a more petulant, self-serving worldview, one that fills him with bitterness instead of joy. When Wonder Woman departs, we are given no inkling that Superman will rejoin the world. In fact, with pessimism permeating his being, he counsels her to return to her island home and leave the world to its own designs.

Superman's predicament is not uncommon, in literature or history. In *The Iliad,* Achilles refuses to fight against the Trojans because he feels dishonored by King Agamemnon. Superman feels equally slighted by the world's dismissal of his ideals and has given up his fight. Achilles retreated to his tent, Superman to his fortress situated at the North Pole. Granted, the cause of the withdrawal of service is technically different as Achilles squabble is with the king, and Superman feels rebuffed by the people, but the communities the two men serve both suffer because of their decisions. Either man could have continued to perform his duties but placed his own needs above those of the community. Much like the heroes of literature, historic figures also face scorn.

In *The Analects,* we learn that the great Chinese philosopher Confucius also faced ridicule. His student Lu spent a night at Stone Gate. While there the innkeeper inquired where he was from. Lu answered that he was from the House of Confucius. The innkeeper's dismissive response was, "Isn't he the one who knows it's hopeless, but keeps trying anyway?"[7] Such ridicule never stopped the self-motivated sage. Superman, unfortunately, appears to be on the gatekeeper's side and decides that trying to help others is a futile expenditure of time and energy. If some students find Superman's response troubling, they would not be alone. Confucius once noted that one of four things he found disturbing was knowing one's duties without following them.[8] Responsibility is a word Superman would rather forget at this point.

The story begins with two very different reactions to the summons. Norman McCay, the elderly pastor, quickly acquiesces to the Spectre's request and steps into the unknown. Superman, the alien of vast power, refuses Wonder Woman's call to arms. By refusing the summons, Superman does not move to the next phase of the heroic quest. Norman, however, does, entering the initiation phase where he will be faced with great challenges. This aspect of the initiation phase is called the "road of trials."[9] In this tale, it is strength of character, not strength of arms, that enables the heroes to accept the summons.

As the story moves forward, Norman McCay and the Spectre find themselves witnessing yet another superhero battle. This time a group of heroes on a bridge are exchanging laser fire with a group standing on an occupied cable car. The car teeters on the brink of falling as the Spectre looks impassively on. Norman McCay, in contrast, is greatly disturbed by the actions he sees and the distressing idea that the "heroes" have, incredibly, grown even more reckless. Most of all, he decries both the lack of hope he sees and the overwhelming need for it.

Norman's words are answered in a blur of motion that saves the bystanders in the cable car and halts the fighting. The panels show wounded and shaken people exiting the car alongside people gazing upward with awe, joy, and hope. They spontaneously utter one of the most familiar phrases in our culture. "Look," one person shouts. "Up in the sky," another adds. (You might know the rest of this famous mantra.) On the bridge, tearful eyes look upward as hope returns to the people of the world in the form of Superman, his red cape flying in the breeze as he unceremoniously holds the combatants in his grip. His face is chiseled with resolve and determination.

Only one man is not cheering, and that is Norman McCay. Norman receives a vision of Superman screaming in agony, impossibly hot flames searing his body. The road of trials is long and dangerous. It would appear Superman, for all his power, may not survive the path he is on.

Superman's return has inspired others to do the same. Wonder Woman works alongside him, as does the Flash and the Green Lantern. These heroes all worked together in their youth as members of the superhero group called the Justice League. The League has reformed and is committed to curtailing the actions of the new breed of superhero. Their ranks grow as new recruits join their ranks. One man—Batman—does not join them, prompting Superman to travel to Gotham City to seek him out.

Not that it was terribly hard to find him, mind you. Bruce Wayne no longer dons his cape, and he does not need to. His secret identity was revealed years before, and his enemies destroyed Wayne Manor. Bruce now lives his life as Batman only, spending his days in the Batcave, maintaining order throughout Gotham without leaving his chair.

Bruce has an army of Bat Robots that patrol Gotham, spreading the fear he understands so well among the criminals and the innocent of Gotham simultaneously. He sees this orderly, nearly crime-free city as Utopia. There is no superhuman activity in the city, and almost every position of authority is under his influence if not his outright control. Superman is not impressed by what he sees, believing Batman's obsession with victory through fear has gone too far.

Batman is equally unimpressed with Superman's return, as he and the Justice League are acting on their own sanctions, creating their own laws and judicial system within the confines of the United States. To Batman, Superman is little more than a totalitarian leader who may well target him next. Both men are too interested in controlling events to see that the very traits they disdain in others are on full display in their own words and actions.

In the end, Batman refuses to join the League, for he has his own plans and his own teammates, both robot and human, to aid him. Batman's comfort in himself is clear throughout the dialogue. He calls Superman "Clark," even when told not to. He mockingly points out that the superhuman problem is not new, adding for no reason other than insult, "Where have you been?" He also dismisses the needs of average people, who decided they wanted "more ruthless" heroes. "Be careful what you wish for," is his assessment of that desire.

For his part, Superman tries to appeal to Batman's sense of duty. This, of course, does not work as Batman sees himself fulfilling his duty. They bicker and squabble, both men unwilling to join the other, just as they, despite Batman's words, are unwilling to let "normal" people solve this problem. They both have the best course of action, just ask them. Superman departs without the one ally he truly wanted. Batman remains, knowing he must work twice as fast now that the Justice League is back, for they could well interfere with plans he has been working on for the better part of a decade.

Undaunted by Batman's position, Superman and the Justice League continue to convert and combat the younger superheroes. Eventually they come to the hero called Magog, who plays a central role in this drama. Magog is the highest-profile hero of the new generation. He replaced Superman as the "protector" of Metropolis and engaged in a battle that killed one million civilians in a nuclear blast. The explosion turned all of Kansas and parts of Nebraska, Iowa, and Missouri into a nuclear wasteland. It was this action that drew Superman from seclusion. As the two confront each other, we learn more details about Superman's departure and gain insight into certain grim realities that have unfolded throughout recorded history.

Magog explains how Superman refused to change with the times. He was increasingly seen as old-fashioned and out of touch with the modern world. Batman's nemesis, the Joker, came to Metropolis and killed ninety-three people at the Daily Planet. Among them was Superman's wife Lois Lane.

The Joker, handcuffed by the police, was shot and killed by Magog's signature energy blast as the authorities were taking him into custody. Superman arrived on the scene and had Magog arrested for murder. Such an act took more conviction than anyone, especially Magog, realized. Superman had to weigh what he believed about justice against the sense of vengeful satisfaction he may have felt seeing the Joker's final defeat. The concept of following one's highest philosophy versus personal desires is a conversation overflowing with possibilities in the classroom. Superman chooses his highest ideals and takes Magog into custody for murder.

Superman finds himself on the unpopular side of this issue. Magog is acquitted as the pie chart on the front page of a newspaper informs us that 77 percent of Metropolitans believe Magog is more suited than Superman to defend their future. Magog, as is his wont, desires a fight with Superman to settle the issue. Superman declines, flying away rather than fighting, leaving Metropolis in the hands of the protector they wanted.

The question could be asked, "Why does Superman leave?" It is doubtful he was afraid of Magog. It is also not reasonable to think he has dramatically changed his philosophy; otherwise he would not have had Magog arrested. Perhaps the answer lies in the words of Mark Waid and his thesis that Superman, like the rest of us, needs a sense of belonging, something the years and Magog have taken from him. His wife now dead and the people of his adopted home city turned from him, he decides to turn from them.

In the *Dhammapada,* Buddha offers both insight about the nature of wise men and a warning to them. "The wise man tells you where you have fallen and where you yet may fall—invaluable secrets! Follow him, follow the way." In Metropolis, Superman is this wise man, trying to show the people, despite the loss of his wife and their disregard for his message, the way of truth, justice, and restraint. Buddha advises people to allow themselves to be taught by the wise man, for he will "keep you from mischief." Buddha also declares, "The world may hate [the wise man]."[10]

This sensation, of being hated and dismissed, is new to Superman. He has always been loved and revered by the people. He has never had to deal with their rancor, indifference, or animosity. In fact, his universal acceptance may be the most unrealistic aspect of Superman. It can be argued that most revered people do not reach that status until after their death.

Martin Luther King Jr. was viewed with increasing animosity between the years 1965 and 1968. During this time, he turned his attention to the inequities of the North and its de facto economic segregation. Many who supported his efforts to desegregate the South were enraged. It was heroic when King sought to change Southern custom and culture but quite another thing when he turned to the North's discrimination. Abraham Lincoln, a president generally held in high regard in the modern world, faced a difficult struggle in his attempt to be reelected and was loathed by people in the North and South alike. Jesus, a man regarded as one of peace, infuriated Roman and Jewish authorities during his life. Malcolm X was viewed as a threat by white America and, as time passed, by the Nation of Islam as well. Socrates was accused of corrupting the youth of Athens. All of these men died violently, at the hands of either individuals or institutions.

This raises an interesting point: do we, at times, despise those who remind us we are not as great as we wish to be? Instead of seeing them as role models or examples to follow or aspire to, do we desire their fall so we can continue to be ourselves without reminders that we could be better? Abraham Maslow regarded such animosity as "common," stating, "The commonly seen hatred or resentment of or jealousy of goodness, truth, beauty, health, or intelligence is largely determined by threat of loss of self-esteem.... Every superior person confronts us with our own shortcoming."[11] Perhaps the real surprise is not that people have turned their backs on Superman, but that it took so long to do so.

The people of Metropolis have spoken, and Superman exits the world stage, but he returns. In the dead zone that was Kansas, he confronts his youthful adversary.* The truth be told, the battle is anticlimactic, as Magog's energies lack the force to harm Superman.

---

* Kansas is the state in which Kal-El's rocket landed, therefore Magog destroyed Superman's first earthly home.

His energy blasts, while visually impressive, do no harm, other than burning off Superman's cape. Magog falls to his knees and reveals his pain with the following words, "The world changed ... but you wouldn't. So they chose me. They chose the man who would kill over the man who wouldn't ... and now they're dead. A million ghosts. Punish me. Lock me away. Kill me. Just make the ghosts go away." Batman 's words, "Be careful what you wish for," can almost be heard whispering over the dustbowl of Kansas.

This event leads to an extraordinary decision by Superman. He decides to build, in Kansas, a huge penitentiary to hold those superheroes that refuse to join the League. The structure is referred to as the gulag, a word most commonly associated with former Soviet dictator Joseph Stalin. The gulag, built without conferring with U.S. authorities, represents Superman's decision to act without consulting or conferring with "normal" people. Evidently Superman's mantra—truth, justice, and the American Way—needs a revamping. It is now his way. The gulag, and its inhabitants, help bring the story to its climax.

The walls of the gulag are torn asunder by Captain Marvel, a hero of immense power and, in his prime, equally immense goodness. He had been brainwashed and twisted, however, by Superman's old nemesis, Lex Luther. The inmates of the gulag break free, and the Justice League, without Superman, stand ready to stop them—and, if need be, to kill them.

Superman is not with them because he is trying, yet again, to gain the aid of Batman. The League, led by Wonder Woman, is resolute in its desire to defeat the young heroes, even if it means killing them. If this sounds odd, it is important to remember that Wonder Woman is a warrior princess, and she sees the events unfolding as a war. In war, as Superman said in an argument with her in the tale, people die. She left that argument to bring war to the younger generation. Superman left their argument with a different mission.

As Wonder Woman demands that the inmates cease their activity or face dire consequences, Superman is in the Batcave, trying desperately to gain Batman's aid. As before, Batman glibly attempts to dismiss Superman's request. Superman nearly persuades Batman to join, using the most important common ground the two have always shared, respect for life. "The deliberate taking of human—even super-human—life goes against every belief I have—and that you have. That's the one thing we've always had in common. It's what made us what we are. More than anyone in the world, when you scratch everything else away from Batman, you're left with someone who doesn't want to see anybody die."

The artwork clearly shows Batman is emotionally moved by Superman's words, as the Kryptonian has ripped through all the clever arguments and precious logic to the human core of Batman. Batman, however, does not say he will enter the fight and Superman speeds off to the Gulag alone, hoping to contain the battle. This hope, however, is lost as Captain Marvel slams Superman to the ground and keeps him engaged in a one-on-one battle as the riot escalates.

The intensifying battle leads Norman McCay to plead with the Spectre to stop the battle. The Spectre cannot, for his job is not to cease the hostilities but to pass his final judgment—and the time is not yet right.

A moment of hope does occur, as Norman McCay again looks upward for help. Batman, in costume for the first time in this saga, arrives at the gulag, accompanied by Batrobots and the allies he has made over the past ten years. Batman and Superman are united again. This is the heroic moment—the crescendo that films and books often build to. This time, however, the heroes fail. Some lives cannot be saved.

The ranking members of the United Nations, terrified by the growing superhuman war, decide to take action. They see that the superhuman battle will spread over the globe, claiming countless lives unless they stop it. Three jets, each carrying nuclear warheads, speed to the riot, ordered to drop their deadly packages. Batman and Wonder Woman prevent two bombs from being dropped, but the third is delivered, spurring the Spectre to speak.

He explains that the evil of genocide is being faced. If the bomb detonates, all the superhumans will die. If the bomb is stopped, their battle continues. Their struggle will eventually consume the earth and its inhabitants. Either way, one race will cease to exist. The Spectre turns to his beleaguered human companion and orders him to aid in the judgment. The question he poses to Norman could be asked to a class as well: "Who shall be held accountable? Whose sin is this? The humans' or the superhumans'?"

When Norman attempts to argue there is "no evil," only "bedlam," the Spectre ignores him and again stresses the need to judge. The Spectre is not present at this moment to hear philosophic arguments or deal in half measures. The violence in which the heroes have been engaging is ending the only way it can—in death and grief. Ultimately, Captain Marvel attempts to stop the third bomb, but it detonates, leaving Superman alone at ground zero, among the corpses of his friends and foes, all whom he sought, and failed, to save. In a fury he races to the U.N.

It is in the U.N. when we see the true return of Superman, the hero instead of world leader or disciplinarian of wayward heroes. Norman McCay materializes and confronts Superman with the only weapon he has, the wisdom of a preacher deeply rooted in the faith that goodness exists in man, especially Superman. As if talking to a member of his congregation, Norman declares that the biggest mistake Superman made was the day he made being "super" more important than being a man. Contemplating these words, Superman witnesses a handful of survivors, carrying Captain Marvel's cape, race into the U.N. This small contingent bears witness to the reawakening of wisdom and humanity in Superman.

The secretary general of the U.N. approaches the Kryptonian, stating, "We saw you as gods." Superman replies," As we saw ourselves … and we were both wrong." He has returned to his roots, looking to work among people again, not dominate or ignore them. He vows to use his power to help humanity solve problems and become trusted again. There must come a sense of unity, no superhuman and human world, only life and the hope that the two worlds can become one again. Superman ties Captain Marvel's cape to a flagpole, reverently recalling that the fallen hero fought through his psychosis and saved both groups. In doing so, they are allowed to face the future together. This hopeful future is the prize, the boon that the world receives as a result of the heroes' quest. Individuals who partook of the quest also receive rewards.[12]

Norman, returned by the Spectre to his church, gains a renewed sense of purpose and faith in his mission. The Spectre notes, "You have watched the titans walk the Earth … and you have kept stride. Perhaps you are more like them than you realize. You exist to give hope." We next see Norman joyfully giving a sermon at his church, his faith strengthened by the trials he has endured.

Superman reclaims his humanity and compassion. This point is made as he is working alone yet again. This time, he is in Kansas building a memorial for all those who died because of the mistakes made by everyone involved in the tragedies of the past. As in the opening of the book, Wonder Woman comes to visit. She delivers a gift, a pair of false glasses. The gentle smile on his face communicates volumes regarding the glasses' meaning to Kal-El. As she departs, kissing him lovingly, she calls him Clark. He does not object.

As the story concludes we find Batman, Superman, and Wonder Woman having a conversation in a hero-themed diner. Batman deduces, being a great detective, that Clark and Diana are expecting a child.[*] Diana surprises everyone by asking Batman to be the god-father. He initially protests, pointing out his deficiencies as a father figure and his reliance on fear. Clark concedes he has a different philosophy but admits there are few people he would trust more than Batman. He accepts, embracing Clark and joining a most unusual family. The three heroes exit the diner into a future where dreams can be pursued, even the dreams of superheroes.

---

[*] Wonder Woman's secret identity is Diana Prince.

# CHAPTER 3

# Batman the Moral Vigilante

In the previous chapters, we briefly contrasted Batman with Superman in the light of the balanced life, something that seems to elude Batman. Batman does, of course, posses multiple strengths, otherwise he would be a poor hero indeed. While considering Batman's strengths, the mind quickly focuses on his physical prowess, his keen intellect, his astounding array of gadgets and crime-fighting paraphernalia, and the legendary Batmobile. Although all of these things are of great importance, they pale compared to what makes Batman, well, Batman, and that would be his heightened sense of morality. It is this moral sense that not only separates Batman from the criminals he pursues, but also distinguishes him from other grim and violent heroes.

The phrase "violent heroes" has an undesirable connotation but encapsulates certain comic book heroes, Batman among them. Batman, more than Superman and Spider-Man, is a violent character. This does not mean that the other two icons do not engage in epic battles, but due to their heroic attributes, their violence is less realistic and haunting than Batman's. In the midst of a battle, Superman may fly, hit his adversary with his heat-ray vision, or deliver the knockout by dropping a crane on his opponent. All the while, he shrugs off attacks due to his almost impregnable alien physiology. Meanwhile Spider-Man climbs a wall, traps one enemy in his webs and, using his "spider-sense" to dodge bullets, renders the other two assailants unconscious with a jumping punch-kick combination only Bruce Lee could hope to imitate.

The victories scored by both Superman and Spider-Man in the previous paragraph have violence in them (gunfire and a dropped crane), but the ferocity of these actions is tempered by a disconnection between the reader and the hero. Most of us have no frame of reference for flight, lifting and dropping cranes, climbing walls, or dodging bullets. These spectacular actions dominate the scene and make it distant from our reality. Batman, however, is not so detached from us. He breaks bones and shatters teeth with ferocious punches and kicks. He avoids gunfire not by superhuman senses and quickness that enables him to dodge, but by misdirection; the fear his presence generates causing the gunman to rush, tremble, or freeze; and sometimes dumb luck. Batman's violence is grounded much more firmly in our reality than other iconic heroes.

A quick evaluation of two scenarios can clarify the depth of Batman's intensity. In Frank Miller's epic story *The Dark Knight Returns*, Batman is seeking information from a petty thug. In the midst of his "interrogation," taking place in a vacant apartment, Batman throws his antagonist through a window. The man sits in a heap, a large pane of glass stuck in his arm. The man, perhaps used to dealing with police, proclaims he has rights. Batman dismisses this claim and focuses on the situation at hand, "Right now you have a piece of glass cutting a major artery. Right now I am the only one who can get you to a hospital before you bleed to death."

Batman is equally intense in the story *Justice*. In this tale, a cadre of villains act as humanitarians, luring people into becoming citizens of intergalactic cities or remaining on Earth. The people taking residence in the cities will become infected by a special nanobyte technology that will turn them into slaves of the robotic villain Braniac. Those staying on Earth will be ruled over by Superman's foe Lex Luther. Braniac, however, hates all humanity. Once he takes his slave cities to space, he plans to use the world's nuclear weapons to destroy all human life left on Earth.

The Justice League captures one super villain, Captain Cold, and they seek to gain information from him. Batman performs the interrogation. During the process Batman talks about the tendency of Superheroes to be a little sentimental, saving personal keepsakes and gifts from appreciative individuals. While conducting the interrogation, Batman is seen examining Cold's ray gun. In frustration, Captain Cold demands to know why Batman is asking these questions. Does Batman want to know if he has sentimental connections to his gun? "No," Batman answers, "I was wondering about your fingers and how many you want to keep." Soon thereafter Batman exits the room with the information he seeks. The assumption made by the gathered heroes is that Batman's threats were a bluff, designed to scare Cold into sharing what he knew. Superman, however, makes a silent observation.

Batman was infected by nanobytes earlier in the tale and even tried to kill Superman with kryptonite. He failed and found himself bound by Wonder Woman's golden lasso. The lasso, however, has magical properties that compel any person snared by it to tell the truth. The magic overrides the nano technology and Batman is unaffected by them so long as he keeps the lasso wrapped around his waist. He was wearing the lasso when he "bluffed" Captain Cold. The threat, Superman concludes, was real, for Batman could not bluff while influenced by the lasso's magical properties. Batman was fully prepared to break or even remove Cold's fingers to get what he wanted. Superman does not share this information with the other heroes, nor does he at any time in the story confront Batman regarding the issue.

At this point, we can easily see that Batman is capable of violent acts, but what about the morality promised earlier in the chapter? We have seen little evidence of this important attribute that guides Batman's actions. There are two popular comic book heroes who are equally, if not more, intense and violent than Batman. They are Wolverine and the Punisher. These two individuals routinely cross a line that Batman does not: they kill their adversaries. Punisher and Wolverine, two comic book characters who engage in street-level violence as Batman does, have no compunction about killing in certain situations.

This essential belief, that he will not be responsible for another's death, is an important aspect of Batman's moral code. Somehow, through the pain of his childhood (even non-comic fans tend to be aware that in his childhood, Bruce Wayne witnessed the mur-der of his parents; young Bruce would eventually become Batman) and the years of walking among the filth of humanity, Batman holds onto the ideal that human life is sacred. This may seem odd to the reader, but the complexity of Batman runs deep and is evaluated and re-evaluated as each new writer accepts the challenge of telling his tale.

The paradox of Batman may be best summed up by Bane, a masked villain who makes his way to Gotham. Bane, a child born in prison and raised within its unforgiving walls, has visions of a terrifying bat creature and comes to Gotham to make the city his. He also seeks to destroy Batman, whom he associates with the creature from his visions. At their first meeting, Bane witnesses Batman battling local thugs and, to his surprise, watches Batman struggle to save his foe from falling to his death. Bane notes, for himself and the reader, "You are strange. A figure cloaked in a nightmare, but you will not break the 6th command-ment." The sixth commandment, however, prohibits killing. Batman goes a step further.

In the *Knightfall* story line, Batman is engaged in a massive melee on a bridge. He is bat-tling an armor-plated usurper to his mantle and local thugs and crime lords. Accompanying him in this struggle are Robin, Nightwing (Dick Grayson, the original Robin), and Catwoman. Catwoman, who often plays the dual role of opponent and confidant to Bat-man, is present because she was seeking revenge against the crime lords who tried to kill her earlier in the story. During the battle a helicopter occupied by a couple of low-level criminals, crashes into the bridge. The men inside the helicopter could die at any time.

Instantly Batman makes a decision and rushes to save the men, ordering Catwoman to join him. Her protests fall on deaf ears, and she joins Batman's rescue mission. She men-tally notes she was not sure if the man she was fighting alongside was even the real Batman, but this action made it clear that it was. Not only does Batman not take a life, he cannot sit idly by and watch someone die. His 11th commandment, evidently, reads, "Thou shalt save any life thoust can."

Does this predilection to preserve and not take life alone make Batman a highly devel-oped moral individual? Lawrence Kohlberg's work on the stages of moral development are very useful in answering this question.[13] Kohlberg identified six stages of moral develop-ment, the final two stages being the most difficult to achieve. Stage four in his continuum can be called a "law and order" orientation. The laws of society are how someone firmly set in this stage defines right and wrong. The legal point of view is very important at this phase. The person in this stage may be aware of certain exemplars of higher mores of mo-rality, but this understanding does not profoundly affect the way they live their lives, re-vealing their loyalty to "law and order" thinking.

When one considers the numerous laws Batman breaks on a regular basis (assault and battery, trespassing, breaking and entering, stealing evidence, etc.), it is obvious he is not bound by devotion to existing laws. The law does not equal justice, and it is justice that is Batman's driving force, his ultimate concern.[14] He is not, at his core, an agent of vengeance, despite the broken bodies left in his wake. If vengeance were his goal, his devotion to pre-serving life would not be so keen.

This does not change the fact that embracing justice as an ultimate concern causes Batman to work outside of the confines of the law. This leads us to the question, "Is Batman a criminal?" In *The Dark Knight Returns,* Batman answers this question, smiling, in the affirmative. It is important to note two facts at this point. The first is the context of the admission: Superheroes were on trial because of their methods. Much like Martin Luther at the Diet of Worms, Batman would not recant. He also knew such an unrepentant answer would be shocking and put others on their heels, something he always enjoyed.

The second issue we face here is whether we would define every lawbreaker as a criminal? Is criminal the first word that comes to your mind when you here the names Martin Luther King Jr. or Gandhi? Both men spent time in jail for breaking the law. Nelson Mandela spent more than twenty years in prison. It is important to note that King and Gandhi are used by Kohlberg as examples of people who have reached stage six of moral development. Is it possible that Batman, the breaker of bones and the thief of evidence, is also functioning at this lofty level?

The defining characteristic of the fifth stage of moral development is the emergence of a "prior to society" perspective. This means the individual—in this case, Batman —looks at human activity and rights through a lens that evaluates these concepts as they were prior to social contracts, laws, or society itself. In essence, there exists a distinct human nature and, by extension, natural rights that society should not violate. The individual at stage five does not—most emphatically does not—use this distinct perspective to endorse anarchy. To the contrary, he or she will appreciate the need for social order (much like someone at stage four) but can move comfortably outside of the law if the law seems to fail in its duty to protect human rights.

Batman exemplifies this dichotomy on a regular basis as he routinely apprehends criminals and turns them over to the police so that society's judicial system can perform its function. Batman even works with a trusted policeman, Jim Gordon, in an attempt to bring law and order to Gotham City. The judicial system may include corrupt cops, paid witnesses, corruptible judges, and disreputable lawyers, but all of this is better than unmitigated anarchy, so Batman works with the system while transcending it, creating the paradox of the moral vigilante.

Does Batman meet the requirements to be considered at the sixth and final level of moral development? The odds seem against this, as men like Gandhi and Martin Luther King Jr. are sighted as examples of this level. The two men, like Batman, may be considered criminals. They also could be seen as tremendously irritating to the moderate position. Gandhi stubbornly refused any compromise position with the British Government regarding India's home rule. King's famous "Letter from a Birmingham Jail" was not aimed at radicals but at local clergy who wanted King to cease his activities so the veneer of peace and calm in the city would not be disturbed. When Batman declares himself a criminal, he is taking aim at moderates who may wish him to temper his activity so as not to challenge them to reevaluate their own orthodoxy.

Thus far it may seem that Batman has more in common with King and Gandhi than originally suspected, but there is one very important distinction: both historic figures embraced as one of their guiding principles the philosophy of nonviolence. Batman, most obviously, has not and will not.

Living the principles of nonviolence and radical love seem out of Batman's reach. So can we find a historic figure who exemplifies Batman's sense of moral outrage but does not shy away from—and in fact seeks out—physical and violent confrontation? Perhaps history teachers approaching the Civil War may want to compare Batman to John Brown and see what conclusions their students make.

# CHAPTER 4

## *Knightsend*: Finding Meaning through Suffering

In the previous chapters, we witnessed Superman's heroic quest unfold in the pages of *Kingdom Come*. For Batman, the heroic quest can be witnessed in the overarching scope of his life. From orphaned boy and witness to his parents' murders to self-made hero and Guardian of Gotham City, Batman's life is a testament to the will to overcome obstacles. This dramatic life can lead the reader to ask a number of questions. How does a person find meaning in life when random, dramatic, and arbitrary events from their childhood have provided destructive evidence that people are helpless when confronted by the whims of capricious fate? Has Bruce Wayne transcended his suffering, or is he merely a product of it? What happens if a carefully constructed life is torn apart by new tragedies, leaving an adult once again facing the prospects of a very uncertain future? The story *Knightsend* provides an opportunity to evaluate these important questions.

*Knightsend* is the third and final installment in the *Knightfall* trilogy. In the first installment, a new threat, Bane, has arrived in Gotham. Not content to merely kill Batman, he seeks to break him completely and make Gotham his own. Detonating a bomb outside of Arkham Asylum, Bane releases the demented inmates on the populace of Gotham. In an exhausting effort, Batman helps capture the escaped psychopaths, from the lower rung criminal to his most deranged opponent, the Joker.

With his prey on the brink of physical exhaustion, Bane confronts the Dark Knight. Bane, who has his physical might augmented by a drug known as Venom, overcomes his depleted foe and breaks his back. He then drags Batman to a rooftop, proclaims his victory, and throws the broken Bat to the street. Part two of the trilogy ensues, with Bruce Wayne choosing Jean-Paul Valley (who had formerly been the hero Azreal) to take up the role of Batman. Jean-Paul, who is tormented by visions produced by his indoctrination into a cult, slowly loses his sense of morality. Jean-Paul defeats Bane when he adds armor plating and a deadly arsenal of weapons to the bat-suit. In his righteous quest to destroy Gotham's criminal element, he ignores the strict codes that guided his predecessor's actions.

Bruce is shocked by the carnage caused by Jean-Paul. He is also disturbed by his lack of judgment placing the safety of Gotham in the hands of someone so unstable and by the defilement of Batman. He decides that he must return to Gotham (he had left to help locate Tim Drake's/Robin's father) and reclaim the mantle of the Bat. This will require regaining the skills, reflexes, confidence, and strength that enabled him to be Batman, attributes that have atrophied in the months of recovering from Bane's attack. As Bruce suffered at the hands of Bane, so now must he endure the strict training and discipline required to regain his full identity and become Batman once more. This chapter does not trace the story from start to finish but focuses on key themes that can be found in the story and brought to students who, in many cases, identify heavily with suffering but lack the balancing force of meaning.

It is with this concept of balance that we will begin our quick study of *Knightsend*. As stated, Bruce Wayne is no longer technically Batman, having been broken by Bane and relinquishing the mantle of the Bat to Jean-Paul Valley. However, Batman cannot be completely removed from Bruce Wayne's psyche for he *is*, in the most private and intimate manner, Batman. Batman is the meaning of Bruce's life. Batman was Bruce's vision of hope as he sought meaning in his orphaned life. Batman was a vision of strength that enabled him to reconcile the horrific reality of his parents' murder and fuse it into a life of serving others in an effort to end their suffering. As Bruce merges with his vision, Batman becomes physically manifest, and Bruce's life becomes secondary to the mission of Batman, but all that is gone now; Bruce is left with a distinct form of suffering, the suffering people feel when they are separated from their mission in life or trapped in a job they do not want. He also suffers because the city he has sworn to protect, the city he loves, is now being threatened by the corrupted visage of his vision, Jean-Paul's ultra-violent and destructive Batman. Compounding this pain is the reality that Jean-Paul has the honor of being Batman because Bruce gave it to him, a terrible choice to say the least. Viktor Frankl observed that people have "the uniquely human potential ... to transform a personal tragedy into a triumph, to turn's one predicament into a human achievement."[15] Bruce has undertaken this amazing endeavor once, but what steps must he take to transform his tragedy a second time?

The first phase of this journey is seeking a mentor, or at least someone capable of pushing Bruce to regain his fighting form, sharpen his skills, and strengthen his body. The seeking or appearance of the mentor, although common to myths and legends throughout history, has an interesting subtext in Batman's case. First, Bruce has to be humble enough to admit he needs such aid, a difficult task for someone who has always sought to face life's worst challenges alone. Maybe there comes a point when even the most accomplished hero (or most jaded teenager) recognizes the need for aid.

The choice Bruce makes for his trainer/mentor is also a source of curiosity. He chooses to approach the enigmatic adventure seeker, Lady Shiva. In Hinduism, Shiva is the aspect of God responsible for death and destruction. This is an appropriate name for Lady Shiva because she is someone who, in Bruce's words, "kills without remorse." He also regards her as, perhaps, the best fighter on the planet—and therefore someone he recognizes as capable of bringing him back, physically, to being the man he once was.

Lady Shiva, who is drawn as an Asian woman, lives in a modest home outside of Gotham. When Bruce enters her dojo, we see a large yin-yang symbol on her wall. Students may recognize the symbol, and its placement in an Asian woman's home will seem sensible. In some ways, the teaching of Lao-Tzu, founder of Taoism, the tradition from which the symbol originated, can be used to give texture to the scene. An important aspect of Taoism is the pulling together of opposites to create a more complete and fully functioning whole. In Lady Shiva and Bruce, we see an Asian woman, raised amid Eastern culture, acting as mentor to the embodiment of the Western male, who has long embraced the cultural archetype of the rugged individual. But now, the man needs the woman, East meets West, and rugged individual becomes willing pupil. All this is possible because Bruce has been broken and seeks to become whole again.[16] Lady Shiva, however, has an ulterior motive that drives her to agree to aid Bruce.

She agrees to train Bruce, and for weeks the training involves Lady Shiva pummeling Bruce because he has lost much of his skill and precision. There comes a point in the training when he finally lands a blow, causing Lady Shiva to declare he is ready to move on in the training. She wants to teach him to kill. Bruce emphatically rejects the notion that killing is necessary. Shiva, in a moment of utter contempt and disgust, declares he is not worth her time. An option occurs to her, and she asks Bruce to return to her home in two nights.

In the interim, she dons the Mask of Tengu (a bat spirit) and kills a martial arts master. She gives the mask to Bruce informing him "field training" begins when he wears that mask at a certain address the next night. Bruce does not know what Shiva has done, but the disciples of the murdered master will seek revenge. One-by-one, from least to most skilled, they will track Bruce down and attempt to kill him. Shiva hopes that one of these masters will force Bruce to kill to survive. Just as Bane broke his body, Shiva would like to be the one who causes Bruce to break his oath not to kill. The training begins in earnest, and we see Bruce's progression as he defeats one master after another. However, these tests are not the only trials Bruce must overcome.

Bruce devises his own test, a private Rubicon that he faces alone, with all his courage, character, doubt, and fear. He stands at the top of a tower in the heart of Gotham, rope and batarang in hand. He contemplates his previous life; when he would fearlessly leap from such a height, throw the line with confidence, swing over the abyss and land on the two-foot perch below. This was once a common activity for him and one he must be able to do now if he is truly to become Batman again. Fighting skills and physical conditioning are necessary, but his fearlessness must be regained as well. This is a test Bruce needs to pass alone.

The first time Bruce ascends the tower is after defeating two of the masters. His fighting skills are sharpening, and he decides the time has come to face his personal test. He holds the batarang over his head but does not throw it. He does not take the leap. Instead he turns and leaves, knowing he has more challenges ahead and he is not ready to take the first step in the process. The fights are a necessary part of the growth process, but the essence of Batman is found on the other side of the personal abyss symbolized by the momentous heights of Gotham tower.

Upon defeating his next opponent, Bruce returns to the tower again. He stands still, recalling the night he first performed the leap. It was the night he became more than Bruce Wayne. It is the night he became Batman. Students may be familiar with this concept, of needing to achieve something for themselves that means more to their identity than the tests created by others. Sometimes the praise of others falls on deaf ears, not because the person is stubborn or diffident, but because what he or she needs to accomplish to believe the words of others is private and unspoken. Self-esteem truly comes from the self, not from the words of others or from awards accumulated.

Praise and awards can build our sense of accomplishment and provide validation, but true self-esteem and confidence is found elsewhere. These things come finally from fulfilling or chasing personal dreams and overcoming personal demons along the way. Standing on the towers of Gotham, Bruce faces the prospect of his true identity and the fears that immobilize him. The second trip to Gotham tower reveals that Bruce can remember what he once did, but he decides not to attempt his leap because "something older and wiser tells him no." What is this older, wiser aspect of Bruce that tells him no, or, more precisely, not at this moment? Is it his soul, his conscience, his subconscious mind, or the part of himself that longed to be Batman from the moment he was born? What is this inner wisdom that causes him to turn his back on the abyss, sadly accepting that he is not ready for the leap, but determined to return?

It is important to note that Bruce's refusal to leap from the tower in that moment is not a refusal to continue the effort to become capable to make the leap. Bruce's determination to continue his efforts is not necessarily a trait we see in our students or ourselves. The determination to continue, to become worthy and ready of the challenges of life, is sometimes lacking. The "no" of the moment becomes a "no" for a lifetime, and our full potential is not realized. This is the intersection where Bruce stands at, the simple choice to stop trying or continue the struggle, even when the end we want is nothing more than a vision.

It is the vision of becoming worthy of being Batman that brings Bruce to the towers of Gotham for a third visit and the knowing that he is not ready that causes him to turn back. This time, however, students might notice the increased intensity Bruce has brought to the tower. As he stands looking over the chasm, knowing he will not leap, he thinks, "God hates a coward." This is a strange thought to appear in a Batman story, as he rarely exhibits any sense of the metaphysical, religious convictions, or spiritual tendencies. But as he stands he considers not only that God hates a coward, but that he may be a coward worthy of eternal scorn.

Students, particularly Christians, may protest passionately the idea that God hates anything, but perhaps Bruce's approach is not that foreign to them. Very little is accomplished by people who are fearful or frightened, and yet people are capable of great accomplishments if they set aside their fears. All religious traditions extol the virtue of letting go of one's fears and doubts, for they inhibit the efforts of people to become fully functioning adults. In the *Bhagavad Gita*, Lord Krishna advises Arjuna to "cut through this doubt in your own heart with the sword of spiritual wisdom."[17]

Cutting through doubt in the heart is a phrase the summarizes what Bruce is doing. By undergoing this difficult process, he seeks to become Batman again just as Arjuna cut out doubt so he could become a great warrior king, guided by spiritual wisdom. The doubts and fears Bruce faces cloud his ability to see his potential, blocking him from his highest self and calling. Perhaps "God hates a coward" because the coward breaks the first commandment, placing his fears above God, worshipping his fears as all-powerful even as he wishes for the strength to overcome these fears. The attributes sometimes attributed to God are in fact ascribed to our fears, and we tremble, helpless before them.

"God hates a coward" could well be interpreted as saying that the hate comes not from a place of personal insult but a place of compassion. Watching human beings succumb to their fears is a terrible thing when we love them. How much worse must it be to a consciousness that recognizes all the glory just beyond our fears, a glory that is our birthright if we are not afraid?[18] The coward, worshipping a false idol of fear, denies not only God, but the glory of His creation as well, causing him to debase both without the counterbalance of exaltation.

Regardless of these and other possible musings, Bruce is using the thought of himself as the hated outcast unworthy of God's attention as fuel to continue his journey. In his next fight, he is being choked by one of the masters seeking revenge and begins contemplating the ways he may die in this battle. A new thought, however, comes to him, and he breaks free: "Hell is for the fearful. God hates a coward."

This proclamation adds depth to Bruce's contention, for what Hell could be worse than wallowing in one's own fear and cowardice, unable to rise up and become a more complete human being? Is it possible that the universe is designed to reward courage and degrade the coward? Is it equally possible that the courageous individual who becomes too proud of his or her achievements must be brought low to truly understand and appreciate the nature of courage and cowardice, therefore becoming whole for the first time? Is Bruce on such a journey? This could be the case, because after he achieves victory in the battle, he barely wins the next confrontation, confessing to himself that he "should feel good about tonight. But I don't. I just feel empty." Ancient sages would claim this is exactly the state we need to be in, completely empty so that we can be filled again with the most precious sustenance.[19]

The feeling of emptiness does not stop Bruce. He merely pushes on, the outcome of his quest still very uncertain. He again finds himself atop the tower and incapable of making the leap. He does, however, secure the rope to the building and slowly lower himself to ground level. His inner dialogue during the descent reveals his motivation, as he proclaims living the rest of his life as merely Bruce Wayne a living death (Hell is for the fearful). Better to struggle and die than send oneself to Hell.

The battle with the last and most skilled of the masters unfolds. Bruce is pushed to his limits, but he not only achieves victory over the ninja, he graduates from Shiva's tutelage as well. The climax of the battle takes place in an empty boardroom into which the combatants have crashed. Bruce delivers a replica of the "leopard blow," a strike Lady Shiva uses to kill. In doing so, it appears he has killed his opponent, thrilling Lady Shiva, for Bruce Wayne has become a "killer" in her eyes; there is murderous blood on the hands of the Dark Knight.

Others do not share Lady Shiva's glee. Before her arrival, Robin (a teenager named Tim Drake) and Nightwing (Dick Grayson, the original Robin) had arrived as the battle ended and saw their beloved mentor deliver the "leopard blow." They think Bruce has cast his life's code aside, making a lie out of a lifetime of work. Robin is shocked, as if trying to piece the scene together and not wanting to believe the pieces fit. Nightwing, who has known Bruce the longest, is outraged. His accusations and questions end with the arrival of Lady Shiva, who has come to gloat, for she believes Bruce has indeed broken his code because of the test she designed. She leaves, taking the Mask of Tengu with her, for Bruce no longer needs it.

Moments after her departure the fallen ninja begins to groan, still alive, but badly hurt. Bruce explains that he will never be free of Shiva until he gives her what she wants, or at least the illusion of what she wants. He finishes his explanation with the directive that the three heroes need to get the wounded warrior to an emergency room. As Lady Shiva personifies Shiva (the aspect of the god in Hinduism that is responsible for death and destruction) perhaps Bruce represents Vishnu, the aspect of God responsible for the preservation of life and the universe.

After this victory, Bruce makes another trip to the tower to look out over his personal abyss. The scene is narrated by Tim Drake, who states that Bruce is not with him and Dick because "He had something else to do. Something to prove." Tim couldn't understand this, saying he did not know what Bruce meant. There is nothing left to prove. Not to Tim, but Bruce's abyss was his own. He stood over it, dressed in his dark ninja's gi, contemplating making the leap. He does not, however, opting to walk down from the heights only to return dressed, for the first time in the story, as Batman. He takes the leap, and a small smile creeps across his face. He is back, complete and whole. He is Batman again; now he needs to defeat the deranged Jean-Paul and complete the redemption of the cowl and mantle of the Bat.

At this point, there is little doubt that Bruce will succeed. It is how he achieves this victory that is worthy of note. The battle between Jean-Paul and Bruce rages from the bridge mentioned in the previous chapter to Bruce's home, Wayne Manor. Beneath Wayne Manor is the Bat Cave, where the battle approaches its conclusion. In the Bat Cave, Jean Paul, who is all rage and fury, proclaims that if he is not Batman, then he is nothing. Bruce's attention slowly shifts from defeating Jean Paul to saving him.

To do this he tempts Jean Paul to chase him into narrow passages surrounding the cave. Bruce is able to squirm through the tight tunnels, but Jean Paul, who has changed the Batman suit into a suit of armor, does not fit. He sheds all the armor, except his helmet with its night vision and continues his pursuit. Jean Paul does not realize he is also the hunted.

Bruce, waiting in the tunnel ahead of Jean Paul, has reached an area where the tunnel opens up. He stands and grips a board in the ceiling that covers a passage to the surface. When Jean-Paul enters the room, he removes the board, and sunlight bathes over Jean Paul, causing him great pain due to his night vision lenses. He throws off the helmet and confesses that Bruce is Batman and he is nothing. Bruce refuses to take Jean Paul to the authorities. He hears in Jean-Paul's voice the same despair and uncertainty he had felt earlier in the tale. Compassion, not punishment, is what Jean Paul needs. Bruce sends him away, warning him that the quest for identity is long and difficult, but something Jean Paul has to try. As he leaves, a remorseful Jean Paul asks for forgiveness. He recognizes how much he has violated Bruce's trust, defiled Batman's integrity, and desecrated something sacred to Bruce. Bruce forgives Jean-Paul. In a manner, he instructs Jean Paul to go forth and not sin like this again.

Bruce will try to avoid his sins as well, faulty judgment and self-doubt among them. But a lesson has been learned, a vital lesson that benefits Bruce and the reader. Although the following passage is from the story *Justice*, it is a fitting summary for the lessons of this tale as well. Speaking to his butler, Alfred, Bruce grows philosophic, stating, "We have all been changed by our tragedies, no matter how much we have tried, and should try to avert them. No matter what cures we seek, or whom we seek them from. Perhaps there exists a possible benefit when hardship is also accepted as part of human life."

When hardship is accepted as a part of life, we may well find strength we did not know we had. Just as Bruce struggles and overcomes obstacles, we can hope Jean Paul can do the same. So, too, can we look at out own lives and seek greater meaning in the face of hardship. Perhaps we can accept deep in our hearts the wisdom of Viktor Frankl, who said, "even the helpless victim of a hopeless situation, facing a fate he cannot change, may rise above himself, and by doing so change himself. He may turn personal tragedy into a triumph."[20]

# CHAPTER 5

# Spider-Man

Spider-Man likely competes with Batman and Superman to be the most recognizable name in comic books. Spider-Man's position as the icon of Marvel Comics has caused his comic to be the vehicle through which important issues are sometimes addressed. In 1971, *The Amazing Spider-Man #96* directly addressed drug use as a destructive, possibly deadly, habit. In 1984, Marvel, in unison with the National Committee for the Prevention of Child Abuse, released a special edition of a Spider-Man comic addressing childhood sexual abuse. In December 2001, Marvel, in the pages of *The Amazing Spider-Man Volume 2 #36*, allowed readers to see how various heroes reacted to the events of 9/11.

Throughout the decades, Spider-Man has been called upon to face difficult situations. What about this character enables him to resonate with readers and viewers alike?[*] The answer may be that Spider-Man is more like us than almost any other comic book hero. This may sound odd considering Spider-Man can climb walls, lift a car over his head, possesses lightning quick reflexes, and has a sixth sense that warns him of approaching threats and attacks. The reader's commonalities with Spider-Man extend far beyond what he can do. They are linked to who he is. Like Batman and Superman, Peter Parker (the teenager who becomes Spider-Man) is an orphan. He lives with his Aunt May and Uncle Ben in Queens. The elderly couple provides a loving, if not opulent, home.

He is, in many ways, a stereotypical nerd picked on by his more athletic peers and generally ignored by girls. He would much rather go to a science lab than a school dance or sporting event. It is at a science demonstration that he is bitten by a radioactive spider and gains the proportionate strength and agility of a spider. Using his scientific mind, Peter will invent the mechanism he uses to shoot webs. The successful film series alters this aspect of his biography, making his web shooting abilities a natural mutation of the bite rather than an invention. Although this type of inventive genius may be beyond the average person, a great deal of Peter Parker's reaction to gaining his powers is exceptionally normal.

When Bruce Wayne was orphaned, an overwhelming desire for justice was planted in his soul. This urge would eventually cause him to become Batman. In the interim, he

---

[*] The three Spider-Man films released in 2002, 2004, and 2007 all appear on the list of the thirty highest-grossing films of all time.

lived a life of material privilege in Wayne Manor. Peter, whose parents died when he was young, is raised by his lower-middle-class aunt and uncle. He has no great drive for justice or for righting the wrongs of the world in a dramatic manner. He loves science and could have an impact on the world through that venue, but being a scientist is not the seat of high adventure.

Superman is also orphaned and raised by adoptive parents from the same economic strata and cut from the same moral cloth as Peter's aunt and uncle. He, of course, always has his powers. It is a part of his life growing up. His mother and father counseled and guided him to, someday, use his powers for the greater good. The call to be a hero was a constant presence in young Clark Kent's life. Peter's Uncle Ben and Aunt May guided him to be a good person but did not consider the fact that they were raising Spider-Man. The Kents always knew they were raising an extraordinary being.

Superman's powers are, for all intents and purposes, natural. The Earth's yellow sun affects his Kryptonian physiology in such a way that grants tremendous strength and talents. Anyone from Krypton who came to Earth would have Superman's power. Bruce Wayne chooses to be Batman. Through effort and force of will, he becomes a supremely gifted athlete and martial artist. He is trained to be a detective. He studies different forms of explosives and armaments. Peter Parker receives the power of Spider-Man through an accident. Upon realizing he has these new powers, Peter's reaction is not that of the natural born hero, but rather the typical America teen. He seeks to become a television star and use his powers to provide for himself and his family.

In disguise, he tests his newfound powers in a wrestling match with Crusher Hogan. The victory earns Peter some money and launches his career. With an agent to promote him, a stage name, and his phenomenal abilities, Peter becomes an instant hit on television. After a particular television special, however, he takes an action that changes his life. A burglar runs past him backstage. Peter could have stopped him but chooses not to, citing that it is not his job. He is, after all, a star, not a policeman. His desire to help improve his life and that of his family is mirrored by a deep apathy for others.

A few days later, the same burglar breaks into the Parker's home. The thief shoots and kills Uncle Ben as he seeks to protect his home. Peter, stricken by grief and guilt, decides he will us his powers to promote the well-being of others, not merely himself. As the famous catchline synonymous with Spider-Man instructs, with great power comes great responsibility.

Being a teenaged superhero raised by a widowed aunt isn't the easiest path to walk. Money increasingly becomes an issue for May Parker. In his dual existence, Peter defeats a host of villains and psychopaths but sometimes fails to pay the bills. His job as a freelance photographer doesn't always earn enough to make ends meet at the end of the month. Adding to his anxiety is the fact that some media outlets tend to portray Spider-Man as a glory-seeking vigilante rather than a hero. Peter earns no money as Spider-Man and receives as much scorn as he does praise. His social life is often in shambles, as he will stand up dates because he is fulfilling his role as Spider-Man. Even his academics, an area of keen interest in Peter's life, suffers because of his secret life. He often wonders why he maintains the two lives, especially when Peter's life seems always to take a backseat to Spider-Man.

Peter's attempt to maintain a personal life is often hindered by the very demanding public life of Spider-Man. This struggle calls to mind the often imperfect balancing act that social activists perform and may call into question what type of world Peter, and we, are living in. Nelson Mandela articulated that every human being has twin obligations: commitments to the family and to the community. He contends that in a civil society, each individual can fulfill these obligations according to their own inclinations and abilities. The more unjust a society, the more difficult it is to meet the twin obligations.[21]

In Mandela's case, a black man living in South Africa could fail to meet his familial obligations, not because of a lack of concern or skill but because the system of apartheid created obstacles too difficult to overcome. Attacking these obstacles could also cause someone to fail in his or her familial duties because the need of the community and nation is so great. What does it say about the society Peter lives in, one created to mirror our own, that it is difficult for him to accommodate both his personal and "professional" life?

Of course, the problem may also lie with Peter. He received his powers at the age of fifteen. This is the age when people struggle to develop their sense of identity. Peter would likely identify himself as bookish, nonathletic, an orphan, an outsider, and a loving nephew. Suddenly he is being asked to integrate the persona of selfless hero into his sense of identity. Even more confusing, he must conceal some of his greatest talents for fear of arousing suspicion.

Peter lives in fear of people discovering he is Spider-Man. Such knowledge in the hands of his enemies could put his family, particularly his beloved aunt, in danger. Therefore, he decides Spider-Man must forever be anonymous, the unknown man behind the mask. At an age when people are often screaming for attention, even for performing the most mundane of tasks, Peter saves lives and performs heroic deeds. He routinely risks his life and is denied almost any reward. Even the simple pat on the back or sympathy for his fatigue is denied as he maintains his secret identity.

He lives an important life completely unnoticed, while less deserving peers gain acclaim accomplishing far less impressive feats. The subjection of his ego is another difficult battle Peter must engage to preserve his secret. It is little wonder that, from time to time, Peter announces to an empty room that he is going to quit being Spider-Man. He always reconsiders, however, personally aware that it is responsibility, not a guarantee of self-satisfaction, that accompany his power.

The reader sees, through Peter's struggles, the difficult decision-making process of choosing the heroic life. When Peter's ego screams "why bother being Spider-Man?" a deeper sense of generativity responds, "Because you care."[22] Spider-Man lives where we live. He lives in a world where responsibilities and burdens feel too great. The option of not applying your full potential to reduce your burdens is a constant temptation. Rarely completely comfortable as Spider-Man but well aware of his talents, Peter grows and evolves. New obstacles, and opportunities, present themselves, and Peter takes each challenge in stride, stumbling at times but always striving to save lives while living his.

# CHAPTER 6

## Spider-Man—The Revelation of Character in Times of Crisis

The story that unfolds in *Kraven's Last Hunt* can be evaluated through a number of lenses. One area of interest can be how, in times of crisis, a person's character is tested and revealed. Peter Parker and one of his longtime foes, Kraven the Hunter, renew their rivalry in this tale. Kraven is a fearsome and proud hunter. Using natural potions and serums, he has augmented his strength, stamina, agility, resistance to injury, and longevity. His exceptionally well-honed fighting and tracking skills, combined with his augmentations, have enabled him to successfully hunt every animal he has ever set his sights on. He often captures his prey by force of arms and traps as opposed to the use of guns. The only prey he has failed to better is Spider-Man.

This inability to ensnare the hero, thereby achieving victory and proving his superiority, has made Kraven obsessed with defeating Spider-Man. This obsession has also caused Kraven to associate the Spider as an image of injustice, darkness, and the depravity that threatens every age of mankind. His sanity, if not already lost, is fading away, replaced with a maniacal, fetishistic desire to defeat his personal Spider.

The opening chapter of *Kraven's Last Hunt* allows the reader to glimpse the primary motives of both Kraven the Hunter and Spider-Man. Born Sergei Kravinoff, Kraven came of age during the Russian Revolution. His parents, aristocrats during the age of the czars, lost everything as a result of the national upheaval brought about by Lenin, Trotsky, and the other revolutionaries. The honor and dignity of the Russian aristocracy was forever lost. Kraven feels the entire world has now, some seventy years later, tragically lost sight of theses concepts as well. Seeing society as irreversibly corrupt, Kraven found meaning and dignity in the jungle. Honor was found in the wild, not in modernized cultures promoting the façade of culture and civility.

Embittered, Kraven considers that the arc of his life, an existence now marred by morose dissatisfaction, may be coming to a close. The mythic vision of the Spider has claimed Mother Russia and trapped most other nations in a web of spiritless and shallow existence. There is no honor in the world. Kraven's one hope for personal redemption is to be found by hunting down and finally defeating Spider-Man. In his growing obsession with the restoration of his personal and family honor, he no longer views Spider-Man as human but rather as a personal manifestation of the Spider fated to torment and humiliate him.

While Kraven prepares to hunt his nemesis, Peter, dressed as Spider-Man, arrives at Jimmy's Corner Bar. A wake is being held for Joe Face, a small-time criminal Spider-Man would pump for information. His appearance causes the other attendees, men of Joe's ilk, to seek to flee the premises. He webs the door shut, for it is not his intention to clear the room but to add money to the collection plate to help buy Joe a coffin and a burial plot. Peter never offers an explanation for this action beyond the simple thought that he cares. The reasons for this compassion are not divulged and are not truly necessary. What matters is the glimpse the reader receives of Peter Parker's compassion for others, even someone like Joe who was technically an "enemy." This sense of caring drives him in much the same manner as Kraven's obsessions motivate the hunter.

Unable to sleep after the wake, Peter dons his Spider-Man costume and goes for an evening swing. Lost in thoughts of life, death, and the outcome of recent adventures, he is ambushed by Kraven. Struck by a poisoned dart, Peter becomes increasingly lightheaded and finds himself entangled in a net. He takes comfort that, assuming Kraven follows his usual tactics, he will be dragged off to some hideout. While en route, he will have time to recuperate from the drugs and plan his counteroffensive. He is shocked when Kraven produces a gun and growls that honor must be restored. Peter notes with horror that the look in Kraven's eyes is completely unfamiliar. His mind races from dead friends to living loved ones as Kraven pulls the trigger. The chapter ends with Kraven burying Spider-Man in a plot on his estate. The tombstone reads "Here Lies Spider-Man Slain By The Hunter."

With Spider-Man defeated and in the ground, Kraven takes to dressing as Spider-Man and patrolling the neighborhood. He has decided it was not enough to defeat Spider-Man, but he now must prove to be his superior by outdoing him at his own work. Returning to his mansion, Kraven's obsession drives him deeper into madness. He crawls on all fours, lapping a poisonous concoction from a bowl on the ground. As he does so a part of him asks, "Why am I doing this?" In confusion he decries his father to be nothing more than a "pompous fool … living in poverty in America" and quickly changes to exaltations claiming his father to be "the last remnant of a world of culture and decency." His father, much like Russian civilization, fell to the Spider and nothing else.

His mind on fire from the potion he drank, Kraven curses the Spider for crushing his father's spirit and taking the guise of the various men who ruined Russia. He shatters a glass enclosure that contains hundreds of Spiders. His intoxicated and deranged mind sees the spiders merge into a single, massive spider with which he wrestles, needing to be consumed by the Spider to truly conquer it.

Once this ordeal is over, Kraven once again goes on patrol as Spider-Man. His evening activity includes witnessing Mary Jane Watson Parker, Peter's new wife, about to be mugged. She was out walking in an attempt to ease her nerves as her husband has been missing for some time. Throughout the story, Mary Jane offers the reader the opportunity to consider the plight of those people left behind by loved ones engaged in dangerous jobs. The spouse of a police officer, firefighter, or soldier surely has nights of uncertainty and fear. Comfort can be found, one hopes, in the company of friends and family. Mary Jane has no such community, for no one knows her husband is Spider-Man. Her fears and nightmares she carries, and faces, alone.

Her hopes, momentarily raised when Kraven/Spider-Man leaps to her rescue, are darkened when she witnesses the brutality of his assault. She knows instantly that whoever is in that costume is not Peter. Of course this only leaves her to continue to speculate, with the worst scenarios her imagination can conjure, where he is. Her desperation will cause her to reach out to Joe Robertson, one of Peter's coworkers. She nearly admits that Peter is Spider-Man, and she fears he is either dead or insane. Both options would explain the recent viciousness exhibited by Spider-Man, which by this point include killing someone. She can't bring herself to confide in Joe and leaves his apartment in a rush. Joe is left confused but contemplative, as he looks at a headline in the daily paper that reads, "Spider-Man Goes Berserk!"

Kraven's rampage, however, has not brought him the final victory he seeks. He must find a way to prove his superiority yet again. To do so, he decides to hunt down, as Spider-Man, the cannibalistic half-man, half-rodent creature known as Vermin. Spider-Man has never defeated Vermin in single combat. He only defeated him in a previous encounter because he had the aid of Captain America. To defeat Vermin will be the final, most important test. In a truly violent slugfest, Kraven defeats Vermin and claims to have become not merely Spider-Man's superior, but superior to the Spider as well. By supplanting the Spider, he claims to have gained special knowledge of fate and humankind. He is triumphant and rises from the sewers where the battle took place, the unconscious man-beast in his arms.

Meanwhile, Peter Parker struggles to achieve his own victory. The rifle Kraven shot him with contained an even more powerful drug, enabling the Hunter to bury him alive. As Peter slowly regains consciousness, he hallucinates, having visions of meeting Ned Leeds, a dead friend. As Ned melts away, Peter balls up in horror envisioning himself as nothing more than a spider. But one constant continues to interrupt his dark fantasies, his love for Mary Jane. Flowing beneath, nearly unperceivable but ever present and waiting to be called upon, is his capacity for love and compassion. As his spider self is gutted by demonic shadows, Peter crawls forth declaring himself a coward even as he fights.

The spider image and shadows gone, Peter crawls alone through a dark tunnel. He is not alone, however, with thoughts of Mary Jane becoming increasingly intense—the gentle stream of his compassion now a raging river pushing him forward beyond his fear, beyond his perceived cowardice, and out of the grave itself as he emerges from the ground, shaken but unbroken. His unease becomes rage as he discovers he has been buried alive for two weeks. While he desires to confront Kraven, he needs to return to his apartment to see Mary Jane, his wife and his strength. He wants to be Peter Parker—not a hero and not a spider, just a man. Their reunion is not long, as Peter knows Kraven is out there waiting for him. As much as he wants to be "just" Peter Parker, he simply cannot. He is, whether he or his wife approve, a hero. He can no more stop being Spider-Man than he can stop loving his wife. Mary Jane protests but recognizes that not only is this what her husband does, but it is who he is—and one of the reasons she loves him. Alone again, she awaits his return hoping for the best and dreading the worst.

When Spider-Man enters Kraven's mansion, he wastes little times before attacking his tormentor. The fight consists of only a single blow as Kraven declares he will take a hundred blows, for there is no reason to fight. The demon Spider has been defeated and

Kraven realizes that Spider-Man is just a man, one in need of the illumination that only he can provide. Kraven briefly summarizes his actions over the past two weeks and invites Spider-Man to join him in his basement.

As he descends to the catacombs beneath his home, Kraven's thoughts reveal he is feeling a deep peace he has not felt in some time. He may even feel happiness. Spider-Man knows no such feeling at this point. He is shocked, however, to see Vermin held captive in an electrified cage. When Kraven explains Vermin's role in their drama, Peter grows increasingly angry. Kraven takes his anger as a sign that the Spider that possesses Peter, but is not Peter, is so enraged that it no longer has power over Kraven.

Kraven then frees Vermin, goading the man-beast into attacking Spider-Man. This is the final test that will provide Kraven the final evidence of his superiority over Spider-Man. As he watches the fight, he begins to feel tired and old, the peace he sought for so long already fading away. As Vermin gains the upper hand on Spider-Man, Kraven intervenes, chasing the vile creature off with a whip and knife. Spider-Man weakly protests as Kraven allows Vermin to flee into the night. He is afraid, rightfully so, that Vermin will kill someone. Kraven's thoughts reveal both a personal lack of concern for Vermin's potential actions and an understanding of what will transpire next. As Vermin leaves he thinks, "The Spider is alive in him; there will undoubtedly be others to rise up in opposition." One would be hard pressed, especially in a world of superheroes and vigilantes, to disagree with Kraven's unspoken assessment.

Kraven turns his attention to Spider-Man. He helps him off the floor and upstairs to the living quarters. Kraven considers the fact that his Spider is finally gone and sees Spider-Man as only a man—and a good one at that. He even considers the possibility that he has been Spider-Man's Spider. As Spider-Man leaves the mansion to pursue Vermin, he promises to return to deal with Kraven. Kraven watches him leave contemplating what a privilege it has been having Spider-Man as a foe, a rival, and as his personal Spider. His sense of honor restored, Kraven wraps himself in a plush housecoat. He positions a picture of himself as a child with his parents in front of a coffin. Standing over it, he shoots himself and falls into the coffin, blood rolling down his family portrait.

Kraven's suicide is immaterial to Spider-Man as he seeks out Vermin. He descends into the sewers where he battles the man-beast to a virtual standoff. Spider-Man abruptly changes tactics and flees the sewers, enticing Vermin to follow him. Unthinkingly, Vermin leaves the sewer to catch his quarry. Vermin does not realize that it is morning. The sewer-dwelling, nocturnal hunter is terrified of the daily bustle of New York City and blinded by the light of day. Spider-Man scoops him up, binds him with webs, and leaves Vermin whimpering at the feet of two policemen. He promises to enlist the aid of the scientific genius Reed Richards to revert Vermin back to human form. Spider-Man dismisses Vermin's protests emphasizing that he is going to help the former scientist whether he wants help or not. The police are amazed that Spider-Man, after all Kraven put him through, still has the capacity to care about Vermin's well-being.

This is where we see that Peter's compassionate core is left undisturbed and perhaps strengthened by his ordeal. His compassion gives him the willingness to pay respect to a simple criminal, to shake off the effects of Kraven's drugs, to crawl from the horrors of being buried alive, and to seek to aid one who seems beyond redemption. It is a quiet but seemingly inexhaustible reservoir of strength. Kraven's obsessions lack this boundless quality. His obsession, once satisfied, leaves him empty and purposeless. His personal quest for redemption on his own terms fulfilled, he takes his life. In the end, he is self-absorbed and unwilling to extend a sense of purpose beyond himself. His intensity has burned itself out, consuming him in the process. Peter's compassion, manifested in a far less intense manner, sustains him in times of crisis and inoculates him against lingering bitterness.

Spider-Man is slightly confused by the policeman's comment, for how could this man possibly know what he has been through? He does not realize the police are in possession of Kraven's final confession. The confession clears Spider-Man of all possible wrongdoings that could be attributed to him when Kraven usurped his identity. The morning paper's lead story is a full report of Kraven's confession.

Peter has not read the paper, and doing so is a distant thought. He just wants to go home where Mary Jane has stayed up all night waiting for him. She embraces him as he returns home, his small apartment filled with love that never had a chance to enter Kraven's palatial mansion.

# Part II

Wisdom and Myth

# CHAPTER 7

## Green Lantern and Captain Marvel

These two heroes, the Green Lantern and Captain Marvel, are both extremely powerful members of the Justice League. The Justice League is a team of superheroes who work together to confront threats too great for a single hero to overcome. The membership in the league is fluid, with regular and reserve members. The reserves are called upon when the regular members are unavailable due to their own adventures and lives.

Beyond being members of the Justice League, Captain Marvel and Green Lantern have something else in common—a shared theme in their origins as heroes. Both men have had their power granted to them by an outside agent. This is different from heroes like Batman or the Green Arrow (who disciplined themselves), Superman or any mutant in the X-Men (whose powers are natural), or Spider-Man and the Hulk (both gained their powers through accidents).

The outside agents who chose Marvel and Lantern are very diverse in origin. A dying bearer of a Green Lantern ring chose Hal Jordan to be the next Green Lantern. In the comic universe of Hal Jordan, there is an intergalactic police force called the Green Lantern Corps, led by a race called the Guardians. The Guardians grant rings of tremendous power to individuals (who become Green Lanterns) and charge these individuals with protecting various sections of the universe. The ring can create any weapon, tool, or object the bearer can imagine. The ring also grants the ability to fly and survive the harsh conditions of outer space. The only limits on the ring's power are that it needs to be recharged every twenty-four hours (by using a glowing, green lantern) and the imagination of the individual Green Lantern. It is fair to say that Hal Jordan possesses one of the most powerful weapons in the universe.

Whereas Hal Jordan's story has a strong connection to science fiction, the emergence of Captain Marvel is linked to myth and fantasy. A mysterious stranger visits Billy Batson, a young, orphaned teen-aged boy. The stranger is, in actuality, a wizard named Shazam. The wizard grants Billy tremendous powers so he can fight injustice and mankind's weakness.

When Billy says the wizard's name, a bolt of magical lightning strikes him, and he becomes Captain Marvel. Captain Marvel's face resembles what Billy's face will likely look like as an adult, but Marvel is as far from being an adult Billy as an oak tree is from being an acorn.

Each letter in the wizard's name represents a mythic power granted to Captain Marvel. Marvel possesses the wisdom of Solomon, the strength of Hercules, the stamina of Atlas, the power of Zeus, the courage of Achilles, and the speed of Mercury. This fusion of attributes makes Captain Marvel worthy of carrying the moniker, "the world's most powerful mortal." There is, however, one last attribute Marvel possesses that is not part of the magic word Shazam —Billy's innocence. Marvel maintains a childlike innocence even as he is imbued with mythic power and wisdom. It is this trait, perhaps, that prevents Marvel from misusing his power.

The unwillingness to misuse the power they have been granted is another commonality that Captain Marvel and Green Lantern share. Both men could, in theory, use their powers any way they wanted, but both choose to do good over and over again. Consider this thought posed to Socrates by Glaucon in *The Republic*, "Suppose now that there were two such magic rings [rings capable of making the wearer invisible], and the just put on one of them and the unjust the other; no man can be imagined to be of such an iron nature that he would stand fast in justice. No man would keep his hands off what was not his own when he could safely take what he liked out of the market, or go into houses and lie with any one at his pleasure, or kill or release from prison whom he would, and in all respects be like a God among men."[23]

Glaucon is challenging Socrates' contention that people will act good for both intrinsic and extrinsic reasons. Glaucon introduces a more skeptical perspective: that people generally do good for extrinsic reasons. If the fear of punishment were lifted (if someone could "be like a God among men"), any individual would act in his or her own self-interests (as no one has "the iron nature" necessary to "stand fast in justice"). Glaucon also posits the idea that acting in an unjust manner leads to greater happiness. Socrates' counter-argument is quite long, as it would have to be, for there is strong supporting evidence of Glaucon's argument readily available in any society.

Captain Marvel offers a literary personification of one aspect of Socrates' response. Socrates contends that the harmonious balancing of the various aspects of the "soul" leads to happiness, "the just man does not permit the several elements within him to interfere with one another, or any of them to do the work of others … when he has bound all these together, and is no longer many, but has become one entirely temperate and perfectly adjusted nature, then he proceeds to act … just and good action, and the knowledge which presides over it, wisdom."[24] If individuals' inner lives are not harmonious, this imbalance will, in varying degrees, negatively affect their disposition, their decision making, and, inevitably, their relationships.

Marvel easily balances six (seven when we include Billy's innocence) very powerful attributes within himself, and the personal harmony he achieves is evident to many who encounter him. It can even be inspirational. When reforming the Justice League, Batman, Superman, and Wonder Woman debated which heroes to invite. Batman was very quick to proclaim he wanted Captain Marvel in the new League. Wonder Woman accused Batman of thinking Marvel was easy to control and therefore would make a good subordinate.

Batman shook this off, not arguing but merely stating that she should not question the Wisdom of Solomon. Superman, who did not interrupt their exchange, held a different and likely more accurate view. He believed Batman wanted Captain Marvel because he was good. Not a good fighter, but just good. Batman, made somewhat dark and distrusting by nature and events, liked having some authentic, unadulterated goodness around.

It is also important to note that the first of Marvel's attributes, the one Batman alluded to in an effort to silence Wonder Woman, is the wisdom of Solomon. Wisdom is the exact virtue that Socrates contends, "presides over" the "perfectly adjusted nature" of one who takes "just and good action." Two questions must be asked; is wisdom alone enough to ensure "just and good action," and can wisdom take root in anyone, or are prerequisites required?

Wisdom requires people to focus on the big picture instead of the claims of the present moment. To embrace wisdom, therefore, requires a predisposition to accept the existence of a bigger picture – a picture beyond the ego or desires of the individual.[25] The idea that people struggle to see a big picture beyond their personal wants and desires is hardly new. Machiavelli noted in his book *The Prince* that people are rather simple and most concerned with their "present necessities."[26]

Wisdom, therefore, seems to be a form of knowing that is at odds with our conscious, deliberately thinking mind. We can always use present necessities (be they personal prestige, present circumstances, or the desire for notoriety) to justify the actions we take. Wisdom demands we move beyond such justifications to a deeper and more inclusive vision of the world. The fact that Captain Marvel accepts the wisdom of Solomon without reservations is not merely due to the magician's spell, but also because Billy Batson's innocence is a part of Marvel. Batson's innocence allows the necessary disposition that enables wisdom to be followed. Wisdom, conversely, allows Marvel to make good decisions and maintain Billy's innocence by virtue of the good choices he makes. It is not, therefore, the innocence of youth that people should outgrow but the arrogance of expertise that effectively prevents the growth of wisdom. This may be why Shazam chose Billy in the first place: because he still had a touch of innocence.

Hal Jordan, however, was not an innocent youth when he gained the ring that made him Green Lantern. Jordan is presented as fearless, someone who was comfortable with the power granted him because he did not fear its power to corrupt him. This description leaves out the fact that the dying alien who granted Hal the ring also sought someone who was exceptionally honest as well as fearless.

Honesty, therefore, may also be seen as requisite to allow wisdom into one's life. Granted, Hal Jordan is not written as a particularly wise character, but he does not allow the power he wields to corrupt him, and there is wisdom in such a choice. Corruption often requires one to believe the lies of others and the ability to deceive oneself. Someone of exceptional honesty would see through the justifications created by the desire to fulfill present necessities and act in a more conscientious and judicious manner.

Curiously, Batman, who has tremendous respect for Captain Marvel, has a certain disdain for Green Lantern. This is because Batman feels Green Lantern does not use the ring to its full potential. Hal Jordan could do almost anything with the ring but tends to limit its uses to making simple shapes and tools. But could it be that Hal Jordan intuitively recognizes that using the ring to eradicate world hunger would open the possibility for using the ring to reshape other fundamental "problems" to coincide with Jordan's worldview? Could Jordan not so much fear the possibility of being corrupted by the power he wields as be wise enough to see which roads lead to corruption, so he chooses not to walk them? Jordan's wisdom seems understated, manifesting itself as an underlying disposition that inoculates him from corruption.

It is not merely conjecture that allows these conclusions about Captain Marvel and Green Lantern to be made. The universe in which they live presents the path they did not take in the form of their arch-nemeses, Black Adam and Sinestro. Black Adam was born Teth-Adam during the nineteenth dynasty of ancient Egypt. The wizard Shazam granted Teth-Adam the power of six gods, but the power corrupted him. Or, perhaps more realistically, the power made it possible for Teth-Adam to fulfill all his present desires (including overthrowing the pharaoh), and he consciously decides to ignore any wisdom the spell granted him.

Sinestro was once considered the greatest member of the Green Lantern Corps but used his ring to place the planets in his jurisdiction under his complete, dictatorial control. The Guardians stripped Sinestro of his ring and banished him to a despotic planet. The inhabitants of the planet, however, despised the Guardians and created a replica yellow ring that had all of the characteristics of a Green Lantern ring without the need to be recharged every twenty-four hours. Sinestro now seeks to destroy the Lantern Corps, but in particular, he hates Hal Jordan. Jordan is sometimes regarded as the greatest of the Green Lanterns, an honorary title Sinestro previously held, and the narcissistic despot is obsessed with killing the man who usurped his position.* Therefore, while wisdom helps Green Lantern and Captain Marvel become heroes, vainglorious pride and the unrelenting need to satisfy personal desires for power and acclaim make Sinestro and Black Adam villains—more than merely rivals, but warnings to Captain Marvel and Green Lantern what they could have become.

---

* Adding to the animosity is the fact that Sinestro trained Hal Jordan when he became a Green Lantern.

# CHAPTER 8

## *Justice* and the Fulfillment of Wisdom

In the twelve-issue series *Justice*, the Justice League faces a dire challenge. One of Superman's foes, an extraterrestrial cyborg named Braniac with a profound hatred of sentient life, has devised a strategy to destroy Earth and provide himself with a population of once-human slaves. He steals technology from the brilliant criminal Siavana and enhances it to create microscopic nanobytes. This technology, when ingested by people, makes them susceptible to Braniac's suggestions and promotes healing of lost limbs or damaged organs. These "healings," however, are only the first signs of a continuous process. The nanobytes will eventually overwhelm the host body, turning it into an organic cyborg, completely subservient to Braniac.

Braniac, realizing that he will need the aid of others to complete his strategy, infects various super-villains with the nanobytes, enabling him to form a Legion of Doom, with himself as the unquestioned leader. The Legion of Doom launches a series of ambushes against various members of the Justice League, incapacitating them. Simultaneously, they present their vision for the future to the world. Some people will accept the invitation to live in intergalactic cities, each city governed by a member of the Legion of Doom. The individuals who become citizens of these cities will eventually be overcome by the nano technology and become organic cyborgs. The members of the Legion of Doom do not realize that they have been infected as well and will eventually succumb to the microscopic parasites.

Lex Luther, who is the only member of the Legion of Doom unaffected by the nanobytes, has been led to believe that only the most industrious people will remain on earth. Sloth, laziness, and apathy will cease to be, and humanity will have the opportunity to reach its full potential. Braniac, however, has no desire to see the human race thrive and has an ulterior plan. Seizing control of nuclear weapons across the planet, he will bring nuclear holocaust to Earth when he departs with his unwitting slave population.

During the course of this saga Green Lantern and Captain Marvel exhibit different aspects of wisdom. Marvel, already possessing the wisdom of Solomon, reveals to the reader what one may act like when they have integrated wisdom into their being. Conversely, the Green Lantern makes it clear that sometimes it requires difficult trials and confronting unconscious weaknesses to first conceptualize and then attempt to actualize the realizations of wisdom. Wisdom, therefore, is far more than facts to be learned, but also truths that are experienced and tested in the laboratory of one's life. Wisdom, in this context, is seen as an unfolding process in which one may or may not be seriously involved.

Both heroes poignantly display their wisdom in conflict with Black Adam and Sinestro, arch-nemeses who also act as shadows to Captain Marvel and Green Lantern.[27] While most super-villains reflect the opposite qualities of the heroes they confront (the Joker an agent of chaos juxtaposed with Batman's intense attempts to bring about order), Black Adam's and Sinestro's physical appearance suggests the shadow relationship. Black Adam's outfit, for example, is a mirror image of Captain Marvel's, merely rendered in black instead of red. Sinestro's garb is also suggestive of his past as a member of the Green Lantern Corps, as is his power ring. In the pages of *Justice,* Green Lantern is more threatened with being overwhelmed by his shadow than Captain Marvel, which may be seen as appropriate because profound wisdom is an attribute Marvel always possesses.

Green Lantern's confrontation with his shadow begins in a devastating manner. Using alien technology known as a "boom tube," Sinestro teleports Green Lantern to a starless region of the universe. Green Lantern's ring, programmed to communicate with its bearer and possessing the vast knowledge of the universe that the Guardians have, informs Hal Jordan that the region of the universe they are in now is completely unknown to the Guardians. The ring does know that Jordan lacks the "will" to use the ring to create another boom tube to bring him home. The rings charge will eventually run out, and Hal Jordan will die in space.

Facing the prospect of his death, Hal Jordan has the ring reduce him to "a series of electronic impulses" so he can be absorbed and maintained inside the ring. The ring concludes this will work and will enable Hal Jordan to survive for an indefinite length of time. Unfortunately, the reality exists that the ring may never be found and Jordan would, in essence, be lost forever—his consciousness alive within the ring. Jordan decides to allow his essence to be integrated with the ring, a decision that quickly threatens to destroy him but could also grant him a greater degree of wisdom.

The process begins with a particular despair, a combination of self-pity and resentment. This starting point of wisdom is found in other literary works, including J. R. R. Tolkien's *The Fellowship of the Ring*. Frodo Baggins, upon learning the immense ramifications of possessing the ring, wishes that history itself could be changed to accommodate his desires. He wishes Bilbo Baggins never found the ring, he wishes he never came into possession of it, and he expresses frustration that the wizard Gandalf gave it to him.[28] Hal Jordan mirrors the crestfallen Frodo, asking, "Why did Abin Sur give me the ring …? Why give me the power of a god?"

Wisdom, therefore, may well begin with the painful realization of how limited one is, despite years of heroic achievements (in Green Lantern's case) or the accumulation of years (Frodo was thirty-three when he received the ring and forty-seven at the onset of his great quest in The Lord of the Rings trilogy). It is worth noting that both these characters experience this sense of inadequacy because their worlds have been expanded by a challenging experience—an experience that revealed the existence of their limitations. The limitations always existed, but they were never brought to the fore. Green Lantern, now feeling exposed, attempts to exert his will on the situation. He uses the ring to create a nonthreatening environment.

This reaction is another step on his quest for wisdom, denial of the need to expand. His response to his certainty that he can handle any situation stripped away, Jordan attempts to regain the illusion of control. He is, in actuality, retreating to a simpler world by using the power of the ring to create a city in which to live. He requests that the ring makes elevators shake like they are old and play Muzak versions of songs when he is in them. His life has been abruptly shaken, and he seeks to find comfort in old patterns and recognizable features from calmer times. This approach does not work, for all he is doing is creating the illusion of serenity in an attempt to ignore his dire circumstance. Illusions, however, eventually fade, allowing the unwanted reality to be revealed yet again. Hal Jordan's illusions fade when he attempts to create people in the city. He is frustrated by the fact that the moment he stops looking at these "citizens," they cease to exist. He contemplates the possibility of abandoning the world inside the ring and returning to space and the countdown to his death. His inability to find solace through control and illusion causes him to approach the dangerous realm of purposeless acquiescence.

Green Lantern refuses to give in to his grief and begins to partake in an important activity. Using the ring to create physical representations of his memories, he relives and analyzes events from his past. In doing so, he confronts key components of his self-image. This self-image, which can be called our "I" self or ego, serves a valuable purpose: it serves as a type of manager that helps people navigate their way through the world as they age and develop. A dilemma occurs when people identify the ego (the manager) as the entirety of who they are. When the ego proves to be inadequate at managing certain situations, people believe themselves inadequate. When the ego is shattered, the belief that one is nothing becomes a strong possibility, primarily because of the lack of realization that people have a deeper grounding or being than ego. A shattered ego, therefore, could lead to a greater sense of being than our old self-image would ever allow. Before expanding one's being can occur, the honest assessment of the "I" self must be undertaken.[29]

In Green Lantern's case, the trait he identifies as being integral to his ego is fearlessness. Fearlessness was the very characteristic that drew the alien Abin Sur to grant him the ring initially. This obviously makes for a strong connection, for it could be said that Hal Jordan would not be a Green Lantern if he were not fearless. The memories he chooses to confront reveal a specific kind of fearlessness, the limitations of this fearlessness, the possible root of evil, and the possibility of finding the greater potentialities of his being.

The first memory the reader sees is Hal Jordan ending a romantic relationship with a woman named Carol. He states that because he is fearless, he is not afraid of losing anyone or anything, including Carol. He concludes that self-centeredness exists at the core of his fearlessness. This theme runs through subsequent reflections about his relationship with his brothers, both as an adult and a child. Self-centeredness is a trait easily identified with Sinestro. It is what enabled him to conquer planets and subjugate populations without remorse. It is what drives his hatred for Hal Jordan, for some consider Jordan the greatest Green Lantern, an honor Sinestro once held. Hal Jordan, through his exile, comes face to face with a trait that could have made him follow Sinestro's path, a path he may have followed if he was not forced to confront his self-image.

In evaluating his self-image, Hal Jordan also allows a glimpse into the nature of his fearlessness. In many ways, his courage, although admirable, is lacking in maturity. His fearlessness gave him "freedom from" but rarely "freedom to."[30] Hal feels freedom from the need for relationships with either Carol or his brothers. He is free from the need for companionship, content to follow his dreams and go "farther and faster" than anyone has before. His deep identification with fearlessness granting him "freedom from," however, has cut him off from the deeper, more mature form of freedom, the "freedom to." The freedom to let someone into the intimate recesses of your life, the freedom to care about affiliations, the freedom to mature, even the freedom to fear the possibility that traits possessed by an arch-rival are also present in oneself.

The realizations Hal Jordan has within the ring do not make him a wise man. For people to truly be looked upon as wise, they must, on a consistent basis, act on their wisdom. Such activity, the actualizing his realizations, is not something Jordan can do, trapped as he is within the ring. Moreover, this shift, from realization to actualization, is not easily accomplished. Consider the life of John Newton, the man who wrote the lyrics to *Amazing Grace*. In 1748, at the age of twenty-three, Newton was returning to England after delivering slaves to the New World. He was comfortable in this profession, and any discomfort with conscience was set aside. A storm struck his ship, and Newton prayed for God's mercy. Surviving the storm, the ship proceeded home, and Newton began his conversion to Christianity. He also began the process of actualizing wisdom.

In his conversion process, he altered certain behaviors, his wisdom leading to actions. The behaviors he changed were the use of profanity, alcohol, and indulging in gambling. He did not, however, find any reason to quit his job as a slave trader, and he continued to make voyages on slave ships. He attempted to allay any guilt he felt by being humane to the slaves on his ships. He was nicer, more Christian, than other slave traders, and this was "good enough." He could break from certain bad habits, but not the job with which he was familiar. Instead, he performed some mental gymnastics and convinced himself that his more enlightened approach to slave trading was a noble alternative to other slave traders' behavior. In this example, it is clear that a realization may take time to reach the depths of being, where it can truly exert transformative power, if it is allowed to sink in at all.

Newton continued his career, but was increasingly aware of the division between his ideals and his actions. It was when he lost the ability to outthink his flaws that his spiritual ideals sank from his head, past his heart and into his very being. A kindly slave trader was still a slave trader, just as a charismatic drug dealer is still a drug dealer, ruining lives to live theirs. It was only when such realities became clear to Newton that he began to feel the regret and shame of his life's decisions (a realization) and worked as an abolitionist (an actualization).

This process begins for Hal when the Phantom Stranger pulls him from the ring. The Phantom Stranger is an enigmatic member of the Justice League with immense paranormal powers. He is not allowed to interfere with conflicts directly but can act as a guide for other heroes. One of the first statements Hal makes upon seeing the Phantom Stranger is admitting that he is afraid. After a brief discussion about the difference between justice and vengeance (begun because Hal expresses a desire to kill Sinestro), the Stranger emphasizes that they must hurry back to Earth because the world needs its hero.

Hal corrects the Stranger, stating that the world needs the Justice League, "almost as much" as he does. Arguments can be made concerning whether this statement is a realization or an actualization, but it is clear that Hal Jordan recognizes he is free to accept the other league members into his life rather than free from the need to engage completely with them. He is not bigger than the League, despite the astounding powers granted to him as a Green Lantern.[31] The Phantom Stranger uses his power of teleportation to return to Earth, reuniting Green Lantern with the rest of the Justice League. He makes the observation that, due to his ordeal in exile, Hal Jordan may actually become the greatest Green Lantern someday.

As the story unfolds, the Justice League becomes embroiled in a melee with the Legion of Doom. In the midst of the chaos, Green Lantern is granted the opportunity to face Sinestro. Engaged as he is, Jordan also witnesses the wisdom of Captain Marvel on full display in a struggle with Black Adam. Black Adam has been weakened by the touch of Parasite, a member of the Legion of Doom. He stands before Captain Marvel, scornful and defiant. He accuses Marvel of wanting to see him in a weakened state, implying his rival must take some pleasure in the situation. The feelings Black Adam attempts to ascribe to Captain Marvel are little more than projections of his own desire to have Captain Marvel at his mercy.

Marvel's answer reveals the deep difference between he and his rival, as well as the difference between himself and most other people. Lifting Black Adam by the neck, he explains, "I don't want to see anyone like this. I hate to see anyone twisted by hate. Or given form and limitation by want. You could have been a great man." Captain Marvel has no desire to lord over Black Adam or celebrate a victory. Rather, we see him filled with remorse that Adam has been corrupted and, he speaks with compassion, even as he seeks to defeat his rival. Black Adam, seeking to be freed from Marvel's grip, says he can't breathe. Marvel says he will let Adam go if he says his magic word and reverts to his mortal form. Adam rejects the idea, proclaiming he has not been in "that form" for a long time. That, according to Marvel, is Black Adam's problem. He has been the powerhouse villain for so long, he has lost touch with the gifts that being simply human grants. Marvel informs Black Adam that surrendering to his mortal form may free him, not just from the Herculean hold on his throat, but from the evil that grips his heart. This is the victory Captain Marvel seeks—one not merely over the enemy before him, but over evil itself. Do words possess the magic needed to bring about this victory?

Green Lantern, witnessing the wisdom of Solomon expressed by Captain Marvel, continues his struggle with Sinestro. Eventually, he gains the upper hand, and Sinestro realizes he is about to be defeated. He goads the Green Lantern, spitefully exhorting him to claim vengeance. Hal Jordan claims victory but states that he does not seek vengeance, only justice. The trouncing of Sinestro and Black Adam does not mean the heroes can claim success in their goal of stopping the master plan of Braniac. Braniac is still free, but fleeing Superman, who proves to be too difficult a foe. Before his capture, however, Braniac launches all the Earth's nuclear weapons. All human life on the planet is minutes away from extinction.

Green Lantern, however, has other plans. He flies into space, ignoring the ring's warning that its charge is nearly depleted. In space he encounters other members of the Green

Lantern Corps whom he had summoned with his ring. The Green Lanterns use their rings to capture all of the nuclear missiles and throw them into the Sun. Hal Jordan does not initially witness the capturing of the missiles, as he is being saved and his ring recharged by a member of the Corps. As he is rescued, Hal Jordan muses, "I knew you'd come when I called. I did not fear. I hoped." Perhaps this is the greatest freedom granted by fearlessness, the freedom to hope. Not a hope for personal acclaim, like being considered the greatest Green Lantern, but for acceptance into "an ever-expanding community in the service of justice." And perhaps the hope that such a community can find the necessary magic words to make the threat of nuclear holocaust disappear in the real world just as the Justice League did in the pages of *Justice*.

# CHAPTER 9

## Thor—Marvel's Mythic Hero

Comic books can be said to reflect myth, but one hero in particular is lifted directly from mythology, the Norse god of thunder, Thor. Although Thor's persona and adventures are creations of the writers and artists at Marvel, a great deal of Norse mythology has been introduced in this long-running series. Furthermore, Thor occasionally engages in heroic quests that lead him into contact with the gods of other pantheons. His most common interaction is with Greek gods, although he does battle the Egyptian god Seth (also spelled Set) when the Egyptian god of darkness and chaos declares war on Asgard, the home of the Norse gods. Thor's stature and tremendous power as a god also allow confrontation with creatures of pure evil, like the demon Mephisto.

Thor's run as a character in the Marvel universe began in 1966 and continues to this day. The series is ripe with fascinating tales and parallels to the mythology that inspired it. This chapter focuses on three areas of comparison: Thor being sent away from his home to learn an important character lesson, Thor as protector of the human race, and stories inspired by the myth of Ragnarok. Ragnarok is an apocalyptic battle between the forces of good and evil. During Ragnarok, Thor engages his greatest enemy, the world serpent Jormungand, for the last time.

When introduced in Marvel Comics, Thor was in a state of exile on Earth. The exile was not merely a question of geography but one of physicality as well. His father, Odin, exiled Thor because he was deemed arrogant and lacking humility. Thor's essence was trapped within the body of Donald Blake, a partially lame physician. Blake was a creation of Odin, not a person chosen to act as a vessel through which the thunder god would experience life. Simply put, Blake was Thor in a mortal form. Blake had no knowledge of his divine creator or of the essence of Thor within him. For ten years, Thor lived as Donald Blake, persevering through his disability and learning to aid others as a skilled physician.

When Odin determined that Thor had learned the lessons he needed, he planted a desire in Blake to travel to Norway. His visit coincides, naturally, with an alien invasion. Fleeing the aliens, Donald Blake becomes trapped in a cave. He finds a wooden stick in the cave, unaware that it is enchanted. The walking stick is actually Thor's powerful magic hammer, Mjolnir.[*] When Blake becomes discouraged by his inability to escape the cave, he angrily slams the cane against a boulder. This action causes him to transform into Thor and the cane to become Mjolnir. Thor easily escapes the cave and drives off the alien invasion.

Although this story is a Marvel creation, parallels can be drawn between it and Norse mythology. Thor is the son of Odin and Jord, the ancient goddess of the Earth. The Marvel universe uses the same lineage for Thor, although Jord is referred to as Gaea. Gaea is based on the Greek goddess of the earth, Gaia. In the Nordic myths, the young Thor exhibits terrible rage and can be very dangerous. He is given to two foster parents, Vingnir and Hlora, who teach him to temper his anger. Both stories consist of Thor needing to learn a lesson that he could not learn at home.

In the comics, he is exiled to Earth, whereas in the Nordic myths, he is given to wise foster parents who successfully teach him what he needs to learn. Both stories also have consequences, for Thor in the myths is well aware of the debt he owes his foster parents. To honor them, he assumes the names Hlorrida and Vingthor, two of many names used to address Thor.[32] In the Marvel universe, Thor becomes deeply attached to Midgard (Earth) and mortals—partially because of his mother, but also because of his Donald Blake persona. A decade spent on Earth, struggling as mortals struggle, leaves Thor with a great deal of admiration for the trials, shortcomings, and glory of being mortal. Thor will split his time between Asgard and Earth, continuing to assume the guise of Blake and maintaining the physician's New York practice.[*]

Thor's affinity for Midgard in the Marvel universe can also be found in his mythic roots. Thor lived in a massive palace called Bilskirnir, which contained more than five hundred halls. The sprawling palace was used to accommodate peasants, farmers, and small landowners after they died. In Norse mythology, Thor was the patron god of the peasant class, putting him at socioeconomic odds with his father, Odin, who championed kings, poets, and warriors—the nobly born.[33]

The tension found between father and son in the myths also appears in the comics. Odin often demands Thor pay more attention to the dangers that threaten Asgard, while Thor demands the freedom to act as the protector of Midgard and its people. When this freedom is denied, the rebellious son will often depart Asgard anyway, leaving behind a father disappointed in his son's decision and proud of his son's strength.

Thor's affinity for mortals is revealed in both grand adventures and small interactions. In one episode, Thor witnesses a purse snatching and intervenes. In an action that can only be described as overkill, Thor sends a lightning bolt crashing in front of the fleeing thieves, sending them toppling to the ground. He then emerges from the middle of the storm clouds he has summoned, brandishing Mjolnir as if confronting giants attacking Asgard. Thor's dramatic entrance, however, gives way to a search for human dignity.

He tells the thieves they face a grave choice between a life of nobility and degradation. The leader of the thieves is dumfounded, inquiring if Thor intends to do nothing. Thor responds by stating he will face his own choice once the robbers make theirs. Although this undoubtedly puts pressure on the criminals, Thor articulates that it does not remove the

---

* Mjolnir is the spelling used in Marvel Comics. Alternate spellings include Miolnir and Mjollnir.

* The Donald Blake persona was written out of the Thor series in the mid-eighties. With the apparent death of all Asgardians (and the actual death of Odin) in a recent story line, he merged with Thor again.

power of choice that the men possess. The purse is returned to the woman, but Thor is well aware of the impact his presence had on this moment. His final words to the leader of the purse-snatchers are, "If indeed heartfelt, thy choice is most wise."

In this moment, Thor is seen expressing concern for the human dignity of both the victim and perpetrators of a crime. The return of the purse is not the only outcome Thor desires. He is also focused on the path the young men are choosing to follow. While he burst on the scene like a storm, Thor also slowed the interaction down, allowing for reflection and action, as opposed to action alone. In doing so, he hopes to teach the young criminals the power of choice and the dangers of living under the delusion that people merely do what they have to without concern for the well-being of others.

Although this scene is small, it does not go unnoticed. Mephisto, the lord of an underworld, is most displeased. Mephisto is a demon who exists in a dimension connected to Earth, and he routinely tempts humans into evildoing so that they become residents of his world after they die. He states, "While man remains a mere educated savage, my ranks of the damned are swelled to overflowing." This may sound like the Judeo-Christian Satan, but Mephisto never claims to be that entity anymore than do any other rulers of various underworlds Thor visits.

In his rage, Mephisto directly entices a number of people to perform random acts of violence. His manipulations lead to the eruption of a riot. The growing disturbance attracts Thor and seeks to quell the mayhem. Thor's efforts fail as the ground erupts. The people fall helplessly into a dimensional vortex. Thor leaps into the chasm and finds himself in the lair of Mephisto. Mephisto expresses his loathing for Thor and the nobility he tries to inspire mortals to attain. He seeks to slay Thor with his hands and magic, but Thor asserts that Mephisto cannot kill him. Although Thor claims this because he is a god, the reader can extrapolate it is also because Thor is being used as a metaphor for goodness and nobility, just as Mephisto is a personification of evil and cruelty. The two forces are locked in a struggle that will not be decided by a slugfest in Mephisto's dark domain.

Mephisto has one last trick to play and he tempts Thor to hurl Mjolnir at him. The crushing hammer strikes true, but the target is an illusion. Mjolnir passes harmlessly through "Mephisto" and becomes imbedded in a wall holding the souls of the people from the riot. They clasp onto the hammer, preventing it from returning to Thor. Part of Odin's enchantment is the stipulation that if Thor should be separated from Mjolnir for more than sixty seconds, he reverts to Donald Blake, and Mjolnir becomes a walking stick. Mephisto cannot kill Thor, but Donald Blake may be a different matter.

Among the trapped souls is one of the purse-snatchers Thor encountered earlier in the story. Despite being captured by Mephisto, he exerts, again, the power of choice. Ripping the walking stick from the others, he tosses it to Blake, who becomes Thor. Thor strikes Mephisto with a furious blow and demands the demon acknowledge the action taken by one of his "claimed" souls. He also demands the release of all the rioters unfairly taken or promises to remain in the dimension and continue the battle.

Mephisto relents, and the battle ends. Mephisto points out that although he cannot slay Thor, the battle proved Thor could not slay him either. He sends Thor and the mortals back to Earth with a final, dire warning: "Work your noble ways upon the woeful, desperate millions of Earth while I work my dark ways ... never farther than a whisper from all the men and women who have ever pondered evil."

The struggle of good versus evil is hardly settled by the end of the story, nor is the question of who is tempting humans to betray their true nature, Thor or Mephisto. Does Thor guide people from their true nature and toward nobility, or does Mephisto cause people to violate their nature and choose evil? What is human nature? That is a question that will take more than a single comic to answer, but it can be used to start the conversation.

The story with Mephisto pits Thor against an alternate dimension incarnation of evil itself. Such a grand setting not only allows Thor to showcase his formidable power but allows for a triumph of the human will as well. Conversely, some stories keep Thor in Midgard to witness the tragedy of human shortcomings and mere glimpses of nobility.

In September 1981, Thor writer Doug Moench penned a short tale that addresses an issue still making news in the United States—tension between the police and the black community. The story opens with a black teen, Jimmy Sayers, shoplifting at a local store. The owner chases him to the street where a passing patrol car spots the disturbance and pursues the young boy.

The boy flees into an alley and the officers, now on foot, follow him. Jimmy slows down, placing his hand in his jacket as he turns to face the officers. The two men do not know the youth has a heart condition and is experiencing chest pains. One officer orders Jimmy to freeze, but the other goes much further. Assuming the boy is reaching for a concealed weapon, he opens fire.

Examining the fallen body, the officers discover Jimmy is unarmed. The officer who did not fire the shots recognizes that Jimmy is badly wounded and declares they need to bring him to the medical clinic a few blocks away. He fears the boy will die if they wait for an ambulance. Local residents see the two cops carrying the wounded boy to their squad car and become enraged. They taunt the cops—"What's the matter pigs—did he threaten you with a slingshot?"—and tell others of their outrage—"They shot that kid for no reason." As the police race off, their car is peppered with debris.

The clinic Jimmy is brought to is where Donald Blake works. Blake performs emergency surgery as a mob gathers in the streets. Just as the police officer acted on an assumption that Jimmy was armed, at least one member of the mob expresses an opinion that justifies his involvement. The rioter proclaims that the police couldn't even be bothered to bring the kid to a real hospital, only a local clinic. Painting the police as completely unsympathetic may make the rioter able to act violently without guilt, but it ignores the reason the police brought Jimmy to the local clinic. Although true it is unreasonable to assume that information is available, it is equally unreasonable to assume the police sat in the car and decided to bring Jimmy to the clinic for malicious reasons. The intent and compassion of the good officer is lost in the turmoil.

The situation intensifies when the rioters occupy the clinic. The leader of the mob reveals political savvy as he explains why the clinic needed to be taken. He does not want to interfere with the surgery, but he hopes this extreme action brings media attention so people can know about the needless shooting of thirteen-year-old Jimmy Sayers.

In surgery, Dr. Blake hears the noise outside the clinic and sends a nurse to find out what is happening. She does not get far, as the chief of staff enters the operating room and briefly tells everyone present about the riot outside and the occupation of the clinic. Riot police arrive on the scene and attempt, unsuccessfully, to talk the leader of the mob into leaving the clinic. He refuses, making another political statement as the crowd starts to chant, "Jimmy Sayers !" The media also arrives on the scene, adding another element to the chaos.

Inside, Donald Blake has removed the bullet from Jimmy's chest and sewn him up. Monitoring Jimmy's vitals is all he and the nurses can do. Checking a window he sees that the situation outside the clinic is growing worse. The police refuse to let anyone else enter the clinic, including Jimmy's mother. The mob responds by throwing bricks and bottles at the officers. Blake realizes lives may soon be lost outside the clinic. He decides to leave a nurse to monitor Jimmy as he transforms into Thor and attempts to subdue the crowd.

Thor attempts to calm the rising storm of violence by illuminating the dark destination to which hate and fear lead. While the choice of using Thor, given that Norse gods were unabashed in their use of violence, to make this argument may seem hypocritical, two points need to be raised. First we need to remind ourselves of Thor's role in the Marvel universe. As one who believes the best aspects of humanity are always accessible, Thor views the violence of the mob as a discredit to human nobility. From a practical standpoint, Thor also sees violence as incapable of helping solve any of the problems raised by the officer's actions. This fits well with the character of a Norseman who had "a large store of good sense" and even "delightful common sense."[34]

In this light, Thor's action can be seen not as forcing the words of nonviolence into a violent Norse god, but as Thor tapping into the common sense of the Norse. Consider this line from the *Elder Edda*, a collection of Nordic poetry and other literature:

> *I once was young and traveled alone.*
> *I met another and thought myself rich.*
> *Man is the joy of man.*
> *Be a friend to your friend.*
> *Give him laughter for laughter.*[35]

The ideal presented here is that man finds great joy in friendship. Friendship, not victory on the battlefield or violence, is identified as something that makes a man feel rich. What Thor views in the streets outside the clinic is the opposite of this ideal because hate and distrust reign supreme. This distrust and hate is aimed at Thor as he attempts to ease the situation.

When Thor calls the use of violence "folly" and asks the rhetorical questions, "Wilt thee fuel the fires of violence with more hate?" he is accused of siding with the police because he is white. The crowd and the police close in on each other, the police brandishing their nightsticks and the mob wielding whatever weapons are at hand. Repulsed, Thor hurls Mjolnir between the two enraged factions. Mjolnir is thrown with such force that a vortex forms behind it, pulling weapons from every hand. Mjolnir, as per its enchantment, returns to Thor's hand, leaving a collection of weapons at his feet. Not satisfied with this action, Thor strikes the ground, vaporizing the weapons and tearing the street asunder.

The fissure Thor created now separates the two combating sides. This action inspires one policeman to decry Thor for destroying public property. This could be seen as a legitimate complaint, but it is more a self-righteous proclamation as the police officer follows it up by asking, "Why doesn't he mind his own business? We can take care of this rabble ourselves!" The officer is far less concerned with the property damage than his own dam-aged ego, as Thor "interferes" when he is not needed. After all, the police had, despite the evidence, everything under control. His condescending reference to his opponents as "rabble" further reveals his sense of superiority. Others in the crowd refer to Thor as a maniac because of his action.

Thor rises above the crowd and continues his impromptu lesson on the limits of hate and violence. He points out that his act of violence merely inspired fear and anger. In the end, these are always the fruits of violence, regardless of what other outcomes accompany violent acts. Hovering above the crowd, Thor delivers his final statement, "Mistakes have been made on both sides, for thou art mortals and fallible, but mutual punishment for those mistakes is a false goal. Prevention of further mistakes is thy only goal—and mine as well!" These words can find echoes in the *Elder Edda*, "None so good that he has no faults, none so wicked that he is worth naught."[36]

The narration boxes inform the reader that some in the crowd begin to become re-ceptive to Thor's message, but Jimmy's mother does not seem to hear. She is quietly weep-ing that she wants to see her boy and is very concerned about his bad heart. Her worst fears are confirmed when, in the operating room, the heart monitor flatlines. The attend-ing nurse and Dr. Jefferies attempt—and fail—to revive Jimmy. The leader of the rioters emerges from the clinic and announces that Jimmy Sayers is dead.

Four distinct reactions follow the grim announcement. Thor, who believed Donald Blake had saved Jimmy's life, is shocked. The police officer responsible for the shooting falls to his knees and screams his guilt to the heavens. Jimmy's mother is struck by profound grief. Some members of the crowd, their anger intensified by Jimmy's death, seem poised to gain retribution. Jimmy's mother shouts in rage at one of these people, demanding he not spoil her grief by adding to it. She begs all who can hear her that they just go home.

The crowd slowly disperses, leaving Jimmy's mother and the officer crying on oppo-site sides of the crevice Thor created. Their eyes lock and they, perhaps, understand each other's grief. Thor, despondent over his own choices, leaves the two alone and returns to the clinic as Donald Blake, the doctor who seemingly walked out on a patient without a reason only to have him die. Blake is placed on suspension, the kind words of the attending nurse failing to lift his depleted spirit.

The two preceding stories show Thor interacting a great deal with mortals on Midgard. He attempts to inspire their innate nobility, whether by struggling against inter-di-mensional demons or the distrust and hate that permeate human relationships. His suc-cesses are often ethereal as his foe Mephisto is not truly defeated, although Thor's resolve is also unshaken. As for the citizens and police who depart the clinic, are they unchanged by the experience, or will they continue exclusively to blame others for the events of the day? How the reader responds to the panel depicting the officer and Jimmy's mother looking into each other's eyes will determine whether any good has come from Thor's intervention at the clinic.

Thor's activity in the Marvel universe often transcends direct interaction with mor-tals. Sometimes they are on the periphery of his tales, and other times they play no role at all. This notion brings us back to Asgard and Odin, Thor's brooding father. Odin is depicted as being on constant guard against the enemies of Asgard and the dangers they represent.

The danger that most consumes the mind of Odin, in both mythology and the Marvel universe, is the coming of Ragnarok. Ragnarok is a final battle between the forces of good and evil. Odin, through a number of quests, has gained knowledge of this final battle and sees omens that foretell its coming. He knows how the battle will unfold, he witnesses the deaths of his fellow gods and the final assault of Surt, a profoundly wicked fire giant, who consumes the universe with flames. Odin dedicates himself to postponing the coming of Ragnarok.[37]

Ragnarok reveals an important characteristic of the Norse gods, one that makes them quite distinct from Greek mythology. Most of the gods will die, including Odin and Thor, in this climatic battle. The Norse gods are immortal when the criterion is longevity of life and resistance to illness and injury. They can, however, die in battle. They can fail, as they are destined to fail in their efforts to prevent Surt from engulfing the universe in flames. The Norse gods, therefore, fight the forces of evil knowing full well that they can, and will, eventually fall before them. This makes them capable of heroism in ways the Greek gods, who can risk neither their lives nor defeat, can never be.

Ragnarok, despite Surt's efforts, does not bring about the final destruction of the universe. A small number of gods and humans survive the holocaust. Over time some will strive to be noble and upright, while others will break promises and commit murder. Some will be philanthropists, and others will be misanthropes. The life cycle continues, one story ends and another begins.[38]

In the Marvel universe, Ragnarok, the cosmic cycle of death and life, comes about much more regularly than its single occurrence in Norse mythology. These occurrences take a number of forms, including Odin surreptitiously using his magic and illusions to seemingly bring about Ragnarok. There are a number of prophecies that need to be fulfilled for Ragnarok to occur. Odin decides to manipulate situations to fulfill the prophecies but allow Asgard to survive. This action served the purpose of weakening the forces of evil and staving off the coming of Ragnarok for "many mortal lifetimes."

Thor is angered when Odin reveals what he has done, for he feels reduced to a puppet in his father's grand scheme. Furthermore, two mortals died as a result of Odin's machinations. Odin imbued one man, Red Norvell, with the power of Thor. Jormungand, Thor's eternal enemy, fulfilled the prophecy of Thor's death by killing Red "Thor" Norvell. That Odin would destroy two mortal lives fills Thor, the protector of Midgard, with great guilt.

Not long after this episode, another near destruction of Asgard and Earth is averted when Thor's mother, Gaea, turns away a group of space gods called Celestials. Odin attempts to stop them through combat, but fails, causing the death of all Asgardians but Thor. Thor, too, will fall to the Celestials only to be revived by Gaea after her intervention placates the Celestials. Gaea informs Thor that the Celestials brought about Ragnarok, the end of the Norse gods, and that he is the only survivor. There is hope, however. Thor may revive the Asgardians if the heads of the other pantheons grant him a portion of their power. This sends Thor on a quest from one divine realm to another in a desperate, and ultimately successful, quest to save his people.

Another cycle of Ragnarok unfolds in a story line called *The Surtur Saga*, written and drawn by Walter Simonson. In this tale, Surtur (Marvel's version of the fire giant Surt) launches a scheme to bring about the end of the universe. Surtur wields a terrible sword called Twilight that he must light in the eternal flame stolen from him by Odin many millenniums earlier. If Twilight is lit, Surtur can destroy the universe. Surtur launches an assault on Earth, causing Thor, the god of Asgard, and the Einherjar to battle his forces in New York City.[*] During the struggle, Surtur's flames threaten to consume New York City. Thor summons a ferocious downpour to douse the inferno. This act, however, also reveals Bifrost, the Rainbow Bridge that connects Asgard to Midgard . Surtur follows the bridge to Asgard and then destroys it, preventing the gods from pursuing him to protect their homeland.

Thor uses the power of Mjolnir to reach Asgard, but he cannot defeat Surtur alone and falls before the giant's power. Odin confronts Surtur next. He is unrestrained as he uses his full power as All-Father in an effort to save the universe from Surtur's dark dreams. Surtur, unable to render Odin unconscious as he did Thor, uses an ancient magical relic to encase him in ice. Surtur hypothesizes that Odin will free himself in time, but not before he lights his sword and destroys the universe. He has one last, unexpected obstacle to face.

Loki, Odin's adopted son in the Marvel universe, decides Surtur must not succeed in his goals. In mythology, Loki is foster brother to Odin and the embodiment of slow, creeping evil. Depicted in earlier myths as merely deceitful, playfully cunning, and unpredictable, he slowly becomes increasingly hostile to the gods. He plays a key role in bringing about Ragnarok by killing the god Balder and will side with the forces of evil at the final battle. Loki's intervention in Simonson's story has antecedents to the Loki of mythology who sometimes "affords them (the gods) real help ... only to extricate them from some predicament into which he has rashly inveigled them."[39]

Loki's intervention shocks Surtur, for he has been told Loki agreed not to support Asgard. In fact, Loki has helped bring events to this point when he offered aid and comfort to an evil elf named Malekith. Loki deduces that Surtur's goal is the destruction of all existence, not merely Asgard as Malekith thought. Loki, whose ambition is to be Lord of all that is, has no desire to see destroyed that which he seeks to rule. Therefore, to preserve his own dreams of dominion, he chooses to prevent Surtur from lighting Twilight.

Despite his mystic might, Loki falls to Surtur as well. Surtur approaches the Eternal Flame, victory finally within his grasp. Mjolnir strikes Surtur's hand, knocking it away from the Eternal Flame. Odin, freed from his icy prison, joins his son, standing between Surtur and his goal. Loki, also, recovered from Surtur's attack, joins them. The three gods let loose separate battle cries as they begin their assault. Odin shouts, "For Asgard!" Thor bellows, "For Midgard !" Loki, suitably, "For Myself!"

The three gods will stop Surtur, but at a high price. Odin purposely falls with Surtur into Muspelheim (Surtur's home). He falls to ensure that Surtur will not return, leaving Thor and Loki to care for Asgard in his stead. Ragnarok is denied again. In its wake, however, Thor must learn to cope with the loss of a loved one.

---

[*] The Einherjar are Vikings who died heroically in battle and moved on to Valhalla, the Hall of Heroes, in the afterlife.

# CHAPTER 10

## The Power of Thor Confronts the Reality of Loss

Death is a subject that is evaded, ignored, and denied by our youth-worshipping, progress-oriented society. It is almost as if we have taken on death as just another disease to be conquered. But the fact is that death is inevitable.[40]

Odin's sacrifice at the end of *The Surtur Saga* allows the reader to witness Thor's attempts to carry on without his father. It is an interesting aspect of education that although many stories and histories include death, little time is spent discussing the process of dealing with loss even though it is one aspect of life all our students will confront at one point or another. Students may learn staggering casualty figures about wars and battles as well as tragic or heroic deaths in works of literature, but often in a tone that makes death seem unreal or something outside our lives. Death is something to acknowledge quickly, intellectually noting its existence and then moving to the next lesson. Witnessing Thor address the loss of his father may well open avenues of discussion that can help a student heal, a weakened individual find strength, or equip students with ideas that help them face one of life's most difficult, and inevitable, aspects with mature feeling rather than shallow bravado.

Upon Odin's fall, Thor instinctively seeks to blast open the ground of Asgard and follow him into Muspelheim. Loki stops him, explaining that opening the fissure between the two realms may well free Surtur. Thor realizes the truth of Loki's words even as he voices his concerns that Loki is likely plotting to claim the vacated throne of Asgard. Loki does not deny the charge as he leaves Thor standing alone in the silent rubble of Asgard.

Thor remembers that he is not alone and begins seeking his fallen comrade Heimdall. Heimdall is the guardian of Bifrost and a loyal subject of his king. He was, in fact, the first god to defend Asgard from Surtur's assault. Being less equipped than Thor or Odin to battle such a foe, Heimdall falls quickly and remains unconscious throughout the subsequent clashes.

Thor finds Heimdall and informs him of Odin's demise. Both men distinctly express their grief. Heimdall expresses the desire to exchange places with his fallen liege, while Thor explains that Odin knew all along the battle would end with his sacrifice. The keeping of a secret that lead to his death, yet another of Odin's concealed plans, leads the grieving son to state, "Father, for that alone I may never forgive thee."

Psychologist Elisabeth Kubler-Ross dedicated her life to the study of death and dying. In her book, *On Death and Dying*, she discussed five stages through which terminally ill patients tend to proceed. The stages are denial (isolation), anger, bargaining, depression, and acceptance.[41] Individuals do not all go through these stages at the same pace or even in the same sequence. Some may skip one stage all together or remain in a particular stage for an extended period of time. Acceptance does (ideally) end the process regardless of the order the other stages are experienced. The stages are also not individual compartments; one can experience two stages simultaneously or leap from stage to stage in no discernible pattern. The variety of manners in which one may experience these stages does not diminish their power or existence but epitomizes the impact individual traits have on how people deal with the reality of death and dying.

It also should be noted that the five stages are not only experienced by the terminally ill, but loved ones and caretakers as well. Upon the death of a loved one, individuals also experience the five stages of death as they grieve their loss so they can continue living. Thor and Heimdall's conversation allows us to glimpse anger and bargaining. Thor is hurt by the knowledge that Odin planned this ending, without consulting him. He believes, as someone with his power would, that, had he been consulted, a plan not involving the sacrifice of Odin could have been devised. Therefore, he expresses doubt concerning his ability to forgive his father. Heimdall appears to be bargaining. While not explicitly calling out to make a bargain for Odin's life, he implies his willingness to do so. The arrival of Hela, the goddess of death, interrupts their grieving.*

Hela declares she has felt a disturbance that sent ripples across the known universe. She proclaims only the death of Odin could cause such an upheaval. This moment introduces doubt into the story. In the Marvel universe, Odin's power is referred to as the Odin Force. Upon his death, the Odin Force is supposed to pass on to his sons. Neither Thor nor Loki has received the Odin Force, creating the possibility that Odin lives. Thor clings to this lack of transference as evidence that his father survives somewhere in Muspelheim. Yet Hela now appears in Asgard seeking the spirit of Odin, certain that he is dead.

Thor lashes out at Hela, physically confronting the personification of death. This can be seen, metaphorically, as Thor experiencing a forceful denial of death and more literally as an expression of anger as he proclaims his father's spirit is not Hela's for the taking. Incapable of withstanding Thor's rage, Hela departs to Hel, the seat of her underworld kingdom.

Not long after Hela's departure, Thor seeks solitude in the mountainous wilderness east of Asgard. Despite his ability to fly and his godly constitution, Thor rides a horse into the snowy landscape. He is in no rush and seems to prefer the slow lope of his steed to the speed of flight. Hela takes note of Thor's solitary brooding and lashes out at him from the safety of her throne room. She causes a mountainside to erode; creating an avalanche that

---

* In Norse mythology, Hel is the goddess of death and Loki's daughter. Hel becomes Hela in the Marvel universe.

threatens to engulf Thor. Refusing to abandon his horse, Thor gallops ahead of the rushing snow. He uses Mjolnir to create a windstorm that holds the snow back while they race to safer ground. Hela, incapable of harming Thor directly from such a distance, lashes out at Thor's horse, dissolving it to dust in a mater of seconds. The sudden loss of his horse distracts Thor, allowing the avalanche to overwhelm him.

When Thor awakens, he is in an icy hall, the guest of a massive elderly man who calls himself Tiwaz. Realizing Thor knows nothing about where he is or who is benefactor is, Tiwaz attempts to ease the thunder god's mind. He states that if he had ill intent he would have left Thor under the snow and rubble of the avalanche. Tiwaz, satisfied with his own explanation, informs Thor they must wrestle if Thor wants to eat dinner. Thor, greatly fatigued by his battles with Surtur and Hela, succumbs quickly, but earns a meal for his efforts.

While eating, Thor expresses his despair at the loss of Odin and what it means to the universe. In his depression, he moans, "What shall we do without him?" Tiwaz, decries Thor for his words. He challenges Thor to "honor his [Odin's] memory in some more graceful fashion." Thor, now angry at Tiwaz's seeming insensitivity, declares that all living things should weep for shame because of Odin's passing. Tiwaz reveals that he has known Odin a long time, longer than Thor has been alive. He will not hear talk of shame for Odin's passing, for Odin lived his life well. Despite the questions he has, Thor falls asleep quickly, leaving his queries unspoken.

Tiwaz, at this point, can be seen as representing acceptance, the final stage of dealing with loss. Far from an impersonal bystander, he has known Odin for over a millennium and yet does not share Thor's depression or anger. Tiwaz, removed from Asgard but still counting himself a friend to Odin, is not indifferent to Odin's passing. As stated earlier, Tiwaz feels Odin lived well, and therefore, he will not talk of his death in terms of shame. Indeed, Tiwaz seems proud of Odin and his decision to safeguard reality by falling with Surtur. Tiwaz holds this pride deep within where shame, despair, and even death cannot touch. This is not merely a device being used to create a sense of dignity in a fictional character but is a reality that can be found in even the most heart-wrenching of venues.

Viktor Frankl, recalling his experiences in a concentration camp, wrote about his feelings for his wife.

> My mind still clung to the image of my wife. A thought crossed my mind: I didn't even know if she were still alive. I knew only one thing—which I have learned well by now: Love goes very far beyond the physical person of the beloved. It finds its deepest meaning in his spiritual being, his inner self. Whether or not he is actually present, whether or not he is still alive at all, ceases somehow to be of importance.[42]

Tiwaz's regard for Odin, much like Viktor Frankl's love for his wife, exists regardless of Odin being alive. Thor, although a loving son, is saddened by what he has lost and does not feel what he still has. The statement could be made that Tiwaz, because of the isolated nature of his existence, is an emotionally remote character. His actions, however, do not support this thesis. It seems more reasonable, but perhaps more difficult, to conceive that Tiwaz represents an elusive level of emotional and psychological development. His style of mourning, therefore, does not fit within expected norms.

The next morning Tiwaz takes Thor for a walk, where he discusses the simple won-ders of his icy kingdom and the ever-present cycles of nature, including death and life. While the concept of "the circle of life" is familiar to almost all students (especially those who have seen *The Lion King*), it is important to remember Tiwaz's character. Many people are comfortable, as a philosophic or intellectual exercise, discussing concepts like death. Feeling everything that accompanies death, however, is something that most would readily avoid. Tiwaz does not merely intellectualize the "circle of life"; as a character, he feels the rhythms of nature and embraces his place, and the place of his loved ones, within those rhythms. He does not stand above nature in an effort to observe and control, he only seeks, and succeeds, to be in a relationship with all the realities of nature.

Thor finds himself comforted by, and exceedingly comfortable in, Tiwaz's presence. He begins to suspect Tiwaz is Odin in one of his many disguises. He expresses this suspi-cion, only to have Tiwaz explain his allegation away before the two wrestle before dinner again. Thor loses again but puts forth a better effort than the previous evening.

The next morning, Thor witnesses Tiwaz chiseling an ice figurine. Tiwaz breathes on her and the figurine leaps to life and begins to dance. Thor proclaims that only Odin is known to have the power to breathe animation at will. He again proclaims Tiwaz must be Odin even as Tiwaz again denies the accusation, reminding Thor that Odin had only one eye and all his disguises shared this trait.[43]

The two men discuss Thor's desperate need for Tiwaz to be Odin. Thor admits that there is much about Odin he does not know and does not understand. He regrets having never learned certain facts about Odin's past and his origin. He feels not knowing his father well is a fatal flaw in his own character. In essence, Thor has lost Odin when he felt they had more to say and learn from one another. Tiwaz, again, cuts through Thor's doubts by fo-cusing on the fact that, despite what is unknown, Odin was the father Thor loved, and this fact exists undisturbed and unchallenged. Done with words, Tiwaz announces it is time to wrestle before dinner. Thor tosses Tiwaz over his shoulder, claiming victory as Tiwaz bursts into laughter at his defeat.[44] Tiwaz then announces the time has come for their last dinner together.

Tiwaz feels Thor is sufficiently renewed, and the time has come for him to return to Asgard. Thor is not so certain; he is still grieving for his father and growing increasingly calmed by his new surroundings. Tiwaz, in an attempt to help Thor see that he can em-brace all of his duties and simultaneously give Odin his due, quotes a "wonderful poet of Midgard" who "spoke through a great book." The book is the Bible, and the words come from Ecclesiastes ("To every thing there is a season and a time to every purpose under heaven, a time to be born and a time to die … a time to kill, and a time to heal … a time to mourn, and a time to dance").

These words can be read as quaint comfort or cynical acceptance of the dreariness of life, or they can allow for transformative reflection on how to live. These words are famil-iar to some Americans because they are Christian, and others may recognize them be-cause they became lyrics in the folk song "Turn! Turn! Turn!" The folk-song interpretation of the passage stresses the more positive aspect of the opposites. This point is driven home by the addition made by Pete Seeger at the end of the song, "a time for peace, I swear it's not to late." This is the time for peace, not war. This is the time to dance, not mourn. This reading seems quite self-centered as the reader decides his or her time is the time for the positive aspects of the poem, and some future generation can deal with the less savory aspects of life.[45]

If one places more emphasis on the less desirable aspects of the poem, the words become a plaintive moan at the repressive crush of life. Biblical scholar Marcus Borg summed up this interpretation as grasping to the thought that "Life is bleak—unbearably so—an endless cycle of meaningless repetition. This is an exaggerated form of scholarly way of reading Ecclesiastes."[46] It is also a way some students would interpret the passage. Such a reading, however, makes it an odd choice for Tiwaz to use. The final reading is how Marcus Borg and Tiwaz hear the words of Ecclesiastes.

The final method of hearing the passage allows for the existence of all the scenarios within the poem as merely a part of life without judgment or preference. Intellectually, this is an easy argument to make, but it is the genuine acceptance of the equal right of the opposites to exist that is difficult. As the tides of life wash over someone, the only consistency is his or her own being. As we experience fear, desire, anger, confidence, and pity, we often feel them in either an exaggerated or muted manner, with both cases being improper. The goal is to feel all life offers to a proper degree neither in a hypersensitive or overly emotional way nor in an overly detached, analytical manner in which we use our intellect to degrade real feelings.[47] In doing so, we experience life fully not just when things are going well, but at all times. This understanding and application of Ecclesiastes is what prompts Tiwaz to urge Thor to return to Asgard. He reminds Thor, "you will not forget your responsibilities even for your grief." This is far from a cynical approach that may sound more like, "You have a job to do, so get over it."

This scene is very interesting, as Thor decides he has a duty as the Prince of Asgard (and the defender of Midgard) that he must fulfill. In many ways, he is acting as his father's son, an action that may bring him peace of mind that solitary brooding will not. In the essay "Funerals: A Time for Grief and Growth," Roy Nichols discusses his role when his father died. Roy, who was also a funeral director, took care of all the details of his father's funeral. He, along with his siblings, even placed their father in his casket and the casket in the ground. Roy found that this level of involvement was more than being a funeral director; he was fulfilling his duty as a son.[48]

Tiwaz examines the concept of a son honoring his father through the actions he can take in the aftermath of a loss. He reminds Thor that Odin would not have wished his son to shirk his responsibilities in favor of prolonged silent brooding. Thor realizes the time has come for him to return to Asgard, even if he cannot claim his hurt is healed. Time may heal all wounds, but living may expedite the healing in a way that waiting does not. Thor, taking such teachings to heart, leaves Tiwaz's icy home with a strength he had not previously possessed. Tiwaz, watching Thor depart, talks to a great eagle that has perched on his shoulder. In this conversation, he reveals that he is Buri, Odin's grandfather and Thor's great-grandfather, and so the cycle of one generation helping another continues.

Walter Simonson's tale is not the only story that allows the reader to witness Thor's grief and growth during a time of loss. *Thor Annual #13* offers an alternative version of events that unfold after Odin's apparent death. Instead of spending time with a long lost relative who offers wisdom and comfort, Thor finds himself engaged in a confrontation with the evil demon Mephisto.

Mephisto, growing bored with the tempting and torture of mortals, seeks more challenging sport. Using his mystic vapors of vision, he witnesses the recent past, including Odin's sacrifice to stop Surtur from destroying the universe. He is confused when he cannot find Thor in the ruins of Asgard . The mists reveal Thor, downtrodden and on the brink of despair, riding his horse in solitude. Mephisto finds the sight teeming with possibilities. He conceives a plan, hoping a foe can batter Thor's body and further weaken his spirit. Mephisto's vile disposition is made clear as he croons, "What greater pleasure than to see one so divine and noble suffer to his soul?"

Mephisto invades the realm of the rock trolls and kidnaps Horth, brother of Ulik. Ulik is the master of the realm and the mightiest of the trolls. Mephisto demands Ulik annihilate Thor, or his brother's life will be forfeited. The enraged rock troll departs his caverns and seeks his foe. Ulik quickly finds Thor and announces his intention to kill the thunder god. Disinterested in combat, Thor attempts, unsuccessfully, to dissuade Ulik. Much to Mephisto's glee, the two become entangled in a furious battle.

Ulik, desperate to save his brother, is relentless in his assault. He uproots trees and hurls them at Thor. He causes a massive avalanche in an attempt to bury his enemy. With the use of Mjolnir, however, Thor repels every attack. The effort required to turn aside the avalanche leaves Thor drained, particularly because he only wants to be left alone to mourn his father. He calls for a cease to their hostilities. Ulik responds by insulting the memory of Odin. Thor, enraged and motivated by Ulik's words, brutally pummels the rock troll. Defeated, Ulik tells Thor of Mephisto's plan to have Thor's body battered so his spirit would be easier to break.

Disgusted by the thought of Mephisto plotting again to claim his soul, Thor turns his back on Ulik and prepares to continue in solitary meandering. Ulik shouts after him, "Go, Thunder God. I'll not beg you to save my brother's life. For what is he to you?" His back still to Ulik, Thor tersely dismisses any implication that a troll should matter to a god of Asgard. Thor pauses and considers what he is doing. Ulik has, in an unorthodox manner, asked Thor for help. Thor considers whether he has become so filled with sorrow that it is acceptable to ignore the needs of another, even Ulik. Thor turns to face Ulik, who is still lying in the snow, and declares the way of Asgard to be the way of life. He will seek to save Horth.

Taking on the quest to save Horth, Thor is also acting as his father's son. The legacy of Asgard, protected and nurtured for so long by Odin, is now in Thor's hands. What will Asgard be without Odin, a place where one's own sorrow causes him to neglect others or where personal needs are met by reaching out to help others in their time of need? Thor's declaration that the way of Asgard is the way of life is also a reclaiming of his own way. Grief does not displace compassion, nor does sorrow prevent meaningful action. For funeral director Roy Nichols, this meaningful action was being intimately involved in his father's funeral. For Thor, it is taking up the mantle of Prince of Asgard and embracing all that the title encompasses.

Mephisto stands unimpressed with Thor's oath and teleports the Asgardian into his realm. The demon quickly announces his intention "to drain your willful spirit 'til naught be left but a naked quivering and despairing soul which I shall clasp to my bosom as the greatest prize of all." Thor, as expected, announces his spirit will never be broken, and the two engage in a dual for Thor's soul.

Using his power of illusion, Mephisto causes "Odin" to appear and call Thor to join him in Mephisto's realm. When Thor declares that Odin's soul cannot be in Mephisto's realm, a harpy is summoned to tear Odin apart. Thor drives off the beastly vulture, as "Odin" becomes a wisp of smoke. Sensing despair in Thor's heart, Mephisto's assault continues.

Next, he shows Thor a scene from his past. Thor presents his beloved, the lady Sif, a rose. Sif and Thor have since parted company, and Mephisto declares the rose now to be a symbol of the death of love. With these words, massive, spiny tendrils engulf Thor, seeking to crush the life from him. Thor breaks free from the iron grasp of the vines. Free, he proclaims to Mephisto, "For life renews itself, through heartfelt loss and dashed hopes ever seek to crush it."

This is the point of contention between Thor and Mephisto. Mephisto believes life must eventually succumb to evil and despair. Life, in essence, is fragile and will eventually be overwhelmed by the obstacles before it. It is inevitable. Thor, standing in the midst of Mephisto's hellish realm, testifies to the seemingly inexhaustible energies of life to endure hardship and be renewed. Mephisto would have Thor believe that to battle the evils of the world is "a vain illusion." Yet there is nothing delusional in Thor's words. He openly admits to the hardships of life and the simultaneous existence of the capacity to strive on despite them.

Thor's resolve still unshaken, Mephisto reveals the collateral damage of his battle with Ulik. The avalanche caused by Ulik claimed the life of an Asgardian family Thor had encountered earlier in the tale. Ulik was defeated, but some of Thor's subjects died as a result of the battle, meeting a seemingly meaningless end. Thor summons a deluge to mirror his outrage as Mephisto mocks this show of power. His evil cannot be extinguished by a mere storm, no matter how powerful. He scoffs at this effort, calling Thor the "portrait of futility."

It is easy to see, and fall for, the point the charismatic demon is making. Mephisto cannot be overcome and, as Thor himself admits, hardships and despair exist in life. All our efforts will not prevent this, so why oppose the inevitable? When viewing the confrontation between Thor and Mephisto in a basic "good guy versus bad guy" sense, it is indeed disheartening. The hero in this instance cannot defeat the villain, so that must mean the villain wins. This is what Mephisto would have us believe, but what of the truths Mephisto either doesn't see or refuses to acknowledge?

Mephisto's stated goal was the crushing of Thor's spirit, something he failed to do. For all his illusion and guile, Mephisto was as much a "portrait of futility" as Thor. Thor, who is often teased by his opponents for having more brawn than brain, is engaging in a more complex mode of living than Mephisto. For Mephisto, the confrontation of life is an either/or proposition. Either you admit his worldview is correct or you cling to the illusion and delusion that love, faith, compassion and perseverance can make a difference in the world and in our lives.

Thor concedes that all the evil and pain of life is very real, but so are their opposites. Hope and despair, courage and fear can and do exist simultaneously side by side. If readers accept that Thor cannot defeat Mephisto, then they also must concede that Mephisto cannot defeat Thor. It is in this moment that the power of Thor truly is seen, as he symbolizes the path of life, even standing in a realm of death and desolation.

Mephisto is granted the last word in the tale, which he uses to prove he does not quite get it. Thor finds the bodies of the family killed by Ulik's avalanche. Thor, who believed the vision of the family he saw in Mephisto's realm was another illusion, finds his resolve strengthened by the discovery of his fallen subjects. He vows to erect a monument to the family, and to Horth, whom Mephisto killed having never intended to return him to Ulik. He also promises to redouble his efforts to resist Mephisto's evil.

Mephisto, sitting on a throne in his realm, laughs at the notion of Thor building a memorial to the dead. The monument will eventually crumble to dust, so why bother? Victory is his. Yet Thor stands unbroken and the survivor of Ragnarok. The eventual fall of his monument would not coincide with the fall of his resolve. If Thor is foolish for erecting a stone monument, then Mephisto must be equally ignorant to relish the idea of its fall.

The stories of Thor dealing with the loss of his father present the idea of opposites existing side by side. The pain of loss and the joy of relationships. The sorrow of never seeing a loved one again and the serenity of realizing you can live without them. The road of despair leading to the treasures of steadfastness. But what bridges these opposites together? What keeps Thor moving throughout the story and real people moving in the face of their own losses? When faced with tragic news, Elisabeth Kubler-Ross identified the different stages people go through. She also stated that there is something available at every stage to offer aid to those coping with death and dying. The one thing that persists through every stage is hope.[49]

# Part III

## Marvel's Mutants, Prejudice, and the Faces of Evil

# CHAPTER 11

---

# Charles Xavier and Magneto

There may be no comic built so firmly on sociopolitical concepts as the X-Men. Introduced in September 1963, in the midst of the Civil Rights movement, the X-Men have become a metaphor for the all-too-real struggle against oppression and prejudice. The comic book series has, both intentionally and unintentionally, become a forum for addressing a variety of societal issues.[50] The social conscience of X-Men is tied to the nature of the main characters. The X-Men, as introduced in 1963, were a group of teenage mutants under the tutelage of Professor Charles Xavier. Mutants are people born with a genetic abnormality. These deviations in their genetic code create latent superpowers.

The appearance of the mutant power usually occurs at puberty. These mutations set mutants (usually at a young and impressionable age) apart from the rest of humanity and cause the average human to distrust, fear, and even hate them.[*] There is blatant persecution fueled by both those in power and mobs in the street. To be a mutant is, at the least, to be viewed with distrust and, at worst, to be hated. Two characters in particular travel over paths that mutants may follow as they confront this discrimination: Charles Xavier (Professor X), and Erik Magnus Lehnsherr (Magneto).

Charles Xavier is the founder of the X-Men and a mutant. Xavier, who is often referred to as possessing the most powerful mutant mind on the planet, is a telepath. His talents include the ability to read minds, control minds, and strike opponents with "psychic bolts," causing them intense mental pain. These talents have taught Xavier the necessity of using his powers wisely, for he could violate the mind and integrity of anyone he meets with minimal effort. In an effort to help other mutants control their talents rather than be controlled by them, he earlier founded Xavier's School for Gifted Youngsters. This is hardly his only endeavor.

Simultaneously, he relentlessly pursues his dream that mutants and "normal" humans will learn to live together in harmony rather than separated by the walls of distrust and hate. To this end, his best students become members of the X-Men, offering an example of

---

[*] In Marvel Comics, mutants are considered the next stage of human evolution. They are sometimes referred to as *Homo superior* as opposed to *Homo sapiens*.

mutants who act on behalf of humanity, protecting them from the threats presented by super-villains. Xavier also appears on television and at speaking engagements where he promotes his ideal of amicable mutant–human relations. Xavier's idealism is juxtaposed with the path offered by Magneto.

Whereas Charles Xavier's mutation gives him mastery of the mind, Magneto has dominion on the physical. Magneto's mutation, which did not manifest itself until he was an adult, grants him the ability to manipulate metal. Events in his life have caused his powers to increase to a seemingly limitless degree, but even without these events, he was immensely formidable. Some simpler expressions of his power include bending metal to bind opponents, emitting bolts of magnetic force, hurling metallic objects at opponents and erecting magnetic force shields that deflect attacks. More dramatic examples of his power include instances in which he redirects missiles launched at him, taking control of a soviet nuclear submarine and sinking it. His vision, however, is far more important than his power.

Magneto believes peaceful coexistence with humanity is impossible to achieve. He suggests an alternative, conquering the world and claiming the position of dictator. By doing so he feels he will not only ensure mutant survival but also guarantee the possibility for mutants to thrive. In the wars to bring about his dominance, untold millions would die, but the end result would be mutants in a position of power and people benefiting from his reign. On various occasions, Magneto mentions the possibility of war ceasing to exist because the entire planet would be under his control. As such all money spent on war could be redirected to education or to fighting poverty and famine. Humans would so enjoy the golden age he ushers in, they would soon forget its bloody origin.

Magneto offers mutants the opportunity to meet force with force and return pain with pain rather than adhere to ideals of better days earned through mutual effort and respect. Mutants, therefore, are presented divergent paths by two distinctive leaders.[51] Because Magneto's message tends to resonate more strongly with mutants than Charles Xavier's, this chapter focuses on his leadership, his vision, and the historic figures we can compare him to first.

On a variety of occasions, Magneto (whether by the media, members of the X-Men, or in his words) is compared to Adolf Hitler. The comparison of Magneto to a tyrant bent on world domination and the destruction of a "lesser" race seems natural. Magneto's history also makes the comparison a warning against allowing anger and rage to make one into something he or she claims to despise.

Born Erik Lehnsherr, Magneto was a European Jew during World War II. He grew up in Auschwitz, and his family died there. He has a tattoo on his arm, an identification number that he carries has a constant reminder of his personal experience with genocide and the evil humans are capable of. He lives in fear that his people, mutants, may also one day face genocide on a worldwide scale. His oft-stated mission is to protect mutants from such a fate. Many actions taken in his world only serve to reinforce his contention that mutant genocide is coming.

There is the island nation of Genosha, an economically prosperous and socially peaceful nation. Unfortunately, Genosha's thriving economy is built on the suffering backs of mutant slaves. Its social harmony is maintained, in part, by the fact that the mutant population provides the existence of a consistent enemy the populace unifies to oppress.[52] The United States also has an antimutant ethos that emanates from both the highest levels of government as well as powerful, private citizens. Dr. Bolivar Trask invented giant robots called Sentinels designed to track down mutants and kill them. The U.S. government will eventually buy Sentinels and use them as a part of Project Wideawake , which utilizes the massive robots now programmed to detect and capture mutants. The U.S. Congress also debates the merits of a Mutant Registration Act to assist in the monitoring of mutant activity.

Looking at the events of Magneto's childhood and the multiple examples of open and government-sanctioned hostility against mutants, it becomes clear that Magneto's concern of a possible genocide are grounded in events all around him. Magneto is driven by rage and hatred, but the threats the world presents to mutants are a present and ongoing reality. Magneto's deep experiences with human hatred have made him unwilling or incapable of considering the possibility that some people are in favor of mutant rights. He chooses to ascribe as a fundamental aspect of all human beings not just hatred but also the desire and willingness to cause violence.

The fact that Magneto assigns such feelings to all humans could be argued as unfair or unjust, but it is a lesser delusion than those we see in Adolf Hitler. Consider the following reflection presented by historian Alan Bullock:

> But "the Jew" as one encounters him in the pages of Mein Kampf and Hitler's ravings bears no resemblance to flesh-and-blood human beings of Jewish descent: He is an invention of Hitler's obsessional fantasy, a Satanic creation, expressing his need to create an object on which he could concentrate his feelings of aggression and hatred.[53]

Hitler, in his twisted imagination, creates a fictitious and dehumanizing personality for Jewish people. He did not, however, limit his false testifying to Jewish personhood. He also assigned to them a most dire intent. Here are Hitler's own words on this topic:

> The ultimate goal of the Jewish struggle for existence is the enslavement of productively active people ... by the denationalization, the promiscuous bastardization of other peoples, the lowering of the racial level of the highest peoples as well as the domination of this racial mishmash through the extirpation of the volkisch intelligentsia and its replacement by members of its own people.[54]

And

> Should the Jew, with the help of his Marxist creed, conquer the nations of this world, his own crown will become the funereal wreath of mankind, and once again this planet, empty of mankind, will follow its orbit through the ether as it did millions of years ago.[55]

Whatever similarities exist between Magneto and Hitler in terms of hatred and rage, there is a vast distance between the grounds from which these feelings spring. Hitler's "Jew" does not exist in the real world. It would be impossible to produce evidence of a Jewish movement seeking "the enslavement of productively active people" or a Jewish conspiracy designed to "conquer the nations of the world." Hitler was, in essence, projecting his own intention into a nightmarish demon he called "the Jew." In doing so, he enabled himself to act as "the hero," saving the world from the parasitic beast that he so clearly saw in the world, for it was ever present in his mind. It was a delusion that he grasped even in his final hours, referring to Jewish people and identity as "the universal poisoner of all people" in his final testament.[56] There was no evidence of remorse in Hitler . The same cannot be said of Magneto.

In a pitched battle with the X-Men, Magneto grievously injures Kitty Pryde, a teenage member of the mutant band of heroes. The sight of the fallen youth snaps Magneto out of his violent rage and causes him to be reflective. In seeking to create a world safe for young mutants, he may well have killed one. His monologue is interrupted when Storm, a female member of the X-Men with the power to manipulate the forces of nature, arrives to find Magneto cradling Kitty's body as a father may hold a fallen daughter. Storm threatens to kill Magneto where he sits, and he offers no resistance. Kitty represents all the innocent people (and the very existence of innocence in people) Magneto would kill, directly or indirectly, via the war he would start in his quest for mutant supremacy. Storm takes Kitty, who has survived, from Magneto, and he flees the island where the battle took place. While Kitty recovers, Charles Xavier notes with hopeful optimism that, for the first time in all their encounters, Magneto's perceptions may be changing. This mental shift may allow Magneto to again act as the good man Xavier remembered him being when they first met.

This process continues to unfold as Magneto allows himself to be arrested and stand trial for his crimes. Magneto views the trial as an opportunity not so much to proclaim his innocence, but to explain his rationale and fears. His commitment to his goal, to protect and preserve mutants, is unwavering, as is his conviction that people hate very easily and that hatred often has disastrous consequences. He maintains the necessity for improved human–mutant relations, regardless of his fate. In a passage that suggests a willingness to become a martyr, Magneto proclaims that he is the very reason mutants tend to be feared and hated. He hopes that by accepting punishment for his past deeds, people will no longer seek to punish mutants as a group.

Writer Chris Claremont presents Magneto as eloquent, dignified, determined, and unrelenting in his view that mutants are in danger. His misdeeds do not eliminate the reality of the dire predicament many mutants find themselves in on a daily basis. Magneto's demeanor reflects little of Hitler's at this point but may well capture the essence of a powerful Civil Rights activist, Malcolm X.

Malcolm X once stated that "objective never changes. You might change your method of achieving the objective, but the objective never changes."[57] Magneto's objective (to protect and preserve mutants) has not changed, but his method has (using the trial to make his case, making himself the target of hatred, martyr himself to protect his people). The comparison to Malcolm X, however, can be seen to run deeper than the application of rhetoric.

Ossie Davis, in response to an editor who questioned why he eulogized Malcolm X, wrote that Malcolm had a way of reminding blacks that they were men. This was not always accomplished through gentle means. As Davis noted, "He would make you angry as hell, but he would also make you proud."[58] It may be difficult to imagine what it feels like to be part of an oppressed group if you have never been a member of one, but most people have felt, at one time or another, a sense of isolation or a sense that one is not worthy of consideration or undeserving of accolades or joy. If individuals find themselves in such a mental state that someone stirs a sense of pride in them, it is easy to see why that person would become admired. Malcolm X did this for thousands of blacks during his lifetime.

In the Marvel universe, mutants are the oppressed group, and Magneto attempts to stir them from their submissive posture, to make them feel like men and stand up to their oppressors. Consider this description of Malcolm X, "Malcolm ... was refreshing excitement; he scared the hell out of us, bred as we are to caution, to hypocrisy in the presence of white folks, to the smile that never fades."[59] One can picture Magneto having the same impact on his fellow mutants, exciting but terrifying them, as he unrepentantly defends the dignity of his people even as he challenges them to find their own dignity and stand up for themselves.

Much like Magneto, Malcolm X's past has unsavory moments. He was a thief, a criminal, and, much like Magneto, filled with hate. When Malcolm X declared white men to be the devil, it was not mere hyperbole. He had a mountain of rage in him just as Magneto is portrayed as having. Both men, the historic and fictitious, mean what they say. This being true, however, also means that a repudiation of particulars from their past is also heartfelt. For Malcolm X, this occurred after his pilgrimage to Mecca. The experience Malcolm had in Mecca was truly transformative. He let go of attitudes and beliefs he once clung to and promoted with a ferocious intelligence.

As Ossie Davis observed, "No one who knew him before and after his trip to Mecca could doubt that he had completely abandoned racism, separatism, and hatred."[60] What he had not abandoned was his intensity, his willingness to fight for immediate freedom for the oppressed, or the joy he took in agitating both whites and blacks who clung to destructive patterns of action and beliefs. Malcolm was decidedly different after Mecca but maintained and used the talents he had developed over his lifetime. An expanding consciousness does not include abandoning the entirety of oneself or adopting a false identity to overemphasize the changes in one's life. Sadly, this is not an aspect of Malcolm's that Magneto shares.

As Magneto's trial continues two genetically altered twins possessing destructive powers assault the courtroom. The twins are the offspring of Baron Wolfgang von Strucker, a Nazi war criminal who sought to complete the work of Hitler. Magneto and Charles Xavier first met in Israel in 1962.[61] Their meeting coincided with a confrontation with von Strucker. During this conflict, Magneto killed the Baron, and his children are seeking revenge. The attempt fails, but the siblings blow up a wall, flooding the subterranean chamber where the fight ends and escape in the chaos. Magneto saves Xavier from the flood, but the fallout from the trial and flood will reverberate for years to come.

Xavier, who had been ill throughout the trial, is near death as he lies in a garden where Magneto and the flood deposited him. Xavier makes a deathbed request of Magneto, asking him to become headmaster of his school, look over the X-men, and teach his newest superheroes, the New Mutants. Magneto resists Xavier's request but eventually relents. Xavier's beloved, an alien empress named Lilandra, arrives and teleports Xavier to her ship, confident that her alien technology will save his life. This interaction, however, does not free Magneto from the vow he took, and he embarks on a new phase of his life.

Before evaluating Magneto's tenure as headmaster of Xavier's school, it is important to consider the man to whom Magneto made this vow and the nature of this chosen path. Charles Xavier's dream is that humans and mutants will one day live together in harmony. His dream is grounded in a belief in the basic goodness of humankind. Such a concept is often mocked by Magneto as being, at the least, hopelessly naïve and, at worst, a lethal miscalculation of human nature.

He, like Magneto, is well aware of the seemingly insurmountable wall of distrust, prejudice, and hate that mutants face. His X-Men have fought the Sentinels on numerous occasions. He is cognizant of the U.S. government's purchase of Sentinels. It is difficult to overestimate the message such an action sends to the mutant community, regardless of the spin-doctoring performed by political operatives. Such realities cause Xavier tremendous heartache and deep doubts about, if not the content of his dream, the possibility of it ever coming to fruition. And yet, he perseveres, never succumbing to, yet occasionally feeling, despair. This begs the questions, what enables a man like Charles Xavier not just to fight for but never to abandon a dream so at odds with the world around him? Figures from history can aid us in our understanding of Charles Xavier and his tenacity.

A reasonable starting point would be to address the accusation that Xavier is naïve, blind to reality because he is lost in his dream. Xavier is in fact operating from a position of naïveté, but not in the blind, childish manner of which Magneto accuses him. An individual's cognitive development can be seen as advancing through three phases: precritical naïveté, critical thinking, and postcritical naïveté.[62]

In a broad sense, this means people progress through a phase in childhood during which they take most anything presented at face value to a phase of critical thinking, where the assumptions of childhood are questioned. The modern and postmodern world encourages people to remain firmly planted in the critical thinking phase. Facts shape reality. The more solid and indisputable the facts, the more secure the grasp one has on reality and the stronger a sense of control over that reality.[63] Fact mistakenly becomes a synonym for truth, though the words have very different meanings. One who progresses to, and remains firmly entrenched within, the postcritical naïveté phase may find themselves at great odds with the world around him or her.

Postcritical naïveté is a disposition that acknowledges the difference between fact and truth, the importance of metaphor and symbolism, the limitations of critical grasping and the illusion of control it grants, and the existence or archetypal truths and symbols as a gateway to a broader, generally unexplored aspect of reality. An individual like Magneto, firmly grounded in the critical-thinking stage, believes individuals like Charles Xavier to be victims of a form of arrested development—trapped in precritical naïveté. In actuality, Xavier has progressed to an internal landscape that in many ways is inconceivable to his critics. One immersed in a postcritical experience of his surroundings, he not only thinks differently about the world but will also embrace a wisdom that can be difficult for others to assimilate.

Societies, particularly Western culture, tend to value greatly and pass on various forms of conventional wisdom. This wisdom is passed on not merely by word but by deed. Individuals, groups, and even a nation's culture pass conventional wisdom from one generation to the next. Espousing high ideals while not acting on them is also a form of conventional wisdom, an unspoken form of the phrase, "do as I say, not as I do." Fighting fire with fire, demonizing the opposition, claiming the moral high ground by immoral means are, in the end, all forms of conventional wisdom.

To be clear, conventional wisdom is the mode offered by critical thinking. It also has great value in certain situations, but is lacking in others. Conventional wisdom employs various methods of grasping or possessing in an attempt to "domesticate reality" and bend it to the individual's will. Subversive wisdom undermines the sense of control and power that conventional wisdom grants and reveals such control to be illusionary or impermanent.[64] Many luminaries who are practitioners of subversive wisdom tend to emerge from spiritual traditions or have some grounding in personal spiritual sensibilities. A radical encounter or experience with a sense of the sacred leaves them unimpressed with conventional wisdom but beyond the nihilistic void that would require someone to declare that if there is no conventional wisdom, then nothing matters.

One does not outthink conventional wisdom; one experiences the shortages within it and the overwhelming mystery beyond it. Subversive wisdom is an experiential reality, not an intellectual exercise. Therefore, subversive wisdom is often found in various religious traditions and texts. This also explains why subversive wisdom often sounds shallow, clichéd, or naïve when parroted by people (religious or secular, scholarly or political) who have read a text (or at least heard it spoken to them) but have limited to no experience with its vitality. One can pinpoint, in history, spiritual geniuses who embodied subversive wisdom and simultaneously envisioned a continuum of spiritual development along which most of humanity falls. One's standing on this continuum coincides with his or her ability to understand, appreciate, apply, and feel the wisdom presented.[65] With these terms in place, we find that Magneto is, in essence, a purveyor of conventional wisdom, whereas Charles Xavier communicates subversive wisdom. This distinction remains despite Magneto's decision to stand trial.

While testifying, Magneto emphasizes that his goal remains the protection and preservation of his people. This goal, although part of the scope of Xavier's dream of mutant–human harmony, does not encapsulate it. Charles Xavier would readily agree with this observation made by Martin Luther King Jr., "segregation distorts the soul and damages the personality. It gives the segregator a false sense of superiority and the segregated a false sense of inferiority."[66] Division creates lies that damage both members of the sundered relationship. Xavier would heal both sides, Magneto only one. This is why Magneto's methods appear doomed to failure. Even if mutants break the lie of their inferiority, humans, clinging to the false premise of their superiority, will remain an obstacle to true freedom and equality. Both sides must be freed from their bondage. It is a lesson Nelson Mandela learned over time as well:

> It was during those long and lonely years that my hunger for the freedom of my own people became a hunger for the freedom of all people, white and black. I knew as well as I knew anything that the oppressor must be liberated just as surely as the oppressed. A man who takes away another man's freedom is a prisoner of hatred.... When I walked out of prison, that was my mission, to liberate the oppressed and the oppressor both.[67]

It is important to note that Mandela, by his own admission, slowly grew into this disposition. The final conclusion was not reached until sometime during his stay in prison. Mandela was forty-five when he was sentenced to life in prison. If we assume he did recognize the necessity of liberating both oppressed and oppressor during his first five years in prison, then it was sometime after his fiftieth birthday that he had the realization he would actualize upon his release. King, by comparison, wrote "Letter from a Birmingham Jail" when he was thirty-nine. In no way is this fact meant to imply some form of superiority in King but rather to illustrate that a process of evolution from conventional to subversive wisdom (critical to postcritical naïveté) does exist and cannot be categorized by the number of years accumulated. For Mandela the process began at a very personal level (a desire for his own freedom) and progressed through various stages until it crystallized in a desire for all people's freedom.[68] Mandela's life is evidence that, contrary to conventional wisdom, people do in fact change and can become receptive of others, even others that seem to deserve animosity rather than generosity.

We are now left with a peculiar predicament: Magneto agrees to inherit all of Xavier's responsibilities even though he is not representative of either of Xavier's dispositions (postcritical naïveté and a practitioner of subversive wisdom). Xavier could be hoping that Magneto will grow as a result of fulfilling his promise. This is a noteworthy goal, but its application may be faulty. When motivating someone to grow, it is essential to be intensely honest in the assessment of the other's station in life. Using the alphabet as markers, if one is at Point B and we simultaneously use inspirational words to motivate, while providing the tools and assigning the responsibilities of Point F, the person will fail. It is necessary, even if it tries one's patience, to make sure Points C, D, and E are in place before assuming the person is capable of Point F.[69] Xavier, while seeing the best in Magneto, may well be setting him up for failure.

Predictably, Magneto's tenure as headmaster of Xavier's school is disastrous, including the death of one of the New Mutants. Xavier makes the following statement as he attempts to convince Magneto to take over his duties: "You say now yours [the life path Magneto chose] was wrong. You seek to make amends—here is your chance!" Although it is true that Magneto has changed, for he realizes that the cost of seeking world domination is too high, he has hardly become one who completely embraces Xavier's vision and methods. He is still more cynical, untrusting, and violent than the professor. He also views his goal as being the protection and preservation of mutant kind, not harmonious relations with "normal" humans. Magneto, who has ever been his own man and blazed his own trail, has accepted the responsibility of stepping into another's shoes and, by extension, an identity he is not comfortable living with. The life of Malcolm X, particularly post-Mecca, provides additional impetus for questioning Charles Xavier for making his request and Magneto for accepting.

Historically speaking, Malcolm X returned from Mecca a different man. As such, he left Elijah Muhammad's Nation of Islam and began the process of establishing his own Muslim organization. As Ossie Davis noted, even after Malcolm's experience at Mecca, he enjoyed, "twisting the white man's tail, and in making Uncle Toms, compromisers, and accommodationists ... thoroughly ashamed of the urbane and smiling hypocrisy we practice."[70] Malcolm X, post-Mecca, needed to follow a path with which he was comfortable. He could not, could never, become another Martin Luther King Jr. That was not Malcolm's way, and to demand it of him, or denounce him by comparison with King, would be a heinous error that diminishes both the struggles and grandeur of Malcolm X.

Malcolm X had to be what he had always been, his own man with his own methods. Magneto, although recognizing his methods were ineffective, adopts rather than develops his own methodology. The error in this is not that adopting a different method is improper but that Magneto's shift comes not from an actualization but more from the obligation of granting a deathbed wish. Magneto's fall, therefore, is almost inevitable. This fall leads to more intense confrontation between himself and the X-Men, conflicts that dramatically illustrate styles of leadership and the burden of pursuing dreams of harmony.

# CHAPTER 12

## *Mutant Genesis* and *Fatal Attractions*: Who Shall Lead? Charles Xavier, Magneto, and the Burden of Leadership

Magneto's disastrous tenure as headmaster of Xavier's School for Gifted Youngsters leads to his eventual decision to live in isolation on Asteroid M. Asteroid M is a base Magneto created early in his career. The base, a combination of an actual asteroid and an intricate living space, maintains a synchronous orbit above the Earth. Magneto chooses this life as an act of resignation, seemingly disinterested in what transpires on Earth, his intensity dampened and his will dedicated to the goal of being left alone.

Magneto's counterpart, Charles Xavier, has returned from his time with Lilandra, and he has reclaimed his position as mentor, leader, and guide of the X-men. He feels some uncertainty as he reclaims this position. Talking to Jean Grey, one of his original students, he confesses, "I look at the world, and cannot help wondering if my dream has any validity anymore."

Both men, because of their past and present circumstances, are riddled with doubt. For his part, Magneto is well aware of his failures as headmaster of Xavier's school as well as the fact that, for all his rage and fury, he has not made the world much safer for mutants. Charles also sees how unsafe the world remains for mutants and how far people are from accepting them. He wonders if he has, or ever will, make any difference. His dream of peace appears destined to be overcome by the reality that many others dream of dominion and superiority. How each character handles his doubts reveals their natures as leaders and people.

In the early stages of the story, Magneto's doubts have driven him to self-imposed isolation on Asteroid M, which is equipped with a cloaking devise, making it virtually invisible

73

to Earth. This locale is important, for it is a manifestation of Magneto's view of humanity —he is above them. He is beyond their reach, beyond their understanding, beyond their laws. His ego, bordering on narcissism, remains intact.

The desire for isolation originates from his frustration over his failure to bring about his own regime on Earth and his disappointing tenure as head of Charles Xavier's school. He is not a man content with his life's work, seeking retirement in old age. Bitterness smolders under the veneer of disinterest, awaiting the opportunity to be unleashed.

Charles Xavier's doubts stem from his full awareness of the lack of progress made in the arena of mutant–human relations. The existence of dramatic and seemingly irrefutable evidence of a lack of progress or compassion has been an obstacle throughout history for every leader who is guided by a vision steeped in subversive wisdom. Those close to Martin Luther King Jr. were well aware of the nervousness and anxiety he felt as the Civil Rights movement progressed.[71] In the nineteenth century, anxiety regarding the chasm between America's ideals and its realities enraged both Abraham Lincoln and Frederick Douglass. The two men communicated their dissatisfaction by using the Fourth of July to exemplify the hypocrisy of American ideals in the face of slavery.[72]

None of these men, the historic or the fictional, succumbed permanently to their anxiety, doubts, or fears. These traits do not signal a necessary extinguishing of faith, hope, and courage. Rather, they can complement the existence of the higher virtues and perhaps are even necessary to their development. Despite his doubt, Charles Xavier still seeks to create community and connection. Magneto's doubt, however, leads him to create a kingdom in the cold, harsh environment of space.

Magneto's "peace" is interrupted by a battle just beyond Asteroid M. A small collection of mutants, calling themselves acolytes, have hijacked a space shuttle and are seeking to find Magneto. Three ships attempting to shoot them down are in pursuit. The acolytes destroy one of their pursuers. Magneto appears and destroys the remaining ships and prepares to transport the crews back to Earth. One of the acolytes, calling him "Lord Magneto," reveals that they are mutants come to serve Magneto and his "glorious cause." Magneto claims the days of having causes are behind him but decides to bring the survivors to Asteroid M instead of sending them back to Earth.

His guests promptly begin fighting amongst themselves, leading to the shooting death of one of the acolytes. The mutant dies at Magneto's feet, running to him as he enters the room. She claims she and her companions came seeking sanctuary and, again, pledges the acolytes' service to Magneto's cause. Magneto again claims to have no cause. The death of another mutant makes him willing to listen to Fabian Cortez, leader of the acolytes, as he speaks of human retaliation for what transpired beyond Asteroid M.

Magneto is receptive to the words of Fabian Cortez and the other acolytes. What is not clear is what influences him more, their argument or their word choice. Repeatedly addressed as "Lord" and told of his "destiny," Magneto's ego, bruised by his failures, discovers there are still those who seek his leadership and protection. His cause is still inspirational to certain mutants. This is understandable, for who has not wished to have the power to lash out and punish those who harm or oppress? Who, at one time or another, has not wished for the arrival of an individual with the ability to save us from our difficulties? Magneto's way promises retribution, revenge, and dominion. It appeals to primal needs for security and safety while offering instant gratification of punishing the enemy without regard to the laws of man or dictates of morality. Magneto finds the aco- lytes see him not as a failure, but as a savior and protector. As he reclaims this position, he not only comes into conflict with the X-Men, but comparisons to Adolf Hitler from the previous chapter must also be revisited.

The Fuherprinzip, the principle that all power be concentrated in the hand of a single individual, was central to Hitler's leadership.[73] The Fuherprinzip can be applied to almost any dictator. Napoleon, for example, once declared, "Do you think, either, that my object is to establish a Republic?... The nation must have a head, a head rendered illustrious by glory and not by theories of government, fine phrases, or the talk of idealists."[74] A single man, a man made great by glorious military deeds, not philosophic musings or clever speech, must rule a nation. While Hitler was no military genius (though he would not admit this), he would readily agree with the sentiment that a single great man must lead. He would also concur with the thought that a Republic, or any government that allows major- ity rule, is not worth establishing. As the dictatorial leader consolidates his power, the proclamations he makes can be truly frightening to a more egalitarian ear.

On July 13, 1934, in a speech to the Reichstag, Hitler declared himself not merely above the law but to be the law in Germany, "in this hour I was responsible for the fate of the German people, and thereby I became the supreme judge of the German people." He also claimed the right to kill political rivals: "And let it be known for all time to come that if anyone raises his hand to strike the state, then certain death is his lot."[75] In *Mutant Genesis,* and with growing intensity in *Fatal Attractions*, Magneto makes and acts on such claims.

As the first chapter of *Mutant Genesis* closes, the acolytes attack Genosha, seeking Rogue, a member of the X-Men.* A small group of X-Men arrive to help their teammate. They have the acolytes all but defeated when Magneto arrives. Magneto claims the acolytes acted with "an excess of zeal" and that he alone will determine their punishment. He also declares Asteroid M, and himself by extension, to be a sovereign world where the laws of human beings hold no sway.

In the ensuing battle, the X-Men are defeated and taken as captives to Asteroid M. In chapter two, Magneto will also kidnap Charles Xavier and his friend Dr. Moira MacTaggert and bring them to his orbiting fortress. This sets up the final battle in chapter three as the remaining X-Men attempt to rescue their comrades and nullify the threat of Magneto.

In the final battle, Asteroid M is destroyed by Fabian Cortez, who seeks to make Mag- neto a martyr and himself the new leader of the movement to safeguard mutants by domi- nating the world. Asteroid M explodes high above Earth with Magneto and all the acolytes, except Cortez, on board. Magneto, choosing to stay on the doomed satellite, uses his power to save the lives of Charles Xavier and the X-Men. Magneto allows Charles to read his mind as his life apparently ends with the destruction of Asteroid M.

One of Magneto's finals thoughts is, "I give you your dream, Charles. But I fear, in time, your heart will break as you realize it has ever been a fool's hope." Before we dismiss this statement as the words of a hateful and bitter man, consider this observation made by the Indian Poet Rabindranath Tagore: "Perhaps he [Gandhi ] will not succeed. Perhaps he will fail as the Buddha failed, as Christ failed and as Lord Mahavira failed to wean men from their inequities, but he will be remembered as one who made his life an example for all ages to come."[76]

---

* At this time, Genosha has changed government and policies, thanks in large part to the efforts of the X-Men.

Tagore's observation bridges the chasm between Xavier and Magneto. Xavier may well not succeed in bringing about peaceful mutant–human coexistence. He will likely die of old age before his dream is realized. He will fail to "wean men from their inequities." For Magneto, this is where the words of Tagore end. Being an example for generations to come is of no interest to Magneto. He wants the change to come about now. Hence, he is fanatical and frantic to see the fruition of his vision. He will brook no opposition, from without or from among his own followers. He is the man of destiny and, as such, will cut a swath through the present and re-create it in his own image. Such a mind-set is seductive for it cries out to our ego and sense of self-importance. Sometimes the personal desire to see the change, to receive credit as the change agent, becomes more important than the change itself. Charles Xavier's ego causes him to question his vision and methods as well, although his evaluation inevitably brings him to a different conclusion.

When the ego's need for instant gratification overcomes Charles Xavier, he finds himself asking if his dream is worth pursuing anymore. But when he surrenders the need to see the culmination of his vision and accepts that his life may merely lay brick in the road future generations will follow, he feels more confident and purposeful. Xavier's work may allow him to be "remembered as one who made his life an example for all ages to come." This is why, when he asked Jean Grey if his dream still had validity, she answered very bluntly, "If it didn't, we wouldn't be here." The X-Men, all strong-willed adults by this time, remain with Xavier because the dream has validity. They are living the struggle and feel its importance even when the world seems indifferent.

This is a difficult position from which to live, for the ego reminds one constantly of the importance of individual glory, to complete a heroic mission, and, therefore, receive a hero's welcome. In this regard, Charles Xavier and the X-Men aren't fighting only for the peaceful coexistence of humans and mutants but also for the shift to the higher consciousness that makes such coexistence possible. It is the shift that Buddha, Christ, and Mahavira failed to bring about, but they did not fail to make the possibility of such a shift known.

Charles Xavier also works to help others see that such a shift is possible and suffers the pain, doubt, and loss of dignity when it becomes apparent that his words and example are being ignored. How he handles this indignation is, in part, what makes Xavier heroic. With his mutant power, he could change the minds of everyone he meets and make them think, even believe, what he wants. If Magneto had Charles's power, he would use it thusly without hesitation. Charles realizes the shift in human consciousness, if it is to be sustained, must be authentic. His mutation grants him the ultimate weapon to win any debate, to change any mind, and he refuses to use it to do so. Charles Xavier may fight the call of the ego on a minute-to-minute basis in ways others cannot imagine. This could well be why he understands both the power and limitation of the ego and seeks solutions beyond its intense, but ultimately unsatisfying, grasp.

As the X-Men return to Earth after the destruction of Asteroid M, Charles Xavier reflects on how the events of *Mutant Genesis* have only strengthened his resolve. He acknowledges that he is haunted by his dream as surely as Magneto is haunted by his nightmare. He concludes rage and despair fueled Magneto's choices, whereas he and the X-Men will be sustained by hope. This hope will be sorely tested, however, when Magneto returns in *Fatal Attractions*.

The return of Magneto, which occurs in the third chapter of the *Fatal Attractions* story line, coincides with a tragic event in the lives of Charles Xavier and his X-Men. Illyana Rasputin, a young mutant under Xavier's care, has died. Charles bears the burden of responsibility of her death and feels a profound sense of personal failure. Magneto, well aware of Illyana's death, chooses to confront the X-Man the day of the funeral to offer a final warning and an invitation. Magneto's arrival is preceded by an exchange between Xavier and Peter Rasputin, Illyana's older brother and an X-Man who goes by the code name Colossus. Consumed with rage and grief, Colossus informs Xavier that his dream has failed him and Illyana. This transgression cannot be forgiven. It is directly after this exchange that Magneto makes his entrance.

The Magneto we see now is even more intense and driven than in *Mutant Genesis*. He has completely embraced the idea that he is a man of destiny, a man who cannot be held responsible for his actions because they are part of a larger, unfolding story that demands he be the savior of mutants. The acolytes, in much greater numbers and with cultist loyalty, accompany him. Fabian Cortez has been dealt with by this new wave of acolytes and the praise of Magneto reflects his growing comfort with the Fuherprinzip. Acolytes declare, as they crash the funeral, "Praise be to Magneto … his word is our law," and "Magnus is our only hope."

Magneto, his power augmented by his near death in the Earth's electromagnetic field, immobilizes the X-Men by manipulating the iron in their blood streams. With the X-Men frozen, Magneto executes Senyaka, one of the acolytes pledged to his cause. Senyaka acted without Magneto's sanction and is punished with death. This action stands in contrast to Magneto in *Mutant Genesis* in which he chastised Fabian Cortez for acting without permission but does not kill him. Magneto claims to offer all mutants salvation in his new orbiting base, a massive construct called Avalon. He proclaims himself to be the future ruler of a world dominated by mutants, the direct antithesis of Charles Xavier and his dream. Any sense that he is the man who allowed himself to be placed on trial or was willing to follow the path of Xavier is gone. Magneto has completely embraced his role as conqueror and future ruler. He even challenges Charles to join him, to show the courage to walk Magneto's path as Magneto had walked in his footsteps. Xavier refuses as the X-Men free themselves of Magneto's control, girding themselves for a battle with their archnemesis.

Miraculously, the X-Men begin to gain the upper hand on Magneto until Colossus turns on them and joins Magneto's cause. Magneto uses the defection to mock Xavier, who responds with an anger he rarely exhibits. His words brand Magneto a coward, someone incapable of rising above the tragedies of his life. Magneto, for all his talk of control and dominion, is controlled by the world and the ugliness of his past. Xavier's actions are even more pronounced. He takes control of Magneto's mind and forces him back to Avalon. He then forces Magneto to hurl Avalon deep into space, knowing this won't end the conflict, but will buy the X-Men time to prepare for Magneto's inevitable return.

Magneto brings Avalon back to its orbit around Earth only to find that the great powers of the world have initiated a defensive plan code called the Magneto Protocols. Strategically placed satellites orbiting Earth send signals to one another, creating a shield that will prevent Magneto from using his power if he returns to Earth. Although not a direct assault, Magneto sees the shield as preventing him from recruiting more acolytes and saving the lives of mutants. Magneto sends an electromagnetic pulse through the shield, destroying it at its source and crippling technology around the globe. Hospitals lose power. Control towers can't communicate with planes. Hundreds, perhaps thousands, die as a result of Magneto's assault. It is under these circumstances that Charles Xavier decides to launch an assault—a final assault—on Magneto's base.

When briefing the fourteen X-Men present, Xavier states that because Magneto's attack did not kill them, it should be viewed as a mistake on his part. He cryptically adds, "We have to make certain it is the last mistake he has the opportunity to make."

Wolverine, the X-Man who feels the least compunction with killing in combat, attempts to force complete clarity from Xavier. The response he receives is a thinly veiled validation of Wolverine's suspicions. Xavier, understanding such a thought coming from him is unprecedented and shocking, offers an explanation. He points out that the fight has escalated beyond philosophic debate, fighting for causes, hopes, or dreams. The fight is now one of survival. If the X-Men, and by extension the world, survive this fight with Magneto then the fight for the dream can continue.

Xavier confronts a crisis that forces him as a leader to make a difficult choice with intense consequences. Charles Xavier has taken responsibility for the protection of the planet, his actions having an impact on the lives of billions. At this point in time, he is as much a world leader as the leader of the X-Men. In this regard, it is appropriate to consider the impact that tense situations have on presidents as they make decisions that affect the lives of Americans, the world, and even the dream that America stands for.

Presidents' decisions are sometimes at odds with American ideals, just as Xavier's thoughts on solving the problem of Magneto are at odds with his ideals. Dire circumstances, unfortunately, force some to live in the pit of despair even as they cling to the highest aspirations. Consider a thread we can trace through American history from Abraham Lincoln to Franklin Roosevelt to George W. Bush to Barack Obama.

The Civil War consumed the life and presidency of Abraham Lincoln. The pressures he faced are unfathomable to the average person. The thought that someone could imagine oneself in Lincoln's shoes and honestly proclaim what decisions he or she would have made boarders on presumptuous arrogance. Lincoln stood daily on the brink of the country's destruction, his decisions affecting its very survival. Two decisions he made that were extremely controversial were the Emancipation Proclamation and the suspension of the writ of Habeas Corpus, which protects U.S. citizens accused of a crime from being held indefinitely by the government. That these two proclamations were made public within two days of each other (September 22 and 24, 1862, respectfully) only underscores the struggle between high ideals and existing, often ugly, realities. Lincoln, almost simultaneously, promised to bring freedom to the enslaved even as he limited it for the free. Both decisions were exceptionally controversial at the time and are still subject to debate today.

Both proclamations, but particularly the suspension of the writ of Habeas Corpus, are difficult to conceive of outside of the Civil War. The Emancipation Proclamation we can at least see as evolving from Lincoln's long antislavery history. His first public denunciation of slavery was made on January 27, 1838, in his famous Lyceum speech in Springfield, Illinois. Any honest assessment of Abraham Lincoln must include the fact that he held the personal desire for all men be free even as his official duty as president made it difficult to act on this wish.[77]

The suspension of Habeas Corpus, however, has no historic precedent in Lincoln's life. It was as act he took because of the Civil War, and he deemed it necessary for victory. If the Emancipation Proclamation was borne from Lincoln's ideals, then the suspension of Habeas Corpus was a product of necessity. That the Constitution allows for this suspension (Article 1, Section 9, Clause 2) does little to alleviate the shock, then or now, that Lincoln effectively limited the civil liberties of every American with the stroke of a pen. Desperate times may indeed call for desperate measures, but can we learn from desperate acts and, by extension, limit them?

Fast-forward to World War II and Franklin Roosevelt. Before entering the war, Roosevelt pushed for the Lend-Lease Act, which allowed the president to transfer title or lend any "defense article" to a country whose defense was also vital to the safety of the United States, to become law. It did so in March 1941. Again we see an act that would be unfathomable without the context of a war. For the most part, this act can be looked on from the present as acceptable, even necessary, as the Lend-Lease program helped sustain the British and the Russians. The alternative outcome, a Nazi victory in World War II, is almost too horrifying to comprehend. Another action taken by Roosevelt is more difficult to see as benign.

On December 7, 1941, the Japanese attacked and decimated Pearl Harbor. They also attacked Malaya, Hong Kong, Guam, the Philippine Islands, Wake Island, and Midway Island. By December 23, the Japanese had taken Wake Island. Hong Kong fell on December 25. The Japanese army was also slowly subjugating the Philippines. The Japanese seemed unstoppable, and Americans were, justifiably, afraid.

On February 20, 1942, President Roosevelt approved the plan that would lead to the internment of more than 100,000 Japanese Americans. Some of those interned were third- or fourth-generation Americans, but this had no bearing on the decision. Japan was effectively pummeling the United States in the Pacific, and Japanese in America were viewed as a possible threats rather than loyal citizens. That 1,200 interned individuals petitioned to serve in the U.S. military did not significantly alter the negative perception. Animosity for the Japanese only intensified when, in late February to early March, the Japanese fleet defeated a joint U.S.–British force in the Java Sea. Then, on April 9, the Japanese took full control of the Philippines.

The racial component of the internment camps is unavoidable, especially considering that German and Italian Americans did not suffer such indignation. Before labeling Franklin Roosevelt an outright racist, however, one should discover if the internment camps were a product of his heart, his head, or a combination of the two. The Emancipation Proclamation was a product of Lincoln's heart and head. He could explain it as a strategic war measure, but it also coincided with his inner desire to end slavery. Did President Roosevelt have a racial distrust of the Japanese or were the internment camps strictly a matter of security? The number of free German and Italian Americans walking the streets in 1942 does not help an attempt to adopt the second option.

When attempting to allay fears and create security, extreme and controversial actions may, and often are, taken. But the contentious question can be asked, are Roosevelt's actions a less extreme reaction than Lincoln's? Lincoln's affected all citizens, and Roosevelt's a limited number. Does the good of the many outweigh the good of the few, or was

Abraham Lincoln more evenhanded precisely because his action affected everyone indiscriminately? Regardless of how one handles these questions, they can be asked only because the United States, and its ideals, survived the crucible of the Civil War . It could be said that Franklin Roosevelt was only able to violate American ideals because Lincoln's violation enabled the ideals to survive. The paradox of America acting as an "arsenal of democracy" through lend-lease while simultaneously acting in a profoundly undemocratic manner toward its Japanese citizens is built on the back of Lincoln's own simultaneous actions of limiting and expanding freedom.

Fast forward to September 11, 2001. It is difficult to overstate the shock and fear Americans felt following the attack on the World Trade Center. On September 20, 2001, President George W. Bush addressed a joint session of Congress. He specifically drew distinctions between Muslims and terrorists, stating, "I also want to speak tonight directly to Muslims throughout the world. We respect your faith. It's practiced freely by many millions of Americans, and by millions more in countries that America counts as friends. Its teachings are good and peaceful, and those who commit evil in the name of Allah blaspheme the name of Allah. The terrorists are traitors to their own faith, trying, in effect, to hijack Islam itself."[78]

There would be no rounding up of Muslims or Arab-Americans to hold in internment camps. President Bush would, however, as presidents before him, reserve the right to act with tremendous authority to ensure the safety of America. In the same address, President Bush said he would use "every necessary weapon of war" to defeat "the global terror network." The Patriot Act and the detention camp at Guantanamo Bay can be seen as two such weapons. Although both these actions have been the centerpiece of heated political debate at various times, the historic evidence clearly suggests that President Bush is not some anomaly in U.S. history violating civil liberties in an unprecedented manner. In fact, he may fit into a larger narrative than we realize.

Move forward to the ascension of President Barack Obama. If the internment of Japanese Americans is a black scar on the record of President Roosevelt and the nation, then President Bush's refusal to detain Muslims and Arab Americans en masse is an improvement of past practices. If so, then we can see President Obama's deeply symbolic decision to close the detention camp at Guantanamo Bay as part of a continued effort to bring America's actions and ideals closer together. Could the continued war on terror, coupled with the Taliban's activity in Pakistan and Afghanistan or the nuclear aspirations of North Korea and Iran cause President Obama eventually to make a decision that future presidents will need to rectify as America staggers toward its promise?

This concept, the process of America staggering toward and struggling with its ideals, brings us back to President Lincoln. He once noted that the greatest glory of the Declaration of Independence was that it established "a standard maxim for free society ... constantly looked to, constantly labored for, and even though never perfectly attained, constantly approximated, and thereby constantly spreading and deepening its influence."[79] America was not just divided by the Civil War. Even then America was, and still is, a house divided—its present reality separated from its lofty ideals that continue to influence and instruct. But if we accept this meta-narrative of American history, how do we connect such a massive story to our own lives? The answer to such a question brings us again to President Lincoln and Charles Xavier.

Much like America, an individual can also live a divided life. Abraham Lincoln communicated such a reality when he would discuss his official duty in contrast with his personal wishes. The divided life can cause someone to maintain silence when speaking out on an issue would be appropriate, to break faith with personal convictions, to deny and thereby strengthen inner darkness, to feel like a fraud or become depressed because the one's selfhood is being actively denied.[80] As an act of liberation, the Emancipation Proclamation freed Abraham Lincoln. His official duty and personal wishes now working in unison, President Lincoln conducted the war with increased decisiveness and vigor.[81] As America exists in a divided state regarding its realities and promises, as President Lincoln could feel the pain of division between his duty and ideals, so, too, does Charles Xavier offer us a vision of the pain one feels when the challenges of life seem to exceed the power of our dreams and the solutions to those challenges, a violation of our ideals.

Xavier's preparations for the invasion of Avalon reveal that, despite the pressure he is under and his own words, his dream is not dead. He has assembled an assault team with his eyes on both the present and the future. The team includes two of the stealthiest X-Men (Wolverine and Gambit), two telepaths to punch through Magneto's psychic defenses and attack his mind (Xavier and Jean Grey), and two individuals with emotional ties to Magneto that they seek to resolve (Rogue and Quicksilver).* Wolverine also has no compunction about killing an enemy in battle and, while lacking Wolverine's reputation, it is not hard to envision Gambit delivering a deathblow as well. The team that remains on Earth is equally important.

When Xavier founded his school, his original class included only five mutants. All five are still with him, holding the distinction of being the "original" X-Men. Only one of the original team, Jean Grey, is going to Avalon. The other four members will remain behind. Hank McCoy, code named the Beast, states a fact in the form of a question, "You don't expect to come back, do you Charles?" Cyclops, another original member who most clearly identifies Xavier as a father figure, adds, "And you need us down here—to stay—to carry on?" Charles Xavier is prepared to sacrifice his life, and that of the assault team, to save Earth from Magneto's aggression. The dreamer may die, but the dream is being entrusted to the next generation so it may live. The dream of mutant–human harmony (like all civil rights struggles) can be seen as a meta-narrative as well, and Charles Xavier has come to grips with the fact that his time on the stage may be ending, but the story goes on. This action could be seen as Charles bringing his divided self closer together, the horrors of what he must do and the significance of his dream occupying his thoughts simultaneously.

The X-Men silently infiltrate Avalon and, usurping control of the main control board, teleport all the acolytes to air-lock pods. The pods are then launched to a stationary orbit around Magneto's fortress. The final battle will be between X-Men and Magneto alone. The battle is truly brutal, both physically and psychologically. Magneto continues to use the horrors of his past to justify his actions. His contempt for human beings is also evident in the venomous words he spews during the struggle.

As the X-Men assault Magneto's body, Xavier and Jean Grey attack his mind. They force Magneto to relive the pain of his tortured past and possibly consider his own destructive choices. Hurt, but undeterred by the psychic assault, Magneto battles on and at-

---

* Rogue had a brief romantic history with Magneto, and Quicksilver is his estranged son.

tempts to kill Quicksilver. Wolverine takes advantage of Magneto's focus on his son and delivers a critical wound to the would-be dictator. Xavier sees Wolverine's strike as an opportunity to break through the last of Magneto's psychic defenses. Jean Grey, however, breaks contact. She claims that the fight can be ended without this psychic violation due to Magneto's wounds.

Magneto, granted a respite by Jean's decision, lashes out at Wolverine. Wolverine's skeleton is reinforced at the molecular level with a metal known as adamantium. This bonding was done to him as part of a government experiment he survived only because of his mutant ability to heal at an exceptionally accelerated rate. Magneto uses his power to separate the metal from Wolverine's skeleton and pull it through his skin. Wolverine falls in agony, his healing factor keeping him on the brink of life.

Charles Xavier, proclaiming himself in some ways a failure because of his willingness to hide behind philosophic differences and forgive Magneto his transgressions, acts in a manner he has not before. Despite this sense of personal failure, Charles articulates, for the last time, the difference between his life's work and Magneto's. Enraged by the deaths Magneto's original assault caused, his failure to stop him in the past, and the sight of one of his X-Men clinging to life, Charles Xavier reaches into Magneto's mind and effectively shuts it off. He takes away Magneto's ego, his rage, and his hate. In essence, he obliterates his longtime rival's mind, leaving the once proud man in a vegetative state. Xavier's decision was most difficult. He sacrifices a piece of himself by violating his ideals in the short term so that his universalizing dream can survive. The future will tell if the actions needed to preserve his dream during a crisis will ever be used again.

# CHAPTER 13

## The X-Men—Group Dynamics and Diversity

The X-Men offer connections to a vast array of real-life and curriculum issues. The team, whose membership has fluctuated and changed over the years of publication, willingly fights for Charles Xavier's dream, even as they experience the cruelty people are capable of. Beyond the daily struggle of being a mutant outcast and superhero are the situational struggles that come with being a part of a team, a team that lives together at Xavier's school. Sharing living space forces them to share daily life experiences as well, including funerals, weddings, dating, mentoring, building friendships, building trust, sibling rivalry, and a litany of common themes that even uncommon characters must confront. The X-Man roster is far too expansive to allow each member a full character analysis in a single chapter, but key members can be introduced to familiarize the reader with them, as well as to illustrate the important role that diversity plays on the team.

The word "diversity" has lost much of its vitality from overuse and buzzword status. When a word is elevated to (or, more accurately, demoted to) the level of bumper-sticker wisdom, richness is often lost. Thankfully, the X-Men were diverse before it was en vogue or politically correct to be so. As a piece of popular culture, the X-Men celebrated diversity well before the concept was institutionalized. The diverse lineup they presented was subtler than the simplistic group status we see diversity reduced to, and in need of liberation from, today.

The original X-Men lineup, presented in 1963, truly lacked visual diversity. Five white teenagers led by a white, male professor hardly sounds like the starting place for an evaluation of a diverse team. Because 1963 is also the year Martin Luther King Jr. requested that we judge people by the content of their character, not merely by the color of their skin, we should look beyond the lack of melanin the original lineup possessed and get to know them a little.

Scott Summers, given the code name Cyclops, is a central figure in the history of the X-Men. Scott's eyes constantly emit a force beam capable of blasting holes in walls and maiming bodies. Only his eyelids and special goggles are able to contain his deadly mutation. Scott exhibited natural leadership qualities and became the field commander of the X-Men. These leadership traits, along with a sullen, introverted personality, were likely all developed in his years in an orphanage. Orphaned at a young age, Scott learned self-reliance. He reminds us that our difficult pasts cut with a twin blade. The methods with which Scott coped gave him strengths (leadership and self-reliance), while simultaneously granting shortcomings (a diffident, untrusting personality with a propensity to brood and remain distant from others). Which side of the coin the reader focuses on greatly shapes the reaction one has to Scott Summers.

Jean Grey, code named Marvel Girl, has telekinetic and telepathic powers. While Jean's powers may be less physically obtrusive than Scott's, they are, in some ways, more difficult to cope with. At the age of ten, Jean's telepathy was triggered prematurely when she witnessed the death of a friend who was struck by a car. Jean telepathically, and quite inadvertently, linked minds with her dying friend. The experience nearly killed Jean as well. Like most mutants, as she ages her powers grow stronger. When she first joined the X-Men, her telekinesis enabled her to lift only objects she could lift physically. As time passed, however, her powers enabled her to lift much heavier objects. As she ages, we see her, at various times, lift cars and hurl them at enemies, hold crumbling aircraft or buildings together, and render foes immobile merely by willing so with her mind. Even as a teenager, the dual ability to strike foes mentally with her telepathy and physically with her telekinesis made Jean one of, if not the most, dangerous members of the team. This is quite a distinction for the only female of the group.

Of course, being the only female on a team with four teenage boys created its own situations to deal with. Jean often finds herself fending off the flirtatious passes of her teammates as well as the attacks of enemies. In the end, the extroverted Jean Grey and the introverted Scott Summers will marry—love finding a way despite the dangers a superhero must face.

Hank McCoy (the Beast), Robert Drake (Iceman), and Warren Worthington (the Angel) rounded out the original X-Men lineup. Hank was born with a great intellect, not his mutant power, and unusually large hands and feet. Upon reaching puberty, his limbs began to resemble that of a gorilla, and his agility, speed, and strength did as well. As Hank matured, he earned a doctorate in biophysics and accepted a position as a research scientist at the Brand Institute. Uncomfortable with his freakish appearance, he developed a serum designed to reduce his oversized limbs. The serum had the opposite effect, causing Hank to grow blue hair all over his body. Along with the hair came sharp teeth and claws, heightened senses, and canine-like ears. Hank now truly looked the part of the Beast. Despite this fact, he slowly learns to accept his appearance and becomes a quick-witted and highly respected hero and scientist.

In Hank McCoy, we see someone of staggering intellectual potential. People's intellect, coupled with how they present themselves, can be the cause of great resentment and animosity. Hank's personality prevents him from being arrogant but does not diminish the reality that, despite the somewhat brutish nature of his mutation, he is the nerd of the group.

Iceman, as the name insinuates, can generate intense cold and ice. He also can mentally manipulate the ice he forms into any shape he can imagine. Unlike Hank, his power does not alter his appearance, so no one would suspect he is a mutant. Also, he has to call upon his power. He can walk the streets unencumbered by average people. In this regard, he is different from Jean Grey, who, despite having no physical mutations must be on guard while in crowds, for the thoughts of others can seep into her mind if she fails to ward them off. In this regard, Iceman has the most benign mutation of the X-Men. He is also presented as the most immature of the group.

The Angel endured a dramatic occurrence when he hit puberty. Whereas many young people are concerned with breaking out in pimples, Warren faced a far more startling change. Wings grew from his back, granting him the gift of flight. He embraced his mutation as a gift and never regretted his mutation, a feeling not all mutants, as the Beast illustrated, share. This is not the only trait that distinguishes him from his peers.

Warren Worthington was born to an exceptionally wealthy family. His childhood, as such, was vastly different than the orphaned Scott or the middle-class Jean. He is from a different socioeconomic stratum, unashamed of it, and not above flaunting it. This disposition —his extroverted ways as well as his wealth—will cause tension, both with original and new members of the X-Men. In particular, it will grate Scott Summers, as Warren becomes an early (but not the last) rival for Jean's affections.

Despite their common ethnic backgrounds, we see a wealth of diversity on display in the original X-Men. These differences include socioeconomics, intelligence, extroversion, introversion, family backgrounds covering the spectrum from orphaned boy to being raised by happily married parents, degrees of maturity, and the role of a female in a largely male group. Also included on the list should be the fact that Charles Xavier is crippled and confined to a wheelchair. This handicap has not limited his passion for social justice or his effectiveness as the driving force behind the X-Men.

The first lineup change in the X-Men's history occurred in 1975. The story line included the original team being captured by a massive entity called Krakoa, the "living island." The creature defeated the X-Men and held them as helpless captives. Xavier embarked on a worldwide recruiting tour, bringing an older and very international cast of characters to the school. John Proudstar (Thunderbird) was an Apache Indian whose mutant powers included superhuman strength and speed. When recruiting Proudstar, Xavier witnessed him wrestle a Bison to the ground with his bare hands. Proudstar joined Xavier despite his reluctance to join another "white man's crusade," as he had served a tour of duty in Vietnam.

From Russia Xavier gains the services of Piotr (Peter) Rasputin (Colossus). Peter is the youngest of the "new" X-Men. He lived as a farmer surrounded by a caring family. The fact he is a mutant did not disturb them. Their acceptance made Peter reluctant to leave, as did his upbringing in the Soviet Union. When Xavier asks him to join the X-Men, Peter's first question regarded the philosophy that powers like his should belong to the state. Xavier responds that they belong to the world.

Peter's mutation grants him the ability to turn his entire body into an almost indestructible steel alloy. Bullets, shells, a fall from a great height, extreme temperatures, and explosives all fail to harm him. When in armored form, he also does not need to breathe, and his metal body does not suffer from rust or exposure. His strength becomes almost incomprehensible when he is in his metal form. An example would be when the X-Men plane was attacked and submerged by Magneto. Following the victory over their opponent, Colossus carried the plane from the seafloor on his back. Despite the awesome physical power he possesses, Peter is a gentle soul. When not knocking down buildings and shattering his foes, he focuses on his artistic gifts and produces beautiful portraits for the X-Mansion.

A Japanese mutant named Shiro Yoshida (Sunfire) briefly joins Xavier's group. Shiro's mother was a survivor of Hiroshima. The radiation from the atomic bomb may have caused her children to be mutants, as Leyu, his sister, is also a mutant. Sunfire has the ability to fly and to fire beams of plasma energy. He is also resistant to radiation. He never officially joins the X-Men, leaving the group after freeing the original members from their captivity.

No X-Man was born as physically mutated as Kurt Wagner (Nightcrawler). The German native was born with blue fur covering his body. His skin also seems to be blue. His hands have only two fingers, and a thumb and his feet only two large toes. Adding to his already unusual appearance are his sharp, canine teeth and yellow eyes. The final abnormality is a pointed, prehensile tail. His parents, unable to cope with their son's devilish form, abandoned him. Taken in by gypsies, he was raised as one of them. As he entered his teen years, his actual mutant abilities manifested themselves. His agility increased dramatically, and he found he could stick to walls in a manner reminiscent of Spider-Man. Nightcrawler also has the ability to teleport. The use of this power is accompanied by a puff of smoke and the smell of brimstone, adding to his demonic visage.

He eventually joins a circus and performs as an acrobat. When a crowd learns he is not wearing a costume, their fear and repulsion grows. Such emotions quickly lead to the forming of a hateful lynch mob that seeks Kurt's death. It is when they have him cornered, too exhausted to teleport, that Charles Xavier finds him. Using his own mutant powers, he grabs control of every mind present, paralyzing everyone but himself and Kurt. Wagner joins the X-Men where we learn of his deep Catholic faith and corresponding belief in the goodness of man. He holds his belief despite the treatment he received. Such determination is easily compatible with Xavier's dream.

Ireland provides the next X-Man, Sean Cassidy (Banshee). Sean was the wealthy heir of the Cassidy fortune, including the historic Cassidy Keep. Sean was, for a time, a member of Interpol and spent time as a freelance operative. He had already seen many years and adventures by the time Charles Xavier approached him. His mutant ability allows him great sonic effects with his voice. He can fly and generate such force with his voice that solid objects are shattered. He can disrupt people's equilibrium and has used his voice to hypnotize individuals.

Ororo Munroe (Storm) comes to the X-Men from Africa. Orphaned at the age of five, she grew up on the streets of Cairo, becoming a proficient thief and pickpocket. It was at this young age that she first met Charles Xavier, picking his pocket in a crowd. He used his power to prevent her escape and realized the powerful mind within the child. She escaped him, however, when an evil psychic, the Shadow King, assaulted Xavier and the two became embroiled in a brutal mental dual.

Ororo's life brought her deep into the Sahara, following a yearning she could not explain. Eventually she would arrive in Kenya, the land of her ancestors. Local tribes worshipped her as a "goddess of life" because of her mutation—the ability to manipulate the weather. Conjuring rain, thunder, cooling breezes, and cloud covers helped the agricultural society thrive. Ororo embraced the role, one that appealed to her for she is often depicted as extremely maternal and caring for the Earth and its residents. It was when she was living in Kenya that she "met" Charles Xavier and joined the X-Men.

Logan (Wolverine) is the last member of the "new" X-Men, coming to the group via the Canadian secret service, among other places. Logan's mutation included heightened senses, strength, and reflexes. His sense of smell and hearing are amazingly acute, enabling him to track down his foes and prevent his teammates from being ambushed. His immune system is also heightened, causing him to heal at an accelerated rate. Broken bones and cuts heal exceptionally fast, a definite benefit for a superhero. Wolverine also ages remarkably slowly. When his complicated origin is finally told, it is discovered he is more than two hundred years old. Not all of Wolverine's attributes, however, are natural.

Kidnapped by the Canadian military, experiments were conducted on his body and, thanks to his healing factor, he could survive, allowing for more experiments to take place. The project, known as Weapon X, eventually laced Logan's skeleton with an unbreakable metal called adamantium. The process caused Logan such pain, he was nearly driven insane. He broke free from his captors and roamed the Canadian wilderness, more beast than man. The experiments created mental blocks and even implanted memories in Logan's mind. As he regained his sanity, he found he had no recollection of the past, as vast as it may have been. He also found he had three adamantium claws that could be retracted into his forearms. Logan always thought they were implants and was shocked to learn he always had bone claws. The process that covered his skeletal system with adamantium also covered the claws.

When Logan joins the X-Men he is very much a loner, ill-tempered and prone to dismissing authority. He is a vicious adversary, one who has no compunction with killing opponents if necessary. Such ferocity causes instant tension among the X-Men, but Charles Xavier will not turn Logan away, he patiently works with his visceral comrade, hoping to help temper his rage.

The new team brings with it a variety of powers and increased diversity. An obvious starting point is the multicultural dimension the new members bring to the team. Not a single one of them is an American of European decent. If we distinguish Native American as distinct from Americans, then we can say there are no Americans among the new recruits. From these divergent origins come a bevy of areas for study. Peter Rasputin opens the door to Communist Russia and collectivism, especially as Xavier recruits him directly from a collective farm. Kurt Wagner brings us religious diversity as one of the few overtly religious characters in comics (comics tend to be very agnostic toward matters of religion). Sean Cassidy and Logan bring years of experience to the table, a form of diversity overlooked and even discarded in our "in with the new, out with the old" culture.

John Proudstar and Shiro Yoshida offer us an anti-American viewpoint, as both men carry animosity because of the suffering of their people. Although this may be uncomfortable to some students, such sentiment is also a reality to be addressed and, in some cases, transcended. This is evident in the two characters as well, for Proudstar will stay with the X-Men while Yoshida leaves after Krakoa's defeat, unwilling to be bound to a team based in America.

Ororo, like Jean Grey, is the only female among the new recruits and may be the most powerful member of the new team. Her weather manipulation makes her capable of using lightning, intense cold, hurricanes, and tornados as weapons against her opponents. Her nurturing and compassionate demeanor also places her in a position of being the total opposite of Logan. It is in such situations, when two people with such contradictory worldviews (Logan the brutal loner and Ororo the compassionate caregiver), that we find the true power of diversity, if we slow down and allow patience to replace judgment.

With the team on a trip to Canada, Logan declares he is going to go hunting. Ororo, the protector of nature, quickly reprimands him for killing for fun. Logan scoffs at her, pointing out he said nothing about killing; he said hunting. He wishes to test his tracking skills by following a deer without being noticed. The goal is not to kill, but to get close enough to touch the animal without it running away. Such an action, he points out, takes true skill. When Storm apologizes, Logan dismisses her, pointing out that she just assumed the worst and didn't bother to ask.

This brief interlude in the ongoing chaos of the superhero lifestyle, illustrates the true power of diversity. Sometimes people have diverse ways of expressing a shared belief. When we push for absolute sameness, we often offend because of the enforcement that our way is the way to express a particular view. Storm and Wolverine actually share a view, a deep respect for nature. Storm displays her convictions regularly—both through her mutant gift and the environment she keeps in her room where she maintains a lush garden. Wolverine reveals little of his inner world when he first joins the X-Men, much more comfortable being the outsider on the team rather than a committed teammate. People are free to make judgments of him, which could be wrong, as this episode proves.

Ororo's need for sameness, for Logan not only to respect nature but also show respect in a way she intrinsically understands and approves of, causes her to categorize her approach as "good" and label Logan's expressed desire (to hunt) as "bad." Logan's explanation, a slowing down of the process because he could have walked out and ignored his teammate, revealed the diversity in their approach, but also a common ground on which they stand. His respect includes a need to walk among nature and be a part of it, whereas Ororo's respect manifests in a desire to care for nature, literally (as she can also fly) soaring above the forest as Logan enjoys pushing through the brush.

Diversity, at its best, isn't just about the differences, it's about evaluating them to discover hidden commonalities. The cycle becomes complete when one authentically respects both the difference and the similarities simultaneously. It is a slow process, one that tears apart the comfortable idea that perception is reality and replaces it with the need to distrust perception and find reality. As the years pass, Logan and Ororo form a very strong bond, grounded on the mutual respect forged both in the hardship of battle and in revealing conversations. Logan, more than any other X-Man, will openly root for Ororo to replace Scott as leader of the X-Men after the trial of Magneto. As leader, she often leans heavily on Logan for support, even as she reprimands him for his propensity to do things his way. For his part, Logan takes her criticisms with much greater grace than he ever accepted Scott's.

In Logan and Ororo, we see the real goal of diversity, the forging of a powerful and enduring friendship. A friendship in which common ground exists, even when hidden, respects the differences even when they are intense, learns consciously and unconsciously from the other, and allows the hardened heart to soften and the nurturing heart to take up the mantle of warrior and protect those in need.

# CHAPTER 14

## Confrontation with Hatred in *God Loves, Man Kills*

*God Loves, Man Kills* opens with three powerful scenes. The first is truly horrific, while the second and third are powerful in a distinctly different manner. The story opens with two young children, age eleven and nine, running in a panic across the playground at their local elementary school. Jill, the nine year old, asks to stop because she is tired. Her older brother, looking over his shoulder with terror, tells her they have to keep running. A gunshot stops him and he falls to the ground, wounded. A group of adults, identifying themselves as Purifiers, surround the two children and, after a cold explanation, execute them. The bodies are then hanged on a swing set with the word "mutie" written across their chests.* The bodies are meant to be an example for all to see come morning, but that part of the plan is interrupted. Magneto arrives on the scene and removes the bodies. Speaking from a place of rage and grief, he swears to avenge the children.

We will learn that the Purifiers work for the Reverend William Stryker, the leader of the evangelical Stryker Crusade.[82] Stryker's goal is to rid the world of mutant-kind, whom he sees as a deviation from humankind and, therefore, an abomination before God. In this moment, he is seen reading the Bible and quoting passages that demand stoning the wicked. This theme, the use of biblical passages to support violent action, occurs throughout the story.

The third scene connects the first two and brings them into a small struggle students will likely be able to relate to. Kitty Pryde, a teenage mutant and recent addition to the X-Men, is enraged and fighting a boy named Danny. The fight takes place outside a dance studio owned by Stevie Hunter, a friend of the X-Men. Illyana Rasputin attempts to break up the fight as her older brother, Peter, arrives to pick her up from class. Peter's arrival distracts Kitty, and Danny lands a cheap shot. The fight is broken up, and the reason for the fight made clear.

---

* "Mutie" is a derogatory word used by those who hate mutants.

Danny claims Kitty started the fight, and she admits to swinging first, but only because Danny mouthed off. Danny was talking about all the good William Stryker's Crusade does, proudly stating that he and his parents are members. He believes Stryker will save humanity from mutants, who are merely getting what they deserve. He goads Kitty by calling her a "mutie-lover." Peter, who is an imposing individual even when not in his armored form, suggests the "conversation" end at this point. Danny leaves, and Stevie offers to bring Kitty inside to clean up.

Kitty, still enraged, wonders how everyone can be so calm. When Stevie offers the thought that it was "only words," Kitty shouts at Stevie, who is black, "Suppose he'd called me a nigger-lover, Stevie?! Would you be so damn tolerant then?!" Kitty turns and runs to Peter's car, leaving him to apologize for Kitty's outburst, claiming she did not mean what she said. Stevie does not respond to Peter, who drives the two young girls home. The scene ends with Stevie standing alone on the street, a tear rolling down her cheek. She considers Peter's apology and thinks to herself that Kitty "meant every word. And she was right."

These opening scenes provide, as does the entire story, ample opportunity for curriculum connections and meaningful conversation. The opening scene calls to mind horrific scenes from U.S. history. It is less than one hundred years since blacks had to live in fear of lynch mobs and the terror they wrought. That the two young children in the scene are black makes this connection all the more frightening. The murder of Emmett Till or the venom spewed at Elizabeth Eckford as she approached Central High in Little Rock, Arkansas, can also be used to illustrate the intense hatred that can reside in the human heart.[83] The murder of Matthew Shepard offers a more recent reminder of the somber reality of hate in America.

Of course, America is not alone in its examples of human cruelty, and the modern age is hardly the birthplace of malice. The treatment of Christians at the hands of the Romans can act as an appropriate segue to the position taken by Reverend William Stryker. Christians were arrested and convicted for hatred against humanity. The emperor Nero, seeking a scapegoat for a fire that decimated Rome, blamed the Christians and "inflicted the most exquisite tortures" on them. These tortures included being torn apart by dogs, nailed to crosses, and being "doomed to the flames and burnt, to serve as nightly illumination, when daylight had expired."[84]

In *God Loves, Man Kills* mutants, not Christians, are the target of persecution. A prominent Christian is the leader of the persecution. Reverend Stryker leads his Crusade from the Stryker Building, a magnificent high rise in New York City. The building and the offices within communicate a sense of power, wealth, and prestige. Stryker is presented throughout the tale as a man of certainty and resolve. He is unwavering in his convictions and hypnotically confident in his mission. It is important to note that the fact a Christian leads the persecution does not make the story anti-Christian. The story is much more anti-zealot. To make this point clear, the reader must understand what type of man William Stryker is and how his sense of identity influences his Christianity.

Stryker quotes the Bible, using passages to justify his hatred and use of violence. His biblical understanding is literalistic and exclusivistic. To be literalistic means seeing the Bible as a divine product with the Holy Spirit directly guiding the hands of the various writers. Fundamentalists and evangelicals tend to have a literalistic view. Passages are seen as factual, unless the metaphor or symbolism is obvious. Equating factuality of the Bible with faith, many fundamentalists come into conflict with science.[85] Focusing on just the literalistic tendencies Stryker possesses will grant insight into his personality. The other qualities that describe his biblical understanding will be interjected when appropriate.

Stryker's literalism extends to the point of using the words of Jesus to goad a brainwashed Charles Xavier to kill Cyclops and Storm (the three mutants were captured by a well-planned Purifier ambush). When asked to do so, Xavier protests, claiming that Ororo and Scott are his children. This prompts Stryker to quote parts of Matthew 10:34–37, "Think not I am come to send peace on Earth; I come not to send peace, but a sword. For I am come to set a man at Variance against his father … he that loveth son or daughter more than me is not worthy of me." Charles then proves his worth by lashing out at his students with a vicious psychic assault. But what is the reader to make of the words of Jesus, particularly these words that seem so hostile, used in this manner?

This is a good example of how quoting a passage while ignoring the character of the speaker and the historical context is misleading. A literalist, be they Christian, Muslim, or an Atheist, could view the passage just as Stryker does, as a test or proof of faith. The Atheist, taking the passage literally, could also offer the passage as evidence of hypocrisy on the part of Jesus and proof of contradictions in the Bible. To attempt to grasp Jesus' meaning, we must look at him in his historic context.

In the first century, Jews were suffering persecution and oppression at the hands of the Roman Empire. The various Jewish responses to this situation were seen in four distinct and established groups: the Essenes, the Sadducees, the Zealots, and the Pharisees. Jesus did not see any of these responses as capable of producing a lasting peace or uplifting those in need. He also viewed them as a causing separation from God. Therefore, he offered a different path. This new path would be recognizable to Jews, but different from the other responses. Therefore, any Jew (or gentile for that matter) who decided to follow Jesus' path, would be forced to break away from the path their parents' had chosen for the family. Such a decision would set parent against child, even if the child had reached adulthood before breaking the tradition of their parents.

As for the apparent conflict between loving God and loving one's children, we must again consider who Jesus was, not how we see the world. Jesus experienced a level of love others did not. This experience of "the constant, unstinted love that flows from God to us" was an experiential reality for Jesus.[86] It was the sacred ground of his life and the reason he was able to express love for the marginalized, ostracized, and ignored. It also gave him the strength to stand against those who created, and even benefited from, the established culture. Having experienced the power of such love, Jesus sought to help others experience it as well. Experiencing this love greatly increases the ability one has to express and feel love for others. Love requires a level of risk. Therefore, Jesus called upon others to take the risk of loving God more than your children and allow God's love to return to you. This will increase your capacity to love others, even your children, whom most people don't think they could love more than they currently do.

It is not an either–or proposition that Jesus puts forth but the beginning of a process that will complete a circuit—dare to love God more than your children and your capacity to love will increase. This will happen not because Jesus said so but because daring to follow the path presented by Jesus can lead to this experiential reality.

Stryker's purposes are not served by lessons of growing love and nonduality. He needs either—or choices (exclusivistic) and violence, so Jesus' words are used to bring about this end. Stryker's goals supplant those of Jesus. This explains why Stryker asks the addled Charles Xavier not only to embrace the word, but also to embrace "myself as the deliverer of the word." Stryker, in a single phrase, elevates himself above the Bible, Jesus, and God.

The kidnapping of Xavier, Cyclops, and Storm are vital components of Stryker's plan to eradicate mutants. Stryker has had a machine constructed that amplifies Xavier's mutant abilities. With the help of this machine, Xavier can detect mutant minds. Once contact is made, Xavier can kill a mutant by destroying his or her mind. The brainwashed Xavier will be strapped to this machine as he seeks and destroys mutant minds. Cyclops and Storm are used to test the effectiveness of Xavier's brainwashing. If he will kill two of his beloved students, he will kill strangers as well.

To reduce suspicion, the kidnapping of the three mutants is designed to look like a car accident that claimed their lives. Three corpses, burned beyond recognition, are found in the wreckage. The police conclude it is an accident, but Wolverine disagrees. Examining the crash site with Colossus, Wolverine states that the accident is a con. He draws this conclusion based on his mutant abilities and his experience as a highly trained military operative. Wolverine's senses are astoundingly acute. The scents of the bodies are not the same as those of his friends. Additionally, he confesses to having staged such "accidents" in his lifetime, and this site carries the hallmark of a professional setup. His experience continues to be of service to the X-Men when he contacts Nightcrawler via a com-link.

While Wolverine and Colossus investigated the crash, Nightcrawler was left behind to watch their car. Wolverine suspected they were being watched and Nightcrawler confirms this suspicion. Their car was checked out while they were gone and is being watched. The three X-Men converge on the Purifiers, two of whom are in heavily armored battle suits. The outcome is uncertain until Magneto arrives, tears apart the battle suits, and declares himself a willing ally in this struggle.

The X-Men take the four Purifiers to Xavier's school and attempt to get information from them. Wolverine, whose claws had cut through a car in the battle, places a fist under the chin of a purifier. He extends the two outside claws, framing the Purifiers face. He threatens to extend the third claw, which would kill his antagonist almost instantly, if answers to his questions aren't given. Magneto intervenes and uses his power to extract information from all four Purifiers. In this scene's final frame, an exchange takes place that is ripe for political and philosophic discussion. Colossus, obviously disturbed by what he has just witnessed, asks, "Was this ... necessary?"

Wolverine, completely undisturbed by the same event, offers a monosyllabic response, "Yup." A cigar held between his teeth only enhances his casual demeanor. Nightcrawler then asks, although no answer comes from the text, "But if we use our foes' methods, my friends, how then are we better than they?"

As the story continues, the surviving X-Men steal Storm's and Cyclops' bodies. Magneto and Kitty Pryde confirm that the two are dead, but Wolverine again intervenes. His senses confirm the two are alive but in a stasis resembling death. Magneto shocks them back to consciousness. He concludes that Xavier, even brainwashed, could not bring himself to kill his pupils. On a subconscious level, he resisted the brainwashing and induced the illusion of death to satisfy his captors. The X-Men and Magneto, knowing Stryker plans to use Xavier to execute mutants during his sermon scheduled at Madison Square Garden, devise their own stratagem to thwart him.

Before this final confrontation unfolds, another layer is added to the reader's understanding of William Stryker's motives. In a flashback, Stryker recalls how, due to a car accident, he had to help his wife, Marcy, deliver their son on a secluded desert road in Nevada. The child, born with physical mutations like Nightcrawler, was a monster to his eyes. William Stryker, who at this time was a master sergeant in the U.S. Army Rangers, killed his son. He handed the body to his wife, held her close, and broke her neck. He placed the two bodies in the car, crawled in next to them, and lit a match.

The car, which was leaking gas, exploded. Stryker survived the explosion, as did his shame. He eventually learns about mutants when reading an article written by Charles Xavier. He realizes that his son was a mutant. Questions about his own wickedness and self-worth rush through his mind. He prays for guidance, and it is granted. He concludes the sin, the birth of his mutant son, was Marcy's, not his own. He survived the explosion because he was chosen by God to lead the fight against the abomination that is mutant kind. Mutants are not made in God's image, but in that of the Devil. Mutants must be evil; otherwise he would be forced to consider his murderous actions in a much different light. Reassured and focused by this "revelation," Stryker begins his crusade against mutants, a crusade that can be completed by using Charles Xavier to eradicate his own kind.

William Stryker, in becoming a reverend, is engaging in a practice that can be called spiritual bypassing. Spiritual bypassing is the practice of using spiritual teachings to avoid dealing with unresolved emotional and psychological issues. Some people, when attempting to implement spiritual teaching in their lives, create a new spiritual identity. This spiritual identity is merely the rearranging of their old, fractured personality into a new, seemingly improved, model. Unfortunately, all the unresolved issues fester under the surface and undermine any authentic spiritual, personal, emotional, or psychological growth. Spiritual teachings and practices are used to rationalize previous and current actions. Traits of those caught in the web of spiritual bypassing include using spiritual ideas for personal gain, narcissism, and delusions of personal grandeur.[87]

In the story, Styker expresses great pride in the fact that for twenty-five years, he was busy "amassing phenomenal temporal power." This line best summarizes Stryker's life mission. He has dedicated most of his adult life to gathering the resources needed to destroy mutants. His goal is not tied to being spiritually uplifted but to gain and wield worldly power free from the moral rigors of the devout Christian. He uses religious language to justify his actions, alleviating any sense of guilt he might feel.

Examples of such activities are prevalent throughout history, speaking to the capacity people possess to creatively justify their actions, rather than an indictment of religion itself. Stryker is a master manipulator, deceiving himself first and then leading others to follow his unsavory path. In this regard, he has been most successful, as evidenced by the words Danny spoke in the opening scenes and by the supportive crowd gathered to listen to him preach at Madison Square Garden.

While William Stryker speaks on stage at the Garden, backstage Charles Xavier begins the process of finding and killing mutants. Mutants first feel headaches upon Xavier touching their minds; they then begin to bleed from their nose and ears and will ultimately die of internal hemorrhaging. The X-Men work to free Xavier from the machine while Magneto makes a grand entrance into the Garden and confronts Stryker. Xavier's primary mission is interrupted, and he is ordered to strike Magneto with a vicious psychic assault. The attack sends Magneto reeling before he falls to the floor, conscious but too weak to even stand. He uses what energy he has to fend off the crowd that, spurred on by Stryker, seeks to kill him.

Xavier resumes his original purpose with surprising results. A senator present in the audience begins to bleed. Anne, the highest-ranking Purifier in the story, also begins to bleed; revealing to her own surprise that she is a mutant. She professes her loyalty to Stryker's cause, but "God's will" needs to be done. Therefore, Stryker shoves her off the raised platform where he delivers his speech. Anne's neck is broken in the fall, and Magneto voices his protest from the floor, questioning the holiness of Stryker's words.

Meanwhile, the X-Men render Xavier unconscious and free him from the machine that made him an instrument of murder. Cyclops destroys Stryker's precious equipment but does not declare victory. He decides that he must stand before Stryker and challenge his ideas, for these beliefs are the real enemy. The other X-Men agree and step onto the stage. Stryker, shocked to see Cyclops and Storm alive, is afraid until Cyclops voices his intention to answer Stryker's charges, not to assault him.

Stryker declares himself nothing more than an instrument of the Lord and reasserts his conviction that mutants are not human. Cyclops counters that his connection to Heaven could be as strong as Stryker's. Stryker has no evidence to the contrary. Furthermore, Cyclops stresses the importance that the actions taken by a person matter much more than the labels placed on them. In this regard, Cyclops could be seen as being more Christ-like than the reverend. Jesus emphasized social justice and worked to elevate all people in the eyes of society, as they were already elevated in the eyes of God. He sought to break down barriers that separated people, not build new ones. Charles Xavier and the X-Men can be seen as far more "Christian" than William Stryker.

Styker, enraged by the insinuation that mutants are human, points at Nightcrawler (with his three-fingered hands, three-toed feet, blue skin, and tail) and shouts, "You dare call that thing human?!?" That singular moment brings us back to Stryker in the desert killing his son. This guilt is unresolved, despite dedicating twenty-five years to hating mutants. Projecting his hate outward at mutants saves Stryker the pain of dealing with his own actions. Mutants can't be human, because if they are, he has been wrong most of his adult life, and he will have to answer for his actions, both to the law and his own conscience.

Young Kitty Pryde vigorously disputes his charge that Nightcrawler isn't human. She proclaims her friend more human than Stryker and worthy of her utmost respect. This scene is rich with symbolic meaning. Nightcrawler is a dedicated Catholic, one of the few comic book characters whose religious convictions are central to his life. It is great irony to see the exclusivistic and prejudiced reverend accusing the devout Catholic, who is a member of a team fighting for social justice, of being inhuman.

No less important is the sight of Kitty leaping to her friend's defense. When dressed in "civilian" clothes, Kitty is often depicted wearing a Star of David necklace.[*] Her Jewish heritage is proudly on display everywhere she goes. Although not depicted as a devout Jew, her faith is very real. This is evidenced in a story where the vampire lord Dracula invades the X-Mansion in an attempt to make Storm his bride.

---

[*] Students may notice the Star of David necklace in the panels when she is fighting Danny.

In an initial confrontation, Kitty attempts to drive off Dracula with a cross. This fails, however, and the vampire lord slaps the religious icon from her hand. He grabs her by the neck, only to have his hand burned by the Star of David, the true symbol of Kitty's faith. The story also shows Wolverine failing to harm Dracula with a cross. Dracula mocks Wolverine's attempt because it is shallow, a physical gesture lacking the inner workings of authentic faith. Nightcrawler produces a cross and succeeds in causing Dracula great pain, precisely because his inner world supports his outer actions.

Stryker, either sensing he is losing the debate or merely enraged by the X-Men's presence, pulls a gun from his jacket and points it at Kitty. As he cocks the trigger, a policeman shoots him. The wound is not critical, and Stryker will stand trial for his actions and those of his Purifiers.

Watching a news report about the incident in the comfort of Xavier's school, Magneto pronounces that no matter how hard Xavier tries, he can never win. Xavier, shaken by his involvement in Stryker's scheme, contemplates joining Magneto's side. Cyclops, speaking for the X-Men, rejects this notion. In a repudiation of Machiavellian thinking, Cyclops states, "The means are as important as the end—we have to do this right or not at all." Joining Magneto to bring about mutant safety through world domination is completely unacceptable to Cyclops.

Magneto, accepting that the X-Men won't join, offers his hand to Xavier one last time. Charles reaches for his old friend's hand, but pulls back. Magneto, declaring the lot of them fools, turns to leave. Kitty suggests he stay and join them, but Magneto rejects this offer far easier than Charles did. He does offer a glimpse into his thinking, hoping the X-Men succeed in their mission. If they do not, he will handle things his way. He then departs, leaving a tearful Charles Xavier ashamed of his weakness and proud of the resolve shown by his students.

Cyclops, as is his way, steps outside to be alone on a balcony. Storm, being the supportive nurturer, approaches him. He does not turn her away. She tells him that she is proud of him and notes how Scott became the teacher for a moment and Charles was the student. Returning to the theme he mentioned at Madison Square Garden, Scott dismisses the use of labels, saying simply, "He was in need. I helped him as he would me. That's what it's all about, really." What if things really were just that simple?

# CHAPTER 15

# Wolverine

The X-Man Wolverine is a complicated antihero. His mutant attributes include his accelerated healing capacity, heightened senses, and retractable bone claws. His healing factor enabled him to survive government experiments that laced his skeletal structure with a nearly indestructible metal called adamantium. The same metal covers his claws, granting him a lethal weapon that he is not hesitant to use. He also has moments when he slips into a berserk fury and fights without restraint. It is not clear whether this berserk fury has always been a part of his psychological makeup, is an aspect of his mutation, or is a by-product of the experiments that nearly drove him completely insane. Regardless of its origin, there exists in Wolverine a fury that is terrible to behold.

Despite his preference to do things "his way," Wolverine joins, and often unwillingly submits, to the rigors of being a part of a team and a community. As a member of the Canadian secret service, he performed many "dirty, brutal, necessary assignments no one else would touch." A subconscious desire not only to break away from such work but to be treated as a valuable human being rather than a valuable commodity may have led to his effortless acceptance of Charles Xavier's offer to become an X-Man. It may also explain why, despite his discomfort with authority and compassionate communities, he remains an X-Man. Inclusion in the team grants him something he has never had: a family to care about and people to support and who support him unconditionally. In the end, Wolverine believes in the good that comes from being part of the X-Men. He allows himself to grow more trusting and less guarded as he slowly embraces the compassionate community of which he is a part.*

This growth does not mean Wolverine ever relinquishes his willingness to wield his claws in a deadly manner, although he does allow his teammates to question his approach. At the end of a particular adventure, he and Nightcrawler watch George Baptiste, a man they helped apprehend, be taken into custody. Having conducted experiments on himself, Baptiste was transformed into a monster called Wendigo. As Wendigo, Baptiste killed a

---

* Wolverine's hesitancy to embrace his place in the X-Men community is quietly demonstrated by the fact that he does not reveal his name to his teammates. Nightcrawler discovers it to be "Logan" when Heather Hudson, one of Wolverine's old friends in Canada, sees him in costume and blurts out his real name.

number of people. Nightcrawler notes that Wolverine has killed as well and yet remains free. Wolverine summarizes his use of lethal force by saying, "A man comes at me with fists, I'll meet him with fists. But if he pulls a gun—or threatens people I'm protectin'—then I got no sympathy for him. He made his choice. He'll have to live—or die—with it. I never use my claws on someone who hadn't tried to kill me first. I call that self-defense." Nightcrawler confesses that the argument is logical but is not convinced that it is right. Nightcrawler does not press the issue, although the reader is told in the narrator's box that Wolverine continues to contemplate his teammate's position.

The brief conversation with Nightcrawler reveals that Wolverine is willing to listen and consider his teammate's perspective. On many occasions, however, Wolverine acts as a mentor to his teammates. His actions in this capacity can help evaluate what it means to be a mentor and how alternative approaches can sometimes yield desirable results.

One occasion in which Wolverine demonstrates his capacity to help his teammates was when Colossus was struggling with a test in the danger room, the X-Men's training facility. Colossus was standing in a powerful hydraulic press. His task was to push back against the walls that were programmed to come together. Physically capable but shaken by his failure in recent battles, Colossus asks Cyclops to turn the machine off. Wolverine, sitting in the control room with Cyclops, notes Colossus' problem is more psychological than physical. Cyclops, watching Colossus struggle, expresses concern that his armored teammate may fold in a fight. Wolverine comments that Colossus would not fold as he quietly pops his claws into the control panel. He leaves the room as Cyclops takes notice of the damage because the panel shorts out, revving the hydraulic press to maximum power.

Wolverine then enters the danger room and stands next to Colossus between the closing walls of the press. Wolverine ignores Colossus' pleas to leave the area as he attempts to get to the root of Colossus' crisis of confidence. Colossus, being told by Cyclops that the press cannot be turned off, pushes back with such force that he breaks the machine. The two heroes are safe and have different reactions. Colossus is surprised at his success, while Wolverine is blasé about the accomplishment, as he knew full well that Colossus was capable of overpowering the machine.

To be sure, Colossus' crisis is not over, and it plays out over the next two issues, but Wolverine's actions bring the problem to the surface so it can be addressed more effectively. He also shows great faith in his teammate by, in essence, risking his life to make a point. This action appears to bring the two teammates closer together, because in subsequent issues, Wolverine openly teases Colossus in the manner of a supportive older brother. Wolverine, although not one to vocalize the thought explicitly, is proud of Colossus for not giving in to his doubts. Of course, one man's mentor may be another man's nuisance.

Wolverine and Colossus are standing in the shattered remains of the hydraulic press when Cyclops angrily enters the room. He dismisses Wolverine's take that all's well that ends well. He hands Wolverine a toolbox so he can dismantle the press, bring it to the repair shop, and rewire the control panel. Wolverine objects but complies with the order. Cyclops admits to Colossus that he "applauds" what Wolverine did but objects to his methods. Cyclops, the field leader of the X-Men, is representative of an authority figure who wants things done in a certain manner.

Cyclops cannot tolerate Wolverine's approach even if it works. He objects to the approach because it could have killed two people. Wolverine would dismiss this argument if he heard it, pointing out that he took a low-risk gamble on Colossus' strength. Wolverine acts quickly but not recklessly. It should be noted that Cyclops, although full of objections, is not full of solutions. He takes no action while Colossus struggles in the hydraulic press and offers no alternative to Wolverine's actions after the incident. He just knows Wolverine, despite his success, was wrong. Wolverine's capacity as a leader and mentor, however, is best revealed when helping the youngest members of the X-Men.

Kitty Pryde comes to Xavier's School for Gifted Youngsters when she is fourteen. As a member of the X-Men, she has battled monsters and evil mutants and traveled to the far reaches of the universe and into other dimensions—all by the time she is sixteen. She had the painful experience of having her heart broken by her teammate Colossus and is equally crushed by her parents' divorce. Sometimes saving the world is easier than dealing with affairs of the heart.

In an attempt to heal from these highly emotional setbacks, she takes time off from being an X-Man and spends time with her father in Chicago. This attempt to escape trouble instead leads to more when she arrives at her father's office to find him arguing with a businessman who represents a corporation that bought his bank. Kitty's father, Cameron Pryde, tells her that he must leave for Japan to meet with the head of the corporation. Ogun, a Japanese representative from the main office, causes Kitty great discomfort. She compares the feelings of unease he generates in her with how she felt the first time she met Wolverine. As her father departs, she suspects that the group represents members of the Japanese underworld seeking to infiltrate American businesses.

Kitty travels to Japan and seeks out her father. At one point, she grows frustrated and embarrassed by the way she is handling the situation. She places a collect call to Xavier's School, and Wolverine answers the phone. She hangs up, too embarrassed to talk to her respected teammate. Wolverine, disturbed and confused to have received a call from Japan, leaves the mansion to seek his teenage comrade. Kitty continues the search for her father.

She finds him in the office of a Japanese crime lord, agreeing to launder money for their syndicate. Kitty flees the room but is pursued by Ogun, who is much more than a criminal mastermind. Although the source of his power is never revealed, Ogun is either a mystical being or a mutant. He is a ninja and a martial arts expert. His agility and speed are beyond the limits of human perfection, and he is hundreds of years old. Wolverine tells a story of a meeting that took place between Ogun and Miyamoto Musashi, a samurai of renowned skill from the seventeenth century.

Ogun kidnaps Kitty and plants a psychic clone of himself inside the young hero. Kitty becomes Ogun's servant while manifesting all of his martial arts and sword fighting skills. Kitty, dressed in full ninja garb, battles Wolverine to a standstill. When he unmasks his adversary, he is shocked to see it is Kitty. As he hesitates, she plunges a sword between his adamantium ribs and cuts his heart and lungs. Cameron Pryde and a female adventurer named Yuriko arrive to see Wolverine fall. Kitty is unaware of their arrival and is struck by four spikes thrown by Yuriko. The spikes are laced with a sedative, rendering her unconscious. They take the unconscious teen and the wounded warrior to the palace of Mariko Yashida, Wolverine's beloved. In this mountain setting, Wolverine dedicates himself to breaking Ogun's hold on Kitty even as he heals from the wounds Ogun inflicted through her.

Kitty can remember what she did to Wolverine but is not completely certain of what she has been through. Wolverine, rather than tell her outright, brings her to a large stone garden. He hands her a rake and tells her to take an hour to herself. When he returns, he finds her meditating on a rock. She glibly notes that meditating just seemed like the thing to do. She continues to be a very typical teen as she invites Wolverine to survey her work. Her invitation includes her own assessment, "Not too shabby, huh?"

Wolverine answers by stating, "You tell me" and implores her to truly look at her own work. Kitty does and is stunned by the beauty she has created. Wolverine notes it is the kind of work a Zen master would take a great deal of time crafting, first in the mind and then with the stones. Kitty accomplished the task in under an hour. She recognizes, for the first time, that Ogun has changed something fundamental at the core of her being. Terrified by this notion, she listens intently as Wolverine clarifies what she has been through.

He explains that Ogun planted a psychic clone that will, over time, overwhelm Kitty completely. Her sudden preferences for meditation and Zen gardening are manifestations of this psychic implant. Kitty believes that the best solution is to go back to the X-Men's mansion and have Professor Xavier erase Ogun's implant. Wolverine does not see this as a wise course of action. His first objection is grounded in the reality that if Ogun wants Kitty, he will keep coming for her. The professor may be able to remove Ogun's taint, but he will be a constant threat to her and the X-Men. Wolverine's true objection is found in his second statement.

Xavier curing Kitty will leave Kitty always dependent on him for a cure. Kitty will lack the confidence that she can resist Ogun on her own. This lack of confidence will leave her somewhat depleted in spirit. Ogun could merely bide his time and reclaim her when he feels the opportune moment has arrived. The only way to be free of Ogun is to prove herself to be beyond his influence. Wolverine's insights are from experience because he had once been Ogun's student, and Ogun had sought to make him the vessel that held his psychic implant.

Wolverine's approach to Kitty at this point causes friction between the two. Wolverine drives Kitty to learn to stand on her own rather than look to others for support when that support is not necessary. Immanuel Kant wrote, "Enlightenment is man's release from his self-incurred tutelage. Tutelage is man's inability to make use of his understanding without direction from another. Self-incurred is this tutelage when its cause lies not in lack of reason but in lack of resolution and courage to use it without direction from another."[88]

Kant is not saying we can reach a level where we need no one but that we sometimes cling too long to another's guidance when we should be beyond the need for our mentor's direction on particular matters. Wolverine knows Kitty needs to reach a point where she can resist Ogun on her own accord, which will free her from his manipulations. He can prepare her for this confrontation, but he cannot fight the battle for her. While these words all make sense analytically, it is far more compelling to experience their power.

Wolverine finds an opportunity to make this point as he and Kitty are jogging through the snowy wilderness. Kitty falls and twists her ankle. In pain, and fatigued from Wolverine's training regimen, she asks him to help her up. He declines to do so. He dismisses her claims to be hurt and demands she help herself. When she says she cannot go on, he tells her not to. When she says that could cause her to freeze, he advises her to get up. When she claims she cannot, he tells her she has a choice, surrender or struggle. He goes so far as to portray how freezing to death could solve all her problems. He makes a final statement about the fact that life is, in fact, rarely fair. In this moment, he addresses her as "Katherine," not "Kitty" or "Pun'kin" as he usually does. The use of a more mature name signifies the need to break free of his tutelage as well and become her own person. He then runs off, leaving Kitty to decide her fate for herself.

Wolverine's departure accentuates Kitty's need to decide to find her own resolve and conviction. The surface cruelty of the act is mirrored by how deeply Wolverine cares about Kitty. He has made a decision, however, to focus on her long-term needs. In many ways, this act is much like his intervention with Colossus. Wolverine knows what his teammates are capable of even when they do not. His methods of bringing this truth to light may be unorthodox and dangerous, but that is who he is. It also reflects how he needs little approval to take the actions he deems necessary. In this regard, he is free from "self-incurred tutelage."

When Wolverine returns to the Yashida estate, Cameron Pryde is enraged that his injured daughter has been left behind. Yuriko declares that she will go out on a snowmobile to find Kitty. She does not need to, however, for the young hero staggers into the compound and runs, without a word, past Wolverine.

Later that evening, Kitty contemplates why Wolverine left her. She realizes Wolverine, for all his efforts to sharpen her skills, continues to give her the power of choice. The power of choice also brings the burden of responsibility, another aspect of Kitty's character that Wolverine seeks to hone. Wolverine does not force Kitty to do anything, whereas that is all Ogun does. In the middle of the night, Kitty makes a fateful decision. She opts to leave the compound and head to the airport. She will return to New York and seek the aid and safety of the X-Men. When the time comes to board the plane, she hesitates, weighing the lessons she has learned from Wolverine. Returning to the X-Men will not do, so she decides to seek out Ogun alone and confront her nemesis and her fear.

Needless to say, Kitty is little match for Ogun, but she does resist his attempt to reassert his psychic hold on her. Enraged by her defiance, Ogun prepares to kill her. Wolverine arrives and confronts Ogun. Their battle rages from the rooftops to the streets, but in the end Wolverine does not fare much better than Kitty. Wolverine realizes he cannot defeat Ogun and apologizes to Kitty for his failure. Kitty, who has been pushed to her limits by both men and has not quit, won't hear it. Ogun mocks Wolverine even as the hero rises to face him. Wolverine makes a fateful decision as he willingly taps into the underlying rage that he works so hard to subvert. Letting go of all restraint, and possibly parts of his humanity, he allows his berserk rage to overwhelm him.

The emergence of his berserker persona is unusual in this context. It usually occurs when Wolverine is provoked to an extreme degree or is badly wounded in combat. He rarely tosses aside his sanity in this manner. A panel depicts Kitty as completely horrified by what she sees as Wolverine, now more beast than man, attacks Ogun. By Wolverine's own description his berserker self "doesn't think. It doesn't feel pain. It kills. And once it's loose, it doesn't stop till I'm dead—or everyone else is." To save Kitty, he risks losing himself.

The feral Wolverine overwhelms Ogun. The miraculous happens as Wolverine subverts his beastly nature before he kills Ogun. He offers Kitty the opportunity to execute her tormentor. Sword in hand, Kitty charges the defeated Ogun but stops before delivering the deathblow. Her inability to kill a helpless foe confirms to herself and to Wolverine that Ogun's taint is gone. The two heroes seek to depart, but Ogun attacks them from behind. Wolverine plunges his claws deep into Ogun's chest, killing his former sensei.

Disturbed by his mentor's death, Wolverine also expresses concern for how the victory was achieved. He did not win as a man but because of the maniacal piece of his psyche. He wonders if the ordeal has made him a worse man than he was before. Kitty quickly points out that Wolverine has been a loyal friend, an unflinching ally, and a source of hope. He risked his very sanity to save her. In every regard possible, he has been a hero, a human, and a man. Comforted by his teammate's words, Wolverine crushes Ogun's mask, and the two depart—both claiming important victories.

The two heroes will return to the X-Men and continue their lives as adventurous superheroes. Kitty's position as the youngest member of the X-Men will be taken up by Jubilee (Jubilation Lee), a mutant with the ability to create explosive balls of energy. She, like Kitty, finds herself seeking the guidance of Wolverine. In a single sentence, she sums up the ironic trait that makes Wolverine a worthy mentor and valuable teammate. After the battle with Magneto at the end of the *Fatal Attractions* story line, the X-Men are racing home from Avalon with a critically wounded Wolverine. There is great concern that he may die.

Dr. Moira MacTaggert is communicating via radio medical procedures to keep him alive. Kitty, who recently had to endure the loss of her best friend Illyana, proclaims she couldn't bear losing Logan, too. Jubilee, concerned about Wolverine in her own right, snaps, "Don't you give up on him! He would never give up on you!" Wolverine, the self-proclaimed loner, teaches his teammates the values of loyalty and perseverance because that is who he is, even when he does not see it.

# CHAPTER 16

## Wolverine—Samurai or Ronin?

In the introduction to the trade paperback *Wolverine*, writer Chris Claremont states that he considers the essence of Wolverine's character to be that of a "failed samurai." Wolverine's gruff disposition and reckless nature are at odds with the control and grace of a samurai. Wolverine may aspire to a certain ideal, but his core nature may be impossible to transcend. These dark and untamed inclinations cause Wolverine to struggle to live up to his ideals just as a samurai can struggle to embrace the duties and discipline codified in the samurai code, Bushido—the way of the warrior.

It is important to remember that a samurai's duty takes precedence over personal desire or preference. Samurai served at the behest of local lords in feudal Japan. Simply stated, "Being a retainer is nothing other than being a supporter of one's lord, entrusting matters of good and evil to him, and renouncing self-interest."[89]

This stands at stark odds with American culture, which promotes individuality and personal freedom as more important than duty and responsibility. A samurai also dedicated himself to rules of decorum and civility. The care taken to foster this civility can be seen in advice ranging from how to properly share one's opinion to how to suppress yawns in public to avoid being rude.[90]

More than mere rules to follow, these dictums are interwoven with the Zen Buddhist worldview that seeks to infuse the practitioner with an overwhelming sense of compassion. Thus, the great paradox of the samurai emerges: they are highly skilled warriors who are influenced by teaching that was originally presented by a man who perceived violence and wanton killing to be a violation of a silent natural law. It is this almost irreconcilable dichotomy that helps explain why the Bushido code became clearer and more organized between 1600 and 1868, a time of general peace in Japanese history.[91] To follow Bushido strictly would have been nearly impossible during the Mongol invasion of the late thirteenth century or the civil wars that erupted following the Mongols' defeat.

It is, in part, the struggle to master the Bushido code that creates *ronin*. A ronin is a samurai with no lord or master. A samurai can become a ronin because of the ruin or death of his master or because he behaves in a manner that causes his master to look upon him with shame and disfavor. Wolverine's disposition and attitude would suggest that the latter reason would make him a ronin.

While Claremont clearly states his view of Wolverine as a "failed samurai," there is another figure in Buddhist lore that the clawed mutant could be seen to represent. The immovable luminary king is sometimes portrayed as a demon standing guard outside a monastery gate. These demonic creatures were converted to become protectors of religion, using their rage and power in the service of Buddhism.[92] Wolverine, with his berserk rage and ferocious fighting style, could cause great harm to the innocent but instead embraces the pursuit of a more moral world. In this regard, Wolverine consciously channels his primal and destructive energies to constructive ends. Although not a defender of Buddhism, he is a defender of virtue. Such a man will inevitably encounter powerful enemies bent on his destruction as they pursue their nefarious goals.

The story that unfolds in *Wolverine* nearly breaks Wolverine's spirit while forcing him to become as self-reflective as he is active. Wolverine travels to Japan to see Mariko Yashida, the great love of his life. She loves him as well. Unfortunately, the combination of his association with the X-Men and her duties as the daughter of one of the oldest and richest families in Japan keeps them apart for long stretches of time. Wolverine is not traveling to Japan merely because he has the time but because he has been cut out of her life. Letters he sends are returned unopened, and when he calls he is not allowed to speak with her. He comes to Japan seeking answers to a very personal problem.

Asano Kimura, a Japanese government agent who Wolverine holds in high regard, meets him upon his arrival. He could even be seen as a friend. The two men have a long history, stretching back to the time when Wolverine worked as a special agent for the Canadian government. Asano aided him on more than one unsavory mission. Wolverine has left the business of espionage and assassination behind, while Asano is still deeply involved in such work.

The introduction of Asano is the first of a series of connections that can be made to *The 47 Ronin*, a legendary story in Japanese literature. Asano is the name of a powerful landowner (a *daimyo*) in the story. As such, he had samurai who served him. The leader of the samurai is a man named Oishi. Although Asano and Wolverine's relationship is different from that of Asano and Oishi's, there are aspects of the lord–samurai relationship at play.

In their initial conversation, Asano attempts to council Wolverine on the proper course of action. He obviously hopes Wolverine will follow his advice. If he were a daimyo and Wolverine his samurai, he would expect compliance. Wolverine, who is already acting the role of ronin (for he left his government "masters," whereas Asano still works for them), does not heed his friend. His anger only intensifies when Asano shares the information that Mariko is now married, used by her father, Lord Shingen, to satisfy a debt.

Wolverine wonders how, considering her professed love for him, she could agree to the marriage. Asano informs him that their love is not the issue. The issue is one of *giri*, not love. Giri is a word that encapsulates a person's sense of duty, justice, obligation, and honor. A person who exemplifies giri can maintain the capacity to inspire and move people centuries after his or her death. A relative's death may not cause someone to cry, but the struggles of a person steeped in giri from the past may move that same person to tears.[93] An exemplar such as Martin Luther King Jr. or George Washington could be said to possess giri. Mariko agreeing to the marriage is a result of her sense of obligation to her father, not love for her husband or a lack of love for Wolverine. Unmoved by this argument, Wolverine departs for the Yashida ancestral home to confront Mariko.

He finds her sitting near a large statue of the Buddha in the compound's gardens. The Buddha can be used to remind the reader of the paradoxical, and seemingly incompatible, demands of the Bushido code. Yamamoto Tsunetomo, a one-time samurai who became a Buddhist monk later in life, noted that a monk needs courage to act on their compassion. A samurai needs compassion to be an upstanding retainer to his lord. A warrior without compassion can become merciless, and such a disposition often leads to his ruin.[94]

The conversation with Mariko goes poorly. She remains steadfast that she is bound by important obligations to remain married, despite the petty and physically abusive nature of her husband. Disgusted, Wolverine leaves the compound with the intention of returning to New York. Distracted by the turmoil in his mind, he does not notice, until it is too late, that a hidden assailant lurks nearby. He barely has time to react as poisoned *shuriken,* multi-pointed throwing stars, strike him.

Wolverine awakens on a dojo floor. The poison was exceptionally potent, almost enough to kill him despite his mutant healing factor. Wolverine's thoughts narrate the scene, and he assumes the poison was meant to kill him, but his attacker miscalculated the strength of his healing factor. He is awake but unsteady and disoriented. Seated on a raised dais is Lord Shingen and Mariko. Two bodyguards and Noburu, Mariko's husband, are also present. Lord Shingen, as the primary antagonist in the story, can be seen to represent one of the aspects of humanity that Zen Buddhism seeks to transcend.

In Zen teaching, all people are said to have a false mind and an original mind. The original mind existed before our birth. It works in accord with nature and is the seat of great compassion, wisdom, and peace. The false mind comes into being as a result of interaction with the world and the embracing of dispositions and philosophies that steer one away from the original mind. When the false mind is powerful, our actions are "warped and polluted" and can cause someone to have a "sullied reputation."[95]

This does not mean that those people acting from the false mind are fools, but rather they are lacking compassion and a sense of equanimity. They grasp and fight for power, using whatever talents they have for their own self-aggrandizement and comfort. They will use their wit and speaking skills to conceal their greed and materialism.[96] Those acting from the false mind may use words such as "honor" and "duty," but only to manipulate a situation or in a way that serves their purpose. Their use of such words lacks authenticity to those who know them or listen attentively. Throughout the story, Lord Shingen uses the vocabulary of enlightened Zen masters but exhibits none of their qualities.

This does not prevent him from building and maintaining a lavish lifestyle. People acting from the false mind can achieve great success in a given field, but they will eventually fall prey to their own cruelty. The Buddha taught, "The evil-doer may be happy as long as he does not reap what he has sown, but when he does, sorrow overcomes him."[97] Wolverine's presence is a threat to the happiness Lord Shingen has obtained through his carefully constructed connections and growing control of the Japanese underworld. Personal power and dominion, artifacts of the false mind, dominate his thoughts. Wolverine therefore must be eliminated. In his dojo, before his daughter, Shingen seeks to finish the poison's work.

Shingen, taking up the role of the honorable father, informs Wolverine that he does not approve of his aspirations to marry Mariko. For reasons beyond his understanding, Mariko has deep respect as well as affection for an unruly foreigner. Shingen offers Wolverine to prove his worth by facing off in single combat wielding *bokan,* wooden training swords. The stage is set, but the deck is stacked against Wolverine.

Shingen is a master swordsman, and Wolverine, by his own confession, was once good, but is now out of practice with swords. Despite his age, Shingen is still graceful and fit. The poison still being expelled from his system slows Wolverine. Shingen takes advantage of Wolverine's inhibited reflexes and strikes him in critical nerve clusters and pressure points. Again, these blows should kill him, but his healing factor enables him to survive the assault. Wolverine, realizing this fight is for his life, extends his adamantium claws. This single act, because it violates the preset conditions of the duel, instantly dishonors him in Mariko's eyes.

This scene is analogous to an event in *The 47 Ronin*. In the Japanese tale, Asano is summoned to the Shogun's castle to learn proper court etiquette. He is to receive instruction from Kira Yoshinaka, a rude, arrogant, and corrupt man who endlessly insults Asano. The usually stoic Asano's patience runs out, and he attacks Kira with his dagger. The drawing of a sword, let alone an act of violence, is forbidden within the walls of Edo castle. Asano is ordered to commit *seppuku*, ritualistic suicide, for his offense. His lands are then taken, his family falls into ruin, and his retainers (samurai) become ronin. Forty-seven of the ronin, led by Oishi, plot their revenge.

Kira, a man of low integrity, is quick to assert the rules of honor and obligation when they suit him. He is much like Lord Shingen in this regard. Kira's crass behavior causes Asano to break the rules of conduct and dishonor himself. Wolverine, goaded as Asano is, breaks the edict of his "friendly" match and suffers a loss of honor before Mariko. Whereas Asano suffers physical death for his infraction, Wolverine suffers a deep emotional blow that threatens to break his spirit completely.

Mariko did not realize the intent of her father's strike. She thought her father was seeking, successfully, to humiliate Wolverine. Wolverine appears so embarrassed by the blows he has received that, in his anger, he turns a "friendly" duel into a lethal fight. Even with his claws unsheathed, Wolverine cannot avoid defeat in the battle.

Sluggish, disheartened, and facing a masterfully ruthless opponent, he is defeated. Worst of all, as he slips into unconsciousness, he hears Mariko declare he is unworthy of her. Broken in body and spirit, he is discarded in an alley. Far from recovered from his wounds and the poison, he is helpless before a group of young thugs who seek to find enjoyment by assaulting a lowlife foreigner. They are stopped by the intervention of Yuriko, a female adventurer who is forever seeking the next exploit worthy of testing her skills. She brings the semiconscious Wolverine back to her apartment to recuperate.

Wolverine's recuperation is interrupted by the appearance of members of the Hand, a group of professional assassins. Wolverine, near full health and alert, tears into the assassins and defeats them. The fight over and his claws dripping with blood, he takes Yuriko to his hotel. She attempts to seduce him, but he refuses, as he is still loyal to Mariko.

Yuriko leaves Wolverine at the hotel, and the reader learns she is an assassin employed by Lord Shingen. Her task is to assassinate a crime lord named Katsuyori. His death will solidify Shingen's hold on any illicit, but profitable, business in Tokyo. We also learn the depths of Shingen's scheming. The Hand has consistently failed to penetrate Katsuyori's defenses, causing Shingen to assign Yuriko, his top assassin, to the task. He doubts even she could penetrate his defenses, so he manipulates events so that Wolverine will help her get close enough to Katsuyori to kill him. Shingen wants Wolverine dead, but not before he is used to eliminate the elusive crime lord. Once Katsuyori is dead, Yuriko is to kill Wolverine as well.

It is no accident that Yuriko finds Wolverine in the alley; it was part of the plan. Shingen anticipated Wolverine surviving his death blows in their duel just as he anticipated the sense of disgrace he would feel after their fight. Dishonored before Mariko and bludgeoned by Shingen, he would be receptive to Yuriko's comfort and aid.

Yuriko's next course of action is to inform Wolverine that Katsuyori intends to kill her. She knows Katsuyori will be at a private viewing of a play. With Wolverine's help, she can infiltrate the private theater and eliminate the threat posed by Katsuyori. She convinces Wolverine that Katsuyori will not be scared off by threats. Only his death can ensure her safety. Wolverine agrees to help, and the two adventurers penetrate the well-protected theater to find an audience of four settling in to watch the play.

Wolverine is shocked when he notes that Mariko and her husband have joined Katsuyori and his wife for the viewing. Shingen has sent his daughter and son-in-law as his representatives. He believes the presence of his daughter will lower Katsuyori's guard, for who would risk their daughter's safety should an assassination attempt go wrong? Katsuyori is not without schemes of his own. He agreed to the meeting because the actors on the stage are also his bodyguards and assassins. The play being performed is *The 47 Ronin*, therefore every "actor" has a sword.

At a key point in the play, one of the actors leaps from the stage, seeking to kill Mariko and her husband. Wolverine leaps from the rafters and incapacitates the attacker. He then leaps on the stage to deal with the rest of the troupe. Katsuyori leaves, congratulating Noburu for anticipating his plan. Katsuyori believes Wolverine is a bodyguard. As Shingen anticipated, Katsuyori does anticipate the danger he is in. Yuriko kills him and his wife as Wolverine battles the swordsmen on the stage.

The fight is going well for Wolverine until one of his foes lands a blow that could have cut deep into his torso. His adamantium bones prevent the cut from doing the damage it would to an ordinary man. The pain of the strike, however, causes Wolverine to unleash his berserker persona. In this mode, he dismantles and, in some cases, disembowels his opponents, all the while revealing in the dark joys of letting loose his feral nature. Mariko, who has never seen him this way, is utterly terrified. She flees the theater leaving Wolverine crushed again by her reaction. Yuriko, witnessing this scene from the shadows, cannot contain her joy.

She and Wolverine become inseparable as they spend the next couple of weeks drinking and partying their way across Tokyo. Any inclination to heroism is cast aside and living for the next night's drunken partying is all that matters. As the boisterous couple leaves a bar, Asano approaches Wolverine. He tells his longtime friend that a new and unknown leader of the Japanese underworld has emerged and is rapidly consolidating enough power to control Japan itself. He needs help to uncover and neutralize this individual. Wolverine dismisses Asano and continues with Yuriko into the night.

Despite his healing factor, Wolverine is inebriated and passes out on the street. The Hand ambushes Yuriko and communicates Lord Shingen's displeasure. She has defied him by refusing to kill Wolverine as ordered. She is given a choice, kill him now or be killed herself. She decides to kill Wolverine and takes out her throwing blades to cut out his heart. Her true intention is quickly revealed as she attacks the five members of the Hand and leaves Wolverine on the sidewalk. She is enraged because, in his drunken slumber, he mutters Mariko's name.

Wolverine wakes up, trying to figure out why five dead members of the Hand are laying around him, and returns to his hotel room. He enters the room and finds Asano dead on the floor, one of Yuriko's spikes in his neck. He hopes it was an accident but quickly dismisses this thought. Smelling the blade, he notices the scent of the poison that debilitated him after his initial meeting with Mariko. He realizes Yuriko works for Shingen and has been lying to him since they met. Sensing her presence, he tells her to kill him now because she won't get another chance. She flees instead.

Wolverine chases her across the rooftops, eventually sending her crashing into a Zen garden. Members of the Hand attack him in the garden. For a moment, he thinks he has been lead into a trap, but the look on Yuriko's face is one of surprise. He defeats the Hand and stands alone in the garden, as Yuriko fled while he fought. Looking around the once beautiful but now damaged Zen garden Wolverine grows contemplative.

He considers the course of his life ("The garden has been wrecked. It's patterns broken. Order turned to chaos. The story of my life.") and his failures ("No matter how hard I strive for inner serenity, I screw up … I lost myself."). He also considers the choices he could make ("I may never be what I ought to be, want to be—but how will I know unless I try? Sure, it's scary but what's the alternative? Stagnation—a safer more terrible form of death. Not of the body, but of the spirit."). He concludes that he is no beast, nor is he a man unworthy of having or chasing dreams. Despite all that Shingen has done to him and all that he has done himself, he is a man and he will challenge Shingen secure in this knowledge.

This scene is representative of some of the highest ideals of the samurai. A samurai is called to maintain a strong spirit. It is considered spiritless to think one cannot attain or do what great masters from the past have attained. The masters, after all, were men. Therefore one man should be able to think it possible to do what other men have done.[98] Shingen had, in essence, stolen Wolverine's spirit. Standing in the Zen garden, Wolverine is reclaiming it.

That he does this alone while contemplating the difficulties of this approach to life also has antecedents in Buddhism. The Buddha taught, "Learn what is right, then teach others, as the wise do. Before trying to guide others, be your own guide first. It is hard to learn to guide oneself."[99] Wolverine could still be seen as a ronin, but he also stands on the brink of consciously pursuing higher ideals than he has before. In Buddhism, there is the metaphor of leaving the shore (of everyday existence) to seek the distant shore of higher consciousness. To go from one shore to another one must cross a vast and dangerous ocean. Wolverine has, to use the metaphor, entered his boat and faces himself. In doing so, he must also confront Shingen.

*The 47 Ronin* can again be alluded to as chapter three of *Wolverine* moves into the story's climax. The first connection is the depiction of Wolverine as a drunken oaf. In *The 47 Ronin,* Oishi plays the role of a brokenhearted, purposeless drunk after the death of Asano. In one scene, he passes out in the street, just as Wolverine did during one of his festive evenings with Yuriko. A man comes upon Oishi and berates him for his complete abandonment of the Bushido code. The man kicks Oishi in the face before leaving. Yuriko also kicks Wolverine in the face after she hears him mumbling Mariko's name. The difference between Wolverine and Oishi is, of course, that Wolverine is not gallivanting as part of a bigger plan. He is embracing, as completely as he can, a hedonistic approach to life.

For two years, Oishi plays the fool. He acts as he does to convince Kira that he has no intentions of vengeance. Kira, initially suspicious that Oishi's behavior was a sham, does not conceive it possible to maintain such a deception for an extended period of time. After two years, the 47 ronin attack Kira's mansion in Edo. Although not waiting two years, Wolverine begins the final chapter of his story with a one-man assault on Lord Shingen's operations throughout Japan. Having damaged Shingen's reputation and power throughout the underworld, he will invade Shingen's home and confront his rival.

The two men engage in a vicious battle, Wolverine using his claws and Shingen wielding a samurai sword. The battle ends with Shingen's death. Mariko enters the room to find Wolverine standing over her father's corpse. She reaches for the blade he had so recently held when battling Wolverine. Wolverine believes she will fulfill her obligation as a daughter and seek to avenge her father. He could easily disarm her but does not.

Holding the sword aloft, Mariko discloses that it is the "honor sword" of the Clan Yashida. The lord of the clan has no special claim to the sword. The sword is to be wielded by the samurai who best exemplifies the qualities to which the clan aspires. Mariko, stating that her father brought only shame to the clan, offers the sword to Wolverine. He declares himself unworthy of this honor, but she presses the issue. In the end, he accepts the sword with a humble heart.

Both Wolverine and Oishi kill their rivals despite knowing that there will be consequences to their actions. Oishi and the surviving ronin have violated the law of the land by executing a government official, but they have also followed the Bushido code by avenging Asano. They are allowed to commit seppuku, an honorable death for a samurai, rather than be tried and executed as common criminals. The fact that their actions would end in their deaths does not stop the 47 ronin from avenging their lord. Wolverine is well aware that killing Shingen will likely end any possibility of reconciliation with Mariko. Despite this fact, he continues on a course of action that will end with the death of this special relationship. That the relationship continues is unexpected and welcome, but winning Mariko's hand is not what motivates Wolverine.

Interestingly, when Mariko addresses Wolverine, she mentions that the honor sword represents "all we were and all we wish to be. It is perfection of form and function." The existence of an original and false mind leads to the great potential and great function. All people have, from the time of their birth, great potential. If this potential is unripe, frozen, undeveloped, or inflexible, great function cannot follow. When potential is developed through disciplined practice and application, great function will follow.[100]

Wolverine, while perceiving himself as struggling to harness great potential in order to manifest great function, is viewed by others (Mariko in this story and Kitty Pryde and Jubilee in the previous chapter) as exceeding others as an exemplar of loyalty, honor, and duty. His compassion, hidden from his own eyes, is on full display to those around him. That he follows his own code of conduct may be a sign of his highly developed character more than a side effect of his difficult life. A samurai who personifies great potential and function is said to act free and independent of rules because of his supreme mastery of his potential.[101] Perhaps the best path to being a true samurai is by walking in the shoes of a ronin.[102]

# Part IV

## American Dreams and American Nightmares

# CHAPTER 17

# Captain America

Steve Rogers, the man who becomes Captain America, is a man with a sense of mission. The roots of his story reach back to a dark time in American and world history. During World War II, the great evil of Nazism threatened to spread across the globe. This is not merely a plotline but the actual history of the character's development. Captain America's first appearance was in March 1941, before America was actively engaged in World War II. The comic routinely depicted Captain America battling the Nazi menace. The first cover of *Captain America Comics* pictures Captain America, in full red, white, and blue uniform, punching Adolf Hitler in the face. Captain America was created to be the defender of America and American values. He would become a symbol of these values as well.

Steve Rogers's transformation into Captain America was a conscious decision. Physically frail, Rogers failed an army physical and was not allowed to enlist. His physical weakness belied an exceptionally strong will. Rogers volunteered to participate in a top-secret government project called Operation Rebirth. Seeking an advantage in the war, American scientists invented the super-soldier serum. Once injected and consumed, this liquid would imbue the drinker with enhanced strength, dexterity, constitution, and endurance. The goal was to generate an army of super-soldiers who would easily overwhelm the enemy and end the war with far less bloodshed and suffering. The experiment proved to be a success, as Steve Rogers almost instantly became the personification of physical perfection. The hope for generating an army of super-soldiers was quickly crushed, however, because a Nazi spy killed the inventor of the serum and destroyed all his notes. Steve Rogers became the only man to take the potion, making him America's greatest soldier, coined Captain America by the government.

Rogers fought the Nazis and the Japanese throughout World War II, before the war claimed him as well. During a mission in the North Atlantic, a plane crash seemingly claimed the life of America's greatest soldier. He survived, however, encased in a block of ice. Eventually he is awakened from his suspended animation and rejoins the world, a man of the present with the ideals of the past. Is he a walking relic or a walking reminder of all that is good and hopeful about America? Do his values hold sway in the modern world? Perhaps some ideas need to pass away, for they have no purpose in the modern world.

Such problems plague Captain America, who is physically young and in his prime, but his mind is from a different era. Most of Steve Rogers's friends are deceased or senior citizens, while he is in his early thirties and in prime condition. Such a paradox causes Steve Rogers some confusion, but Captain America is his stabilizing force.

In comics, as evidenced by the X-Men and the Justice League, sometimes superhero groups are formed. These groups are formed for a variety of reasons, and the ties that bind them are equally diverse. The Avengers was one such group, and they are credited with finding Captain America, but he quickly puts his stamps on the team, and, although he does not always lead them, they often follow his example. Such is the strength of his character, even if he, at times, seems displaced in time and the least powerful member of the team. The Avengers lineup has included some of the most powerful heroes in comics, including the technological wonder called Iron Man, Thor the Norse god of thunder, the Beast (from the X-Men), and Zeus' son, Hercules. All of these incredibly powerful heroes listen to and follow orders from Captain America, not because of his power but because of who he is. It is most definitely not the starred and striped uniform and indestructible shield alone that make Steve Rogers the respected hero Captain America. Many could wear the suit, few could be the man, and fewer still could lead the Avengers so effectively. This truth raises up the good Captain and, at times, threatens to wear him down.

Because it is not his powers so much as who he is that makes Captain America special, it is important to understand how he views his mission and how successfully he pursues it. Captain America's own words can be used to begin this process. In a startling chain of events, Captain America is killed in March 2007. The Avenger Thor was not on Earth during this episode but upon his return seeks to say goodbye to his friend and comrade in arms. Using his mystic hammer, Mjolnir, Thor recalls Captain America's soul from the afterlife. During the brief conversation, Captain America declares, "All my life, I fought to become a symbol. A symbol of all the things that were right about this country. All the things I loved." An important question that this raises is what are America's greatest virtues? We also need to evaluate whether Captain America successfully symbolized these virtues. Any number of lists could be generated, but for this chapter, the list of American virtues presented by Jacob Needleman in the book *American Soul* are used.[103]

Needleman discusses not only American virtues but also the accompanying shadow. Needleman's list begins with the very American ideal of liberty.

> Political liberty means first and foremost the social conditions necessary to allow this search for one's own moral or spiritual light. But this ideal and right has been taken to mean merely the right to satisfy one's own subjective desires, whatever they may be, without any reference to the existence of the moral law within.[104]

This definition of liberty speaks to the heart of Captain America's original mission. The Nazis could be seen to symbolize the worst possible scenario of a political party dedicated to satisfying one group's subjective desires. Although not all personal desires are as destructive, America has seen its share of the elevation of personal wishes above the existence of any moral law. Liberty debased to a "do what you want, when you want" slogan lacks the power to inspire people to stand up for others for a prolonged period of time. Reducing liberty to such a simple base, in fact, saps the momentum out of any civil rights movement or desire for self-improvement. A segregationist in 1962 or an alcoholic in 2009 could both claim to be merely "doing what they want, when they want." Meanwhile, the black families in the South or the family members affected by the drinking suffer. When the liberty embraced by an individual or group causes or intensifies the suffering of another, then liberty is being threatened, not celebrated.

True liberty demands not only that we act on our individual desires but develop the compassion to see that others have the same rights as well. The defense of liberty demands that stands be taken, some struggles being more obvious than others. In one story line, Captain America attempts to thwart the schemes of the evil Dr. Faustus. Faustus, an arrogant and well-educated man, invents a unique gas. Whoever inhales the toxin becomes a thrall to the whims of Faustus. At one point, Captain America becomes intoxicated but is freed by the intervention of the superhero Daredevil, who helps awaken his core values.

It is worthwhile to note that Captain America does not free himself from the brainwashing concoction by mere force of will. As Faustus's pawn, Captain America's starred-and-striped shield is painted over with a blazing swastika. While battling Daredevil, oil spills on the shield, causing the swastika to erode. The stars and stripes now visible, Daredevil exhorts Captain America to look at his shield. The narration box informs the reader that "The light from above glistens across the starred and striped surface seemingly boring deep through the layers of his befogged mind and into his innermost being!" The symbolic meaning of his true shield awakens within Captain America his "moral or spiritual light." The symbols that inspire sometimes are far more liberating than mere human will. Captain America's shield, a symbol of liberty, liberates his mind. As the story continues, we see that true liberty as a liberating force is a theme of the story arc and Captain America's life.

Faustus walks along a catwalk in his zeppelin, gloating to a captured foe that he will soon begin the process of releasing his gas in New York City, placing the entire population under his control. From that point, he will patiently allow his influence to spread until he controls the country. Naturally, Captain America arrives and stops the release of the gas. In the struggle between Captain America and Faustus's mind-controlled goons, the aircraft crashes into New York Harbor (near the Statue of Liberty). Captain America emerges from the crash, dragging Dr. Faustus behind him. Faustus cries out, "Why ... didn't you let me drown? Faustus ... cannot be saved ... by you!"

On one level Faustus's dismay at being saved by Captain America is merely the disgrace of being saved by an archenemy. On another level, however, Captain America is now taking the place of his shield as a symbol of the power of liberty to elevate hearts and minds. Faustus represents the lowest form of liberty, seeking his own gratification at the expense of the populace of New York City. His refusal to be saved by Captain America can be seen as quite odd because he is in the process of being saved, at least physically, by the star-spangled hero. What he won't be, what he refuses to let Captain America do for him, is raise him up from his level of thinking. He will not be saved; Captain America and his symbols will not alter his worldview. Faustus's will and the power to lord over others gives him meaning and he refuses to see meaning, or salvation, beyond those desires. This shortsightedness mirrors the lack of vision exhibited by the title character in *The Tragical History of Dr. Faustus*.

Dr. Faustus's refusal to be saved by Captain America does not come as a great shock. It also does not disturb Captain America very much that Faustus remains true to his malevolent inclinations. There are times, however, that the refusal of others to pursue the highest virtues of liberty causes Steve Rogers such distress, he questions the value of being Captain America.

An example of this distress is found in the aftermath of *Operation Galactic Storm*, a story line that brings Captain America and the Avengers into an intergalactic war. In Galactic Storm two extraterrestrial empires (the Kree and Sh'iar) fight a bitter war, a war that could consume the Earth. The Avengers act on Earth's behalf, hoping to intervene as diplomats and negotiate the war's end or, at least, prevent the use of stargates that could threaten Earth. Their negotiations are unsuccessful, and various teams of Avengers find themselves in small skirmishes and battles. The war continues until the Shi'ar ultimate weapon, the Nega-Bomb, is detonated. This action is taken by the Skrulls, a third alien empire with a long history of hostility with the Kree. The Avengers had once intervened in a Kree-Skrull war years before. The Skrull, a race with shape-shifting abilities, had infiltrated the Sh'iar court with the intent of escalating the war. Their use of the Nega-Bomb kills billions of Kree. This devastating explosion ends the war. Sh'iar Empress Lilandra, although not authorizing the bomb's use, takes advantage of it impact. She declares that the remnants of the Kree Empire will be annexed by the Sh'iar.

Adding to the dreadful conclusion of the war is the discovery of the machinations of the Kree Supreme Intelligence. The Supreme Intelligence is an organic computer life-form that is over a million years old. The being is an amalgamation of the greatest mind since the history of the Kree. Upon the death of any exemplary Kree thinker (scientist, philosopher, general, etc.), the brain patterns are assimilated into a computer and added to the consciousness of the Supreme Intelligence. The Supreme Intelligence orchestrated most of the events of the war, including the use of the Nega-Bomb, because he believed that the Kree had reached an evolutionary dead end. The radioactivity caused by the bomb's fallout would enable the Kree to evolve further. Therefore, the Supreme Intelligence sacrificed the Kree's present (including the billions of lives lost in the explosion and their independence) for the hopes for a better future.

The Avengers, outraged by this thought, seek to kill the Supreme Intelligence for the crime of genocide. Captain America points out that the Avengers are not executioners. The Supreme Intelligence should be brought before a war crimes commission, not hunted down and executed by a superpowered mob proclaiming to be pursuing justice. Iron Man disregards Captain America's orders and heads a group of Avengers to execute the Supreme Intelligence. This action leads to Captain America questioning his capacity to inspire, lead, or even fit in with the Avengers.

His sense of alienation begins with his orders being ignored and a group of Avengers seeking vengeance on the Supreme Intelligence. It deepens when, in the aftermath of the war, the Avengers vote not to have disciplinary action taken against the members who killed the Supreme Intelligence. Captain America's dejection reaches a nadir when only three superheroes show for a seminar he is giving on superhuman ethics. He apologizes to the three attendees and leaves the dais.

Later that night, Clint Barton (a member of the Avengers who goes by the moniker Hawkeye) invites Steve Rogers out for a drink, hoping to cheer up the living legend. Tony Stark (Iron Man) discovers where the two heroes are and meets them at the bar. Tony, who led the rebellion against Steve's authority, declares he and Steve need to talk alone. Clint leaves to play pool, and the two estranged heroes exchange words.

As the conversation progresses Tony confesses that there was a point during Galactic Storm when he believed Steve was dead. In that moment, Tony realized that he would miss Steve Rogers greatly if he died. He confesses, "You're an inspiration to me, Steve. To a lot of us. We may not think like you or act like you—but we still respect you and appreciate what you do and the way you do it." With these words, Tony Stark expresses an unfortunate truth: the best role models often can seem daunting because they do things in a way we cannot. Whereas Faustus refused to be saved by Captain America, Tony Stark's awe expresses it is not his refusal but a sense of inadequacy that prevents him from being as good as Captain America. He even asks Steve for forgiveness. Steve quickly points out his own shortcomings and compliments Tony on his courage (Tony is a recovering alcoholic and still entered a bar to meet with Steve). This scene is a great reminder that one never knows for certain how his or her presence inspires another. Steve is comforted by Tony's words, just as Tony is inspired by Steve's capacity to live his ideals even in situations that are far from perfect.

Fittingly, it is the American virtue of independence that causes the relationship between Tony Stark and Steve Rogers to weaken. The highest manifestation of independence is the ability to move beyond the conditioned self and the conditioned response to events. This conditioning comes from our society, culture, family, and friends. The conditioned self becomes subject to evaluation, and, possibly, fidelity to these exterior factors becomes subject to a growing interior conscious self. At the basest level, independence is nothing more than fidelity to one's own ideological position and "egoistic idiosyncrasy."[105] An authentic sense of independence balances the desires of the individual with the needs of the community, and the independent person can freely choose loyalty to the common good, the country, and a cause. Independence does not mean isolation and dismissal of moral law.

Perhaps the best example of Steve Rogers exemplifying the ideal of independence is when he tenders his resignation as Captain America. The president had formed a commission that includes, among other U.S. government officials, the heads of the FBI and CIA. This commission discovers a document Steve signed in 1941 in which he agreed to participate in Operation Rebirth. By the terms of the document, Captain America works exclusively for the U.S. government.

Captain America points out that, since his revival from suspended animation, he has been serving the country as a member of the Avengers and as an independent agent. The commission dismisses this argument and states its position that Captain America must have all his activities and assignments cleared by their office. Steve takes twenty-four hours to consider the commission's demands.

Alone in his apartment he muses that "going back to my wartime role as a glorified agent of America's official policies, I'd be compromising my effectiveness as a symbol that transcends mere politics." This thought makes it clear what Steve Rogers is going to choose. He returns the next day, dressed in civilian clothes, not his Captain America uniform. He acknowledges that Captain America was originally a soldier, bound by a strict chain of command. In the years following his return, Steve Rogers made Captain America much more than that. To become a government agent would force situations in which Rogers would have to compromise his ideals for orders. This is a completely unacceptable situation. Therefore, he turns in his uniform and shield. The American ideal of independ-ence, and his effort to live those ideals, prove more important than even the persona he adopted and molded to best inspire others to recognize and live the true American dream.

It is important to note that Steve Rogers does not bear his country malice for the gov-ernment's role in his resignation. Taking the title "The Captain," Steve Rogers resumes be-ing a superhero and works with the Avengers. Thor, returning from a mission in space, visits the Avengers and is surprised to see the changes in Steve Rogers's costume. Upon hearing what has happened, an enraged Thor declares "madmen" run the U.S. government and that he will go to Washington to overthrow them. Steve calms Thor down, emphasiz-ing he still believes and respects in the American system of democracy. His issues with a single administration do not negate his love of country just as his love of country does not dictate the need to be a pawn.

The next American virtue is practicality. Practicality can also be viewed as a form of honesty, an honesty forged in experiential reality. Needleman sees American practicality as rooted in ancient Athens and Socrates. This practicality, although it had no influence on the founding of America, also exists in Christianity and Buddhism. One's inner search to achieve a level of honesty (which would only strengthen one's liberty and independence) "must be experienced, and not only believed in as dogma or inferred on logical or concep-tual grounds."[106] This form of honesty, openly seeking and evaluating the truths of life, has, in Needleman's estimation, greatly degenerated, and American "honesty" is most commonly expressed as a form of cynicism.

Captain America faces this cynicism on a regular basis. Many people, be they govern-ment agents or policemen, view him as a glory-seeking individual. This is an unfortunate as-pect of cynicism—the projection of the onlooker's motives onto the actions of others. If people cannot conceive of themselves acting without self-aggrandizement as a primary mo-tivator, then they fail to see, or dismiss as delusional, that trait in others. If cynics decide al-truism is disguised selfishness, this enables them to belittle the helpful individual and enables the capacity to comfortably do nothing.

Captain America portrays the higher aspect of this virtue, the experiential reality that expands the scope of one's vision, in subtle ways. An example of this can be found in the quiet aftermath following a battle. Captain America, the government agency S.H.I.E.L.D. (Supreme Headquarters, International Espionage, Law-Enforcement Division), and the Hulk dismantle a vicious organization called the Corporation. One of the villains, a woman who goes by the code name Vamp, was rendered mentally incapacitated by the battle. A S.H.I.E.L.D. agent, perhaps angered by all he had to endure to achieve victory, is seen ver-bally abusing the woman. He calls her "Tramp" instead of Vamp and threatens to hit her with the butt of his gun if she does not follow the other captives being lead away.

Captain America snatches the agent's gun and breaks it. He proclaims the woman de-serves pity, not abuse. The agent can only see a helpless enemy, one easy to demean and push around. Captain America sees a defeated person. Captain America, who witnessed the cruelty people can heap on the helpless when he freed Jews from concentration camps, does not tolerate the abuse of others, even defeated enemies. With the battle over, he feels malice for none. The agent attempts to hit Captain America, calling him self-righteous as his hand nearly breaks on the hero's shield. Other agents look to intervene but are stopped by a stern warning from Captain America, who proceeds to take Vamp into custody.

The action of taking a criminal into custody is an apt introduction for the next American virtue—the rule of law. In Needleman's analysis, as in the life of Captain America, the rule of law is meant to enhance people's liberty and independence. The laws created by the government are often punitive, designed to punish those who harm the common good. This punitive function of the rule of law is also protective. Government laws protect society. This is done to help create an environment that allows society to orient itself toward the greater dictates of the conscience.

Ralph Waldo Emerson also noted the existence of these two forms of the law, stressing that the laws of man are subservient to a deeper, eternal law. When Emerson wrote, "Be it known unto you that henceforward I obey no law less than the eternal law," he was not dismissing the laws of man, but merely voicing the desire to see them reflect a greater purpose. This is why he would continue to aid his parents, support his family, and be a good husband, but do so in "a new and unprecedented way."[107] He would not be a slavish follower to the laws of man but joyfully surrender himself, after putting forth the serious effort demanded by the highest dictates of liberty and independence, to the moral law of conscience.

The opposite of this position is to allow laws and statutes to replace the conscience. This position demands the acceptance of what is legal as being the equivalent of what is good. In such a system, people surrender the highest form of liberty and independence because there is no system above the works of human beings. This is surely not what the founders of America, who routinely broke the laws of England during the years leading up to the American War for Independence, sought to create. It is a thin line that separates the rule of law from the tyranny of the law. It is also not Captain America's understanding of the law, as he stated when he resigned, "My commitment to the ideals of this country is greater than my commitment to a 40 year old document."

Captain America exhibits his respect for both forms of the law in the field as well as when standing before a government commission. In a dramatic story with a simple beginning, Steve Rogers moves into an apartment building. One of the tenants, Anna Kapplebaum, always invites new arrivals to dinner. Steve, who has a strong respect for traditions, accepts the invitation. He and Josh, a resident who extended the invitation for Anna, have dinner with her that evening.

When Steve meets Anna, he sees numbers on her wrist, a souvenir from World War II. In a flashback, Anna explains that her family had been sent to Diebenwald, a concentration camp invented for the story. They were taken captive after Kristallnacht. Her mother and father died in the camp when she was twelve. She stayed in the camp throughout the war, but her death seemed imminent as the war neared its conclusion. The commandant of Diebenwald ordered all records in the camp to be destroyed and all remaining prisoners to be executed. Anna was poised to share her parents' fate, but Captain America arrived and saved her. She never realizes that she is sharing a meal with Captain America in his civilian clothes. Nor does she or Steve realize she will soon meet Captain America again.

Leaving a butcher shop a short time later, Anna bumps into a man she recognizes —not only recognizes, but whom she is terrified to see again. She faints, and Josh rushes her to a hospital. The man she encountered was Dr. Mendelhaus, a man known as the Butcher of Diebenwald.

In the hospital Aaron Heller, a Nazi hunter, and his daughter, Marie, visit Anna. He shows Anna a cane that has notches carved in it, one for every Nazi upon whom he has visited justice. Aaron, who also bears a concentration camp brand, is in poor health. He wishes to bring Dr. Mendelhaus to justice before he dies. Anna agrees to help punish the man directly responsible for her parents' death. A neo-Nazi working in the hospital as a janitor sees Aaron leave Anna's room and quickly plans for her to be kidnapped.

Anna is brought to an abandoned church, where she sees Dr. Mendelhaus kneeling before a picture of Adolf Hitler. He tries to explain that he has been forced to the church and is as much a prisoner as Anna. His past, and his inability to remember Anna, earns him no sympathy. As the Nazis prepare to take their two prisoners to a boat, Captain America makes a dramatic entrance. He is once again battling to free Anna from the Nazis.

As Captain America routs his foes, one Nazi leads Anna and Dr. Mendelhaus to the boat in an attempt to escape. Aaron and Marie Heller intercept him, but Aaron suffers a heart attack, and he drops his gun. The lone Nazi gunman takes aim at Aaron, only to be disarmed by Dr. Mendelhaus. The doctor proclaims that there has been enough killing, that it has to end. Anna picks up the gun and prepares to shoot Mendelhaus, even as Captain America arrives and objects to the execution. Much as he did during the Galactic Storm story line, Captain America seeks to bring the villain—in this case, Mendelhaus—to the courts. Good people, like Anna, shouldn't need to kill to feel safe. Captain America's understanding of the rule of law as a protector of citizens is on full display in this scene, although the reader may wish to see Anna pull the trigger. In the end, Captain America's words cause Anna to hesitate.

Marie Heller, cradling her dying father's head, does not hold back. She shoots and kills Mendelhaus. His last word is "Anna." Marie then tells her father, "The Butcher of Diebenwald is dead … it's finally over." Captain America does not echo this victorious sentiment. Justice that is not balanced by mercy cannot bring about release from the vicious cycle of violence. The story does not reveal, although readers can certainly discuss, what action Captain America takes in regard to Marie. Would he arrest her for the murder of Dr. Mendelhaus, or let her go free with a caustic warning?

The final virtue of America to be covered is the freedom of speech. Needleman stresses that freedom of speech is necessary to allow people to discuss, evaluate, and build a community's conscience. Freedom of speech is also dependent on freedom of thought. Thoughts churned and reflected on in solitude can be brought to the community, allowing our inner and outer worlds to coalesce with those of others. This process is not without tension but can increase the sense of partnership as truths are sought among societal and familial norms.

Needleman's assessment of the current state of freedom of speech is a scathing indictment. Freedom of speech has descended to a level that caused him to write the following:

> How much of what we prize as the right to free speech is based on a loneliness that makes us yearn for others to pay more attention to us? How to understand the decay of this ideal into the sanctification of superficial opinion, on the one hand, or commercial communication on the other? How to understand that we are losing the *knowledge function* of the

community, that the hard work of thinking together is being eclipsed by the addiction to information ... and by our society's attachment to applications of knowledge that bring only egoistic and often illusionary gain?[108]

The phrase "sanctification of superficial opinion" speaks directly to the level of discourse that can be found in society. It also recognizes the existence of expertise, something that speaks to the reality that some "opinions" are more valuable than others. The sanctification of any opinion, however, enables expertise to be sneered at and experts to be dismissed as elitists. It also enables individuals to hold their own opinion as sacrosanct and not engage in open or honest dialogue. Why would someone need the input of others when he or she already possesses the final word?

Captain America rarely addressed this issue in life, although we do see him support freedom of speech as a matter of course. From beyond the grave, however, he echoed Needleman's sentiment. As the evaluation of Captain America as a standard to evaluate America virtues started at his grave, so there shall it end. Thor, much as he was when Steve Rogers resigned, is outraged. Thor proclaims murder to be unforgivable. He states with unshakable conviction, "if you would have me take action against those responsible for your death—you will be avenged in full." What it means to a Viking god to avenge a fallen friend in full is left to the reader's imagination.

Captain America, as he had done before, turns down Thor's offer. He expresses one regret, that his life is now being used to advocate whatever is most convenient or to serve a political agenda. He bemoans the fact that he can hear the media talking nonstop about something they don't understand. Captain America was always about the best virtues of America, not a particular political stance or the advancement of one's career and notoriety. The media "can't hear that truth above their own voices."

Thor honors his friend's wish to not seek revenge and says goodbye, allowing Captain America to return to the afterlife. He does offer a gift, however. Flying into the upper atmosphere, he summons an intense electrical storm that interrupts all newscasts, radio stations, and satellite and cable broadcasts. He does this at the precise moment that Captain America had died the year before. His anniversary gift to his comrade is a true moment of silence, freeing him from the numbing effects of freedom of speech manifested as the sanctification of superficial opinion. The moment of silence lasts a minute before Thor allows communication to continue. This action may speak to an important aspect of freedom of speech, which is the necessity of silence to ponder the value of what we say. Perhaps even to learn to enjoy saying nothing as we allow our thoughts to age slowly and become something worth sharing.

# CHAPTER 18

## Civil War and the Struggle for Freedom and Security

In 2006, Marvel Comics launched a momentous seven-issue series titled *Civil War*. The series had crossovers with multiple Marvel titles, making it the focal point of the Marvel universe at that time. As the name implies, the series places Marvel superheroes at each other's throats over an issue that can divide the opinion of readers as well. Captain America, as one might expect, plays a prime role as the leader of one of the superhero factions.

The story opens with a scene that speaks to the lowest manifestations of American virtues. Members of the New Warriors, a group of young superheroes, have decided that being regular superheroes lacks a certain appeal. While some cynics wrongfully claim Captain America's primary motivator is the desire for glory, the New Warriors are all about glory and fame. The team works with WTNH-Channel 8 to bring viewers a reality television show much like *Cops* or *Dog the Bounty Hunter*. Ratings are down, but an opportunity for a great show presents itself.

Four super-villains who recently broke out of Ryker's Island prison are laying low in a nondescript house in Stamford, Connecticut. One of the New Warriors mentions that the four villains are "totally out of our league," but the team decides to attack them because it would be great for ratings. Adding to the surreal scene is the decision to delay the attack so that one of the New Warriors can have makeup applied to cover a pimple. One must look his best when fighting for truth, justice, and the Nielson Ratings. As the makeup artists prepare the hero for the big shot, one of the villains spots the New Warriors, forcing them into action.

The raid actually begins well for the New Warriors. They take down three of the villains in short order, while making smart quips for the camera crew and requesting a villain's putdown be edited out of the episode. The fourth villain, Nitro, is stopped near a school as he attempts to flee. His retreat may be halted, but he is far from helpless. Nitro has the ability to explode and then reform himself. He generates a massive explosion, killing an estimated eight hundred people, including the New Warriors, children at Stamford Elementary, and citizens in the surrounding community.

A number of the most experienced heroes converge on Stamford to help with the cleanup and the search for survivors. Among the heroes on site are Captain America, Iron Man, the X-Men, and the Fantastic Four. Goliath, a hero with the ability to grow to a massive height and have his strength increase accordingly, predicts dire consequences for the superhero community. A series of events, including a rampage by the Hulk in Las Vegas, causes him to believe that a witch-hunt is about to begin. His prediction proves to be prophetic.

Public outrage against superheroes hits an all-time high. The concept of unlicensed and untrained people running around in masks fighting crime, without accountability to a hierarchal chain of command, becomes unpalatable to a growing number of Americans. Tony Stark (Iron Man) is verbally accosted and spit upon by Miriam Sharpe, the mother of one of the deceased Stamford children. Johnny Storm (the Human Torch from the Fantastic Four) is assaulted outside a nightclub. His injuries land him in the hospital. Congress begins debating a Superhero Registration Act that would require all heroes to register their secret identities with the government, be trained by the government, and take orders from the government officials. Superheroes would become federalized.

A group of heroes meet in the Baxter Building, the home of the Fantastic Four, to discuss the Registration Act. Some heroes, like Iron Man and Mr. Fantastic, see the Act as perfectly reasonable. Their thinking is, in light of the Stamford tragedy, people deserve to have their concerns about superheroes allayed. Becoming public employees, submitting to governmental training and restraints, can help calm the public and allow the heroes to continue their work.

Superheroes opposed to the Registration Act have their own concerns. One of these concerns is the idea of being turned into "Super-Cops" and the necessity to relinquish secret identities. Some heroes, particularly those who do not hide their identities from the public, do not think the secret identity issue is a big deal. Others, like Spider-Man, see it as very important. Sue Richards, the Invisible Woman from the Fantastic Four, attempts to make Spider-Man (Peter Parker) understand that secret identities are not essential to being a superhero.

Spider-Man responds by pointing out that if his identity were known, then those closest to him, Mary Jane and Aunt May, would be in grave jeopardy. He does not say, although students may point out, that Spider-Man's concerns are not as easily dismissed as Sue Richards would like. Sue Richards's family are all superheroes and capable of defending themselves. Spider-Man's family members are not, and this is a serious concern. It is a concern made all the more prevalent when Peter's aunt is struck by a sniper's bullet at the end of the saga. The conversation also reveals the impact that personal perspective has on individual outlooks. It, along with a conversation simultaneously unfolding on the S.H.I.E.L.D. Helicarrier (the flying home base of S.H.I.E.L.D.), also reveals how big a picture people can see and how willing they are to consider flaws in what seem like the best-laid plans.

Captain America is on the Helicarrier discussing the Registration Act with Commander Hill. Hill recently replaced Nick Fury, longtime S.H.I.E.L.D. director and trusted ally to Captain America. Captain America states that the Registration Act will split the superhero community down the middle, with most of the resistance coming from heroes who tend to work closer to the streets, like Daredevil and Luke Cage. Commander Hill doesn't see this as a big deal, because Captain America can help lead an Anti-Superhero

Response Unit to bring in the objectors. Captain America refuses to participate in arresting superheroes. His objection, which goes unconsidered, is that the Superhero Registration Act allows Washington to tell the heroes who the super-villains are. Even though Commander Hill did not find this thought-provoking, it allows the reader to consider why Captain America opposes registration.

As his history has revealed, Captain America believes in American ideals, not American bureaucrats. If superheroes took their orders from the government, what would prevent the heroes from being used as foreign policy leverage or even as spies to steal other states' secrets? What type of action would the president of the United States be tempted to take and be willing to make with an army of superheroes bound by legalities to follow the commander in chief? Conversely, what limitations would superheroes find themselves subject to as the result of being public servants?

On one occasion, S.H.I.E.L.D. was ordered by the U.S. government to prevent the Avengers from interfering with problems in Genosha, the island nation know for its tension between mutants and humans. It was a "bad" move politically to intervene directly with the events that were unfolding, even as people died. The Avengers fought through a blockade and went anyway because politics matter much less than human lives to superheroes. Superheroes traditionally are free to act without borders for the good of the world, even if they are not making the world safe for political egos. Free of a chain of command, they can be where they are needed when no one else can be there. To be limited in his ability to act on his conscience is a position Captain America has opposed since his revival from suspended animation. It is the driving force to his opposition to the Superhero Registration Act.

When it becomes obvious that Captain America will not lead an effort to apprehend other superheroes, Commander Hill orders his arrest. Captain America pummels the Anti-Superhero Response Unit sent to subdue him and escapes the Helicarrier. The anti-registration heroes have an inspirational leader and a figurehead in Captain America. The supporters of registration, led by Iron Man, Mr. Fantastic, and Yellow Jacket (Hank Pym), prepare for open conflict with their peers and friends. The civil war has begun.

The two sides of the civil war represent the desire for security and control versus the desire for freedom of conscience and civil liberties. It is worth noting that many of the pro-registration forces are heroes whose secret identities are already known to the public and are used to a certain level of public acclaim. A powerful exception to this generalization is the presence of Spider-Man, convinced by Tony Stark to join the pro-registration side. This is noteworthy because Spider-Man has protected his secret identity more carefully than almost any superhero in the Marvel universe. If he can accept the demands of registration, then others can as well. He also brings an iconic presence to the pro-registration side, counterbalancing Captain America's inspirational allure.

The level of security people feel when trusting superheroes to protect them is always at the fore of Iron Man's mind. He emphasizes the central importance of public security in a statement he makes to She Hulk. She expresses, after a team of pre-registration heroes has just defeated a Doombot in New York City and stand before a cheering crowd, concerns that they are no longer superheroes, but agents of S.H.I.E.L.D. Iron Man interprets the cheers as a sign that people are starting to "believe in superheroes again" when the statement about being S.H.I.E.L.D. agents is made. Overstating his position slightly, he says,

"The only thing changing is that the kids, the amateurs, and the sociopaths are getting weeded out."

Captain America's statement on the Helicarrier would suggest that Iron Man's list of the only things changing would need to be expanded. Regardless, the idea that those three categories would be eliminated from the ranks of the heroes does allow for a greater level of security when considering who is allowed to be a superhero. In a world where people with immense superpower move freely and unchecked in society, sometimes causing great harm, it is little wonder that public opinion leans heavily in favor of monitoring all superhuman activity.

The idea of "weeding out" certain people who are not cut out to be superheroes can also cause concerns, for what is the criterion for deeming an individual a sociopath and unfit to be a superhero? Hypothetically, would Batman be a sociopath and therefore unfit? Would merely being uncomfortably intense and having a predisposition to question authority be deemed unacceptable and therefore grounds to receive the sociopath label? Would a hero with the temperament of a General Patton or William Tecumseh Sherman be cast aside? Who, in the end, makes these decisions? Are certain heroes, although dark in their approach to crime fighting, necessary when battling super-villains?

A trait shared by the three leaders of the pro-registration forces is their connection to the field of science. Hank Pym and Reed Richards are both scientists, and Tony Stark is an inventor. To bolster his argument for registration, Reed Richards even worked out a logarithm that projects the social danger created by the opponents of registration. The pro-registration argument must be correct, for science is on their side, and the logarithm proves the righteousness of their cause. It does not appear, however, that Reed worked out a similar projection for the dangers created by the pro-registration forces. This can give rise to an important observation about science and scientists.

To say science deals with objective facts is an overstatement. Although true that proven scientific laws and overwhelming evidenced theory exist, this does not mean that scientists live in a world of monolithic thought dictated by agreed-upon facts. For example, one can find multiple reactions by scientists regarding the severity, cause, and long-range implications of global warming. If there is one thing these scientists share, it is the certainty they feel in their position, for both sides are supported by science. The simple, and very human reason, for this is the fact that although science may aspire to deal with objective facts, scientists are often far from impartial. Consider "Planck's dictum," a maxim named after physicist Max Planck: major advances in science occur not because the proponents of the established view are forced by the weight of evidence to change their minds but because they retire and eventually die.[109]

Efraim Fischbein articulated this tendency by noting, "A scientist who has formulated a certain hypothesis did not formulate it by chance; it optimally suits his general philosophy in the given domain.... He will be unwilling to give up this first hypothesis because by renouncing it he had to re-evaluate a whole system of conceptions."[110] Interestingly, Fischbein also mentioned that scientists are "anxious to preserve" their original hypothesis because they want to maintain their prestige. This in no way downgrades scientists; it merely reminds us of their humanity and all its wonderful flaws. Using science to achieve certainty has lead to disastrous results in history, particularly when addressing societal issues.

Social Darwinism and the use of natural selection to justify the mistreatment of other people, deemed "inferior," as necessary for the advancement of the "superior" group is a prime example of the dangers of using science to support a particular worldview. Karl Pearson, a German scientist, was a strong proponent of social Darwinism and natural selection as a guiding force of civilizations. While extolling the "natural" superiority of the white race over all other races, he also coldly summarized the subjugation or elimination of other races as necessary, and an almost inevitable consequence, of the process of evolution. Consider this description of the struggle in North America between European and Native Americans:

> I venture to assert, then, that the struggle for existence between white and red man, painful and even terrible as it was in the details, has given us a good far outbalancing its immediate evil. In place of the red man, contributing practically nothing to the work and thought of the world, we have a great nation, mistress of many arts, and able, with its youthful imagination and fresh, untrammeled impulses, to contribute much to the common stock of civilized man. Against that we have only to put the romantic sympathy for the Red Indian generated by the novels of Cooper and the poems of Longfellow, and then see how little it weighs in the balance![111]

While the scientific minds of the pro-registration forces would strenuously object to Pearson's thoughts, there is a curious observation to be made regarding the sides in the civil war. Goliath, the Falcon, Luke Cage, the Black Panther, and Storm —all prominent black superheroes—become members of the anti-registration movement. Two lesser-known black heroes, Shroud and the Patriot, also join Captain America's contingent. Only one prominent black hero, the X-Man Bishop, joins the pro-registration forces. The reason for and implications of this racial divide is not evaluated in the story but definitely can be used to generate discussion in the classroom.[112] It is also worth noting that the first page of issues 2–7 of Civil War all open with a brief synopsis of the previous issue and a reminder of the conflicting positions taken in the conflict. The reader is told that Iron Man sees registration as "a natural evolution of the role of superhumans in society, and a reasonable request." The use of the phrase "natural evolution" can be used to help make the argument that, on some level, Iron Man may adhere to some form of Social Darwinism.

Reed Richards's projections aside, Captain America continues to build the resistance. Using a secret S.H.I.E.L.D. safe house known only to thirty-third degree S.H.I.E.L.D. officers as a base, he continues to act in the traditional superhero role.* Newspaper headlines dispersed throughout the story communicate that Captain America's "Secret Avengers" successfully thwart a scheme hatched by the upper-villain team, the Sinister Six.

Using the Secret Avengers' desire to do good against them, Tony Stark intentionally sets fire to a petrochemical plant near the Hudson River. The unregistered heroes arrive and find a lack of trapped victims or security alarms. One member of the team sees a sign that reads "Geffen-Meyers: A Division of Stark Industries" and realizes they have stumbled into a trap. An ambush renders the team's teleporters unconscious, leaving them trapped to face the registration forces.

---

* The only thirty-third degree S.H.I.E.L.D. officer is Nick Fury. He also supplies older S.H.I.E.L.D. technology to their cause.

Iron Man seeks to persuade Captain America to join the registration movement. He extends his hand and offers to explain to Captain America the "twenty-first-century overhaul" he is bringing to the superhero community. It is difficult to imagine Iron Man's tone not being slightly condescending as he mentions, "we aren't living in 1945 anymore." Captain America does take the outstretched hand, if only to place an electron-scrambler designed by Nick Fury's team to render Iron Man's arsenal of weapons useless. The first battle of the civil war erupts.

The battle's outcome is unclear, despite a spectacular onslaught by Spider-Man. The recovery of Iron Man, however, seems to signal the turn of the tide. He pummels Captain America, enraging the Greek demigod, Hercules, who levels She Hulk and Spider-Man as he rushes to Captain America's defense. Hercules is stopped in his tracks by a violent lightning bolt as Thor arrives on the scene.

The arrival of Thor shocks the anti-registration forces, as rumor was that he was dead. Thor's immense power enables him to begin to single-handedly crush the anti-registration forces. He ceases his assault when Iron Man activates a high-frequency weapon designed to put the human brain into shutdown. His team is equipped with audio-blocks, allowing the heroes to stand down and a S.H.I.E.L.D. squadron to bring the fallen heroes to a detention center. Iron Man's weapon did not fell Hercules, who recovered from the lightning strike and resumed his quest to protect Captain America. He hurls an oil truck into Iron Man, disabling his weapon.

The ceasing of the crippling pitch enables the anti-registration forces to resume their struggle, although they are more interested in escape at this point than victory. Goliath charges Thor as the melee resumes, only to be killed by a lightning strike from Thor's hammer, Mjolnir. The sight of their comrade's death intensifies the attempt to escape the battle. Thor, however, has other plans as he sends another vicious lightning bolt at his opponents. The lightning never strikes its target because of the interference of the Invisible Woman. Despite the fact she is a member of the pro-registration team, she generates a force field around the anti-registration team and beseeches them to use their teleporters to withdraw. The Falcon thanks her as the team disappears. It is also revealed that "Thor" is some form of technology created by Reed Richards. Sue, enraged at her husband for what his creation wrought, demands he not speak to her when he tries to explain himself. The aftermath of the battle has a profound impact on both teams.

Iron Man's team members find they, at best, achieved a Pyrrhic victory. Hank Pym, who considers Goliath (Bill Foster), one of his oldest friends, is completely distraught. He helped create "Thor" and feels intense guilt. Spider-Man, always concerned about living up to one's responsibilities, openly questions the actions taken by the pro-registration team. Sue Richards leaves the team, which also means she leaves her husband, to join Captain America. The Human Torch joins her in defecting.

During this time, it is discovered that Thor is a clone. Tony Stark had collected skin cells and hair follicles by combing his couch following his first meeting with the original Thor years ago. These samples provided him the DNA that made the cloning process possible. Hank questions why the Thor clone did not act like the real Thor. The clone, a perfect physical copy of Thor, lacked Thor's restraint, conscience, and sense of equanimity. It is occasionally noted in the Marvel universe that Thor rarely used his full power for fear of killing a mortal. He would even risk defeat, or at the least take some damage and deliver restrained blows to calculate the measure of his foe so he could strike accordingly. The clone lacked similar concerns and processes. Thor developed this inclination over time, whereas the clone had no previous experience; it was merely programmed to act a certain way. Evidently, the nuance of thought Thor employed was difficult to replicate.

The death of Bill Foster causes a growing number of heroes to question joining the pro-registration force. Spider-Man defects as well, citing Foster's death and the building of a prison in the Negative Zone to hold captured superheroes.* His departure leads to another fateful decision. Captured super-villains are implanted with microchips that allow S.H.I.E.L.D. agents to monitor their movements and shock them should they disobey orders. These villains become S.H.I.E.L.D. operatives working under the code name "Thunderbolts." Two of the Thunderbolts hunt down and pummel Spider-Man, who was fleeing the pro-registration headquarters. The Punisher intervenes in the battle. He kills the two criminals and brings the wounded Spider-Man to Captain America's headquarters.

While the addition of Spider-Man, Human Torch, and the Invisible Woman are most welcome, Captain America's forces are dwindling because of the continuous efforts made to apprehend anti-registration forces. An increasing number of heroes are being captured and sent to the Negative Zone prison. The highest-profile hero apprehended is Daredevil.

After his capture, Tony Stark and five heavily armed S.H.I.E.L.D. agents escort Daredevil to the Negative Zone. As they walk the prison corridors, Tony Stark explains his position to his silent captive. He claims to be backing the registration reforms because the only alternative is a complete ban on superheroes. This argument, while sounding quite strong, has a weak foundation, for in a world of super-villains and alien invasions, there is almost no possibility that superheroes will not be needed. Stark also explains the plan to have a superhero team in every state. Each team will be a federal force, licensed and accountable to the taxpayer. In an attempt to bring Daredevil to the registration side, Stark even offers Daredevil the position of leading his own team.

Throughout Stark's monologue, Daredevil is silent. The guards confirm he had not spoken much since his capture. One of the few things he did say was that a silver dollar found under his tongue when he was captured was for Tony. Tony, looking at the piece of silver states what some students may be thinking at this scene, "I don't understand." Daredevil, who through all his struggles remains Catholic, tells Tony he now has thirty-one pieces of silver and wishes "Judas" to "sleep well." Students may not realize the importance of Daredevil's use of allusion, but it succinctly communicates the strength of his resolve and the contempt he has for Tony and his arguments.

Daredevil's capture does, however, display the effectiveness of the pro-registrations' attempts to apprehend rogue heroes. This reality causes Captain America to launch a strategy to infiltrate the Negative Zone prison and free the captives. Iron Man's team intercepts his in the prison, but fails to prevent him from freeing the prisoners. The fully loaded teams begin the final battle, teleporting to Earth where the chaotic battle tears across New York City.

Citizens of the city flee the battleground as the arrival of reinforcements for both sides only intensifies the chaos. Hercules destroys the Thor clone, and Mr. Fantastic is

---

* The Negative Zone is an alternate dimension that can be entered through specially designed transportation portals.

wounded while protecting his wife from a surprise attack launched by one of the Thunderbolts. Most important, Iron Man's armor is compromised, and Captain America begins a vicious assault on his rival. A group of bystanders and rescue workers pile on Captain America in an effort to protect Iron Man. Captain America demands they let him go and that he does not want to hurt them. One man responds by saying, "It's a little late for that, man!"

These words cause Captain America to look around and realize the damage this fight—both the skirmish and the superhero civil war—has caused. He admits they are no longer fighting for the people, they are just fighting. Spider-Man tells Captain America, "We were beating them, man. We were winning back there." Captain America responds, tears now rolling down his cheeks, "Everything except the argument."

It is in this moment that Steve Rogers realizes he was failing to live up to the highest virtues he had always embraced and had descended to embracing the shadow of his virtues and his ego. By surrendering, he was again acting as Captain America, but Steve Rogers needs to be punished for his role in this folly. Taking off his mask, he turns himself in to two police officers and orders his troops to stand down. This scene does not mean Steve Rogers has changed his position on registration but has merely re-embraced his ideal that the means through which one achieves victory are as important as the victory itself. Realizing his means were faulty, he cannot continue them. Daredevil called Tony Stark Judas, but Captain America betrayed himself and the American ideals he strives to emulate. His surrender could be the first step to redemption, but he will be shot on the steps of a federal courthouse and die in a hospital—a casualty of the war.

Tony Stark reaps tremendous benefits from his victory, not least of them being named the new director of S.H.I.E.L.D. As he gives Miriam Sharpe, the mother of one of the many children killed in Stamford when the story began, a tour of the S.H.I.E.L.D. Helicarrier, he explains parts of his vision for the future. He wants to clean up S.H.I.E.L.D., use the Negative Zone prison to house super-villains and, of great importance to himself, safeguard his friends' secret identities. There is one issue that can be raised in this scene of looking forward to the future with hope. It is clear that Tony Stark trusts no one else to handle the responsibilities he has taken on. He needs power over the orchestration of the war's aftermath, for there is no one else as capable as he. His ego still demands sophomoric satisfaction as he smugly instructs Deputy Commander Hill to bring him a cup of coffee. His will has brought him to power, but does he have the wisdom to use it well? Can a system devoid of trust remain healthy? Captain America paid a price for his role in the war, what price will Tony Stark pay? This is one of the joys of comics; the end of one story line only opens up possibilities for the future.

# CHAPTER 19

## America's Shadow Confronted in *Uncle Sam*

In the striking graphic novel *Uncle Sam,* the reader is taken on a whirlwind tour of the failures and faults of American history. Uncle Sam is a mystical being in DC Comics who personifies the highest ideals of the American spirit. In *Uncle Sam* that spirit seems completely broken, and Sam is hanging on to the edge of sanity. He is dirty and homeless. He speaks in incoherent rants and political sound bites. Eventually other voices come through him, like John Brown and Mark Twain. As he struggles to gain a sense of equilibrium, he slips in and out of time and dimensions.

One moment he finds himself walking down the street of a modern city, the next he is tending to the wounded and dying in Andersonville Prison. Sometimes he is a witness to history, as he views a lynching in the Deep South. Other times he is directly involved in history, as when he finds himself seated next to Jackie Kennedy in the fateful motorcade on the day of John F. Kennedy's assassination. On other occasions he slips into alternative dimensions, encountering other beings like himself—personifications of a nation's aspirations, history, dreams, and sorrows. All the while the reader, like Sam, is bombarded with frightful images from U.S. history that simultaneously deepen and challenge one's understanding of patriotism.

The fact that Uncle Sam is a symbolic and metaphoric personification for America may cause confusion in some students. It may help these students to discuss how metaphors are used to illustrate deeper truths that are not readily apparent. To help students understand this concept, teachers may want to use a metaphor to describe America and explain all the information hidden within the simple statement. A metaphor I have used, with great success is, "America is a crack baby."[113]

Students are always much more curious than outraged when the statement America is a crack baby is written on the board. I do not know if this is from pure surprise or some form of trust that there is an explanation coming. Either way the statement has generated far less outrage than one might imagine. America as a crack baby compliments the journey

Uncle Sam takes, so the metaphor will be explained and then used to present some information in the graphic novel.

When examining the metaphor "America is a crack baby," the best place for the students to start is with a definition of crack baby. If asked to define the phrase, most students present some form of the thought that a crack baby is born addicted to drugs because of the parents. This definition reveals a central theme in the metaphor—addiction—specifically, addiction to something to which the parents exposed the child. If America is, in fact, a crack baby, then the process that infected the crack baby must be at work in America, or the comparison fails. America is the "child" of a parent, England. This parent must also have an addiction that is passed on to the child. Just as the parents' history is important to the birth of their addicted child, so, too, is England's history important to the birth of America.

One of England's addictions in the seventeenth century, the one pertinent to the metaphor, was imperialism. Students may or may not be familiar with this word, so a simple operational definition is often needed to keep everyone on the same page. A definition that fulfills this purpose is simply defining imperialism as a contest for world power and influence. European nations began a process during the age of exploration in which they competed to be the world superpower. England actively and enthusiastically engaged in this process.

Power, of course, is difficult to quantify, so the signs of that power are important to note. If asked how a nation marks its standings in the contest, students inevitably say "money." Although this is true, nations were not establishing colonies because money was found in ready-made bundles. Once a definition for colonies is clear to all, the important marker of land is made clear. Of course, not any land will do. No one becomes a superpower by laying claim to the Sahara Desert. Lands rich in natural resources are most desirable. The resources can be used to produce goods that in turn produce money, which is reinvested in the imperialistic contest and keeps the participant viable. Winning feels good, and success breeds the desire for more success. Of course, sometimes the competition is not cordial, and wars erupt between imperial powers.

These wars allow for some evaluation of the unwritten laws of imperialism. The first rule is, imperial nations may fight wars against each other but never claim the other's homeland as a prize. Colonies change hands in imperialistic wars. The politicians squabble at the negotiation table as their armies had fought on the battlefields, ending the conflict with the victor increasing their holdings and the loser smoldering and planning future campaigns to reclaim glory, honor, and power.

Despite the wars they fight with each other, imperialistic nations view each other with some form of respect. There is the respect granted in the rule forbidding the claiming of the other's homeland as a prize of war. Nonimperialistic European nations are also granted a form of respect, because they are not made the target of this contest. The targets, of course, are Asian, African, North American, and South American regions. The indigenous populations of these places all share one important trait in common: they are not European. They are also not white, and a second addiction made necessary by imperialism begins to rear its destructive head.

What is an imperialistic nation to do with the indigenous population of the lands they acquire? How should they be treated? The answer is revealed again and again, be it in the broken treaties and bodies of Native Americans, the enslaved Africans, or the marginalized laborers of India. These populations can be treated as less than human, as a resource unto themselves, as cattle. Racism comes hand in hand with imperialism because it has a distinct benefit to the racist. It is a salve for guilt and a balm that washes away the need for human dignity. It makes perfect sense for students to look at even the briefest explanation of the African slave trade and ask, "How could they do that?" Once one decides the person they are snatching, shipping, abusing, and selling is not completely human, it becomes much easier. Racism prevents the calls of conscience from being heard even as imperialism and the call of duty drown out other objections.

It can be said, therefore, that America was born of parents addicted to imperialism and racism. Evidence of this is found in the existence of slavery before the nation was founded and in the treatment of Native Americans as the centuries passed. Thirteen colonies became fifty states, not because of thirty-seven birthday gifts but because the acquisition of land and power was a goal woven into the lifeblood of the nation. America sought power and proved highly skilled in its acquisition, becoming the world superpower by the mid-twentieth century and surpassing its "parent" along the way.

Thus far, the metaphor has created a rather bleak picture of America as a nation driven by the quest for dominion and steeped in racist ideology. To think of one's nation this way can be uncomfortable or distasteful, but it is a good place to begin, particularly as a transition to *Uncle Sam*. As the story begins, Uncle Sam is clinging by a gossamer thread to his rapidly declining sanity. The reason for this is that the horrors of America's past are ripping through his consciousness, shattering his illusions of America as a pristine nation worthy to be acclaimed, without contradiction, as the greatest of nations. He is bombarded by images of the present suffering in America as well as subject to time slips where he falls into the past. He is, to use our crack baby metaphor, in the throes of addiction or perhaps more accurately, experiencing the wretched pain and confusion of people trying to break their addictions. Like a recovering alcoholic seeing the pain he has caused and seeking forgiveness, Sam is witnessing the pain he has caused, and continues to cause, with no one around to offer support and comfort him. He is alone on the brink of madness.

His first time slip brings him back to the American Revolution. He is an aged soldier discussing with a woman named Bea his desire to fight in the Continental Army. Bea objects to him leaving to fight but knows she can't stop him. She won't, however, hear talk of Sam not coming back to her. She reminds him that he has always come back after his expeditions, including the time he spent fighting the French and Indian War. Back to the present, Sam finds himself being assaulted by a homeless man who is trying to steal his shoes.

Sam's time slips begin to happen with great frequency. He shifts from walking the streets of New York with newly arrived immigrants in the early twentieth century to the present to the 1832 massacre of Black Hawk Indians and back to the present. The present is not a source of comfort for Sam, as he struggles to come to grips with a sense of self amid the voices in his head. He also slips into a different dimension, staggering into an antique store cluttered with American memorabilia. He picks up a record and reads, "I'm Gonna Slap a Dirty Little Jap" leading him to mumble, "And that was the good war."

It is in the antique shop that he finds himself guided to a lynching by a minstrel toy come to life. Sam confesses that he has never seen a lynching. This is an expression of his denial. As the embodiment of America's spirit, he can see anything in America's history he chooses but has never looked at such a scene. His consciousness returns to the antique shop, and he sees Bea is its patron. Confused, he turns away from her and slips back through time, eventually returning to a present-day city. Images of modern suffering assault him again, and he quotes Thomas Paine in an effort to reclaim his fortitude.

He becomes lucid enough to notice a newscast proclaim that a senator who has recently won a difficult race will be holding a parade. The parade will feature Uncle Sam. The newscast quickly shifts to a report on dandruff, leaving Sam to wonder what qualifies as news in the modern era. A breeze whips into a sandstorm as Sam slips back in time to the Dust Bowl and, again, encounters a woman who could be Bea. Back to the present, Sam finds himself on the floor of a bathroom where he meets the candidate defeated in the recent Senatorial election. The man bears a resemblance to Abraham Lincoln, and another time slip occurs, albeit a short one. Back to the future, and Sam decides he needs to attend the parade and meet Uncle Sam. Uncle Sam will have the answers he seeks.

The Uncle Sam at the parade is a man on stilts, but Sam sees a giant striding proudly and confidently across the land. He is unhampered by doubt and is a vision of strength. Planes soar all around him. This is the Uncle Sam that Sam remembers, the embodiment of the great arsenal of democracy. Sam, despite his ragged appearance, enters the hall where the senator delivers a speech. Sam hears the politician's true thoughts, which stand in stark contrast to his words. Sam begins to raise his voice in objection to what he hears when "Uncle Sam," a gleam in his eye, tells him to leave it alone. Sam stands simultaneously in the arena and in the alternative dimension he can enter. The Uncle Sam before him is a usurper of his title and power. The replica states that he is Uncle Sam and that Sam is nothing. Sam is informed that he used to be someone, but the time has come for him to accept that things are over. His time has passed. Enraged, Sam leaps to tackle his cocksure doppelganger, only to find he has attacked the man on stilts. The police escort Sam away as he watches police battling unemployed workers in Dearborn, Michigan, during the Great Depression.

Sam is locked up for the night but flees the police station when he is brought to talk to the captain. The police let him go because the senator (for political reasons) will not press charges. A mystery woman (Bea) sits in the captain's office having posted Sam's bail. As far as the captain is concerned, Sam is her problem now.

Sitting in an alley, Sam unwittingly slips dimensions and is visited by an old woman holding a trident and a shield bearing the Union Jack. A lion accompanies her. She is the once regal and powerful Britannia, the national spirit of England. Her trident, which once represented dominion over the seas is now rusted and broken. Her youthful features are aged, her hair gray and barely kept. She admits that she, like Sam, once thought she had everything under control. The superpower of the world that fell behind in the competition for world power. Far from bitter, she offers Sam council. Their conversation is interrupted by events in Earth's dimension.

Young ruffians are pouring gas on Sam's body and light it on fire. They do this for no reason other than it seems to amuse them. Sam panics for a moment, wondering if this is how the American dream ends. To the shock of his assailants and himself, he does not burn. He is more than he appears. Images of present Americans suffering again pound him, causing him to stagger into another alley. Barely able to stand, he slips back in time again. This time he is a soldier staring down Revolutionary War veterans at Shays' Rebellion.

Holding his musket, the one he just fired to drive off Daniel Shays and his men, Sam considers a chilling proposition. The American dream of building a land based on the highest ideals died in Springfield that day. The American dream never had a chance. It was killed before its infancy. It was stillborn. Worst of all, Sam fired the shots that caused this to happen.

Terrified, Sam bends down to apologize to a dying homeless man. He wants to make amends to someone, but his thoughts are interrupted when he sees a hat stored in the man's jacket. Sam recognizes it as an item from the mystic antique store he had recently visited. He demands to know how the homeless man acquired it. He points to the antique store, now situated at the end of the alley. Sam races into the store, only to find it deserted and almost empty. On the back wall is a painting of the Columbian Exposition, a painting that Sam enters as he again moves to an alternate dimension.

Bea maneuvers an impressive boat, identified as the ship of state, into the harbor to greet him.[114] Sam greets her as Columbia, the female personification of the spirit of America. She, like Sam, is aged but far more at ease with herself than he is. She claims the coming of World War I forced her to reconsider if she wanted to remain the spirit of the country. She did not. Instead she retired from the position, whereas Sam continued to embody America throughout the violence and upheaval of the twentieth century.

Sam confesses that he met the doppelganger that claimed to be the spirit of America. Columbia, not offering coddling comfort, merely states that the imitation is the spirit of America. The waters get rough as the sky darkens. Columbia explains that, as time passed, people came to want an America, and an Uncle Sam, cast in their image. Thus, the alternative Uncle Sam was born. The original spirit of America, however, could not be completely denied, but it could be channeled into other endeavors while the new spirit held sway.

This notion brings us back to our metaphor of America as a crack baby. Just as the crack baby has the stain of her parents' addictions, so, too, she possesses an undeniable inner strength. A longing for self-respect, pride, and dignity resides in every person. In some it is so buried by the hardships of life, poor personal choices, and unplanned disasters that it does not seem to exist. And yet, many an alcoholic has reported a moment of clarity where an inner voice has cried out to them, "Aren't you better than this?"

America's inner voice, the quiet strength that stands as a stumbling block to racism and imperialistic drives for power, is the Declaration of Independence. If taken seriously, the ideals of the Declaration force the country to correct its own errors. If we solemnly commit to the idea that "all men are created equal," where is the room to endorse racist acts? Where is the impetus to manipulate other nations and claim their resources as our own? The challenge of the words may be too much to bear, but they cannot be wiped from existence. They were presented as the ideal of the nation, and the choice is not whether the claim was made, it is whether we will keep striving to make them a reality or if the time has come to say we have done enough.

In the story, Sam may be ignored, but he is not forgotten—even if he struggles to remember himself. Still frustrated, Sam declares that he betrayed America because of his actions in the past, particularly those aimed at Daniel Shays. Columbia admits that bloodshed was unfortunate. She also reminds Sam that the battle was only part of the story, not the end of it. The Articles of Confederation, deemed unfit to govern a nation, were replaced by the Constitution of the United States of America. Sam begins to recite the preamble to the Constitution as the sky clears.

Columbia leaves Sam with a final thought, "and if America sometimes fouled up along the way—and it did—that was the fault of the dreamers. It wasn't the fault of the dream." She walks through an archway into a dark building, leaving Sam to await the arrival of others from whom he must learn.

First the spirit of Russia arrives in the form of a massive, talking bear. Even though Sam is initially dismissive of his longtime opponent, he contemplates that the bear "doesn't look like an evil empire any more than I look like a symbol of democracy." Confounded, he stays with the Russian Bear as Britannia arrives on the scene. She tells Sam he is more than the spirit of a nation, but the spirit of freedom. He is a grand experiment, and some experiments fail. To accentuate the point, she walks to a gazebo where Marianne, the spirit of the French Revolution, sits. Her mind and spirit were shattered by the Reign of Terror, and she weeps, clutching a tattered French flag. Britannia helps Marianne to her feet, gently guiding her to a more comfortable resting place.

Sam slowly slides from this extra-dimensional locale to another, Britannia's words about working to preserve freedom rather than succumb to fear echoing in his head. He finds himself face to face with his dark reflection. His opponent reclines on a throne of televisions, his feet resting on the U.S. capital building. This version of himself is arrogant, aloof, supra-capitalistic, and seemingly devoid of a moral compass. Sam is instructed, in a mocking tone, to go back to his cardboard box. Sam responds that he has come to get his hat, the red, white, and blue top hat his opponent wears that is rightfully his.

Sam lunges at his clean and pressed mirror image, forcing some of the dark realities of present-day American life into his consciousness. The images are rejected as "nitpicking" even as Sam attempts to explain to his shadow that he is the spirit of a nation, but not America. Sam receives a powerful right cross for his trouble. Getting off the deck Sam discredits his opponent as nothing more than an empty and shallow thug, earning himself another thunderous blow. Another and yet another hit Sam, who has decided the only way to win is to absorb all that this wicked being has to offer until it is revealed to be as ethereal and unstable as Sam thinks it is. With each strike, the malevolent spirit becomes increasingly incoherent, sounding as Sam did at the story's opening. Sam lets loose a gust of wind from his lips, blowing his depleted foe into dust.

As the winds subside, Sam finds himself again homeless on the streets of a modern city. A passerby asks if he is all right and says he left a dollar in his hat. Sam mumbles as he looks down that he doesn't have a hat. To his surprise, he finds his red, white, and blue top hat on the ground. He picks it up and walks off happily, still dirty and banged up, but with hopeful determination in his step—just like America.

# Section II

Teachers' Tools

# Introduction

This is the "nuts and bolts" section of the book. The materials here are designed to be useful in the classroom, either as presented or after some personal tinkering. The three tools provided in this section are vocabulary lists, general curriculum connections, and lesson plans. Tools are provided for each character and story mentioned in Section I.

The first tool is a vocabulary list of words found in the story that students will need to know to keep the story or their reading moving unabated. When working with students who struggle with vocabulary, it would be sensible to have them define all of the words and review them before starting the story. Student groups with stronger vocabulary skills could be allowed to self-select the words they need to look up. It would be reasonable to quiz such a group on the entire list prior to reading to gauge how precisely the students assessed their vocabulary skills.

The second tool is a brief list of general curricular connections for each story or character. Great detail is not given on how to use the connection. These details are left to individual styles and needs. Seeing the list of curricular connections could spur the imagination and lead to even more personalized ideas and lesson plans. The connections could also allow for colleagues to brainstorm possible uses of the story.

The last tool is the premade lesson plans. Even a premade lesson plan can (and likely should) be altered to better accommodate individual classrooms and teaching styles. Having these lessons, however, will provide teachers (especially those unfamiliar with comics) a grounding that is often necessary when working with new materials.

I hope these tools will be useful. Good luck in the attempt to bring the wonder and wisdom of the comic book curriculum to your students.

# Teacher Tools for Superman
## *Kingdom Come*

**Vocabulary List for *Kingdom Come***

| | |
|---|---|
| Prophecy | Pinnacle |
| Initiative | Tethered |
| Commodity | Paradox |
| Despondence | Cadence |
| Paramount | Nihilistic |
| Armageddon | Exacerbating |
| Delusion | Camaraderie |
| Exile | Protégé |
| Solitude | Fascism |
| Agrarian culture | Milquetoast |
| Clandestine | Acquitted |
| Utopia | Default |
| Aerie | Aberrant |
| Sanctuary | Usurped |
| Verdant | Despotic |
| Disoriented | Fellowship |
| Wretched | Manifest |
| Phalanx | Gulag |
| Vigilantes | Inexorably |
| Sanction | Ragnarok |
| Delegation | Belligerent |
| Validation | Pollyanna |
| Cacophony | Invulnerability |
| Condone | Catastrophe |
| Meticulous | Acclimate |
| Methodical | Schizophrenic |
| Police state | Hephaestus |
| Totalitarian | Aristocratic |
| Urban | Genocide |
| Zenith | Denouement |

# Curriculum Connections

Please note the type of class for which a connection seems most natural precedes each idea.

1. **World History.** Chapter 1 includes some discussion about the nature of goodness. The Greek philosopher Socrates and the Chinese philosopher Confucius are used in this discussion. This invites the possibility of using Superman as an example of different aspects of both men's philosophies.

2. **Civics.** In Chapter 1, a summary of Mark Waid's assessment of Superman's ability to integrate with the world is presented. He concludes that, because Superman is comfortable embracing his heritage, he is more comfortable embracing the culture of his new home. The idea of Superman assimilating to life on Earth can be used to begin a conversation about modern immigrants to America and what factors make integration possible.

3. **English/Literature.** The concept of the heroic quest was introduced in Chapter 2. This introduction was not a thorough examination of the heroic quest. Teachers could give students detailed notes and readings about the heroic quest and allow students to trace the heroic journey taken by Norman McCay and Superman.

4. **English/Literature.** In *Kingdom Come,* Superman establishes the gulag (as mentioned in Chapter 2) and attempts to educate the inmates. Are there similarities to Superman's efforts and the efforts to indoctrinate citizens used by the Party in *1984*? Students could also be provided copies of the article "Mind Control in Orwell's *1984*: Fictional Concepts Become Operational Realities in Jim Jones's Jungle Experiment" by Philip G. Zimbardo to enhance their analysis.

# Lesson Plan for *Kingdom Come*

This lesson is most easily incorporated into a civics or history class.

## Prior Knowledge

Students should have completed a unit on the types of government (civics) or on World War II (history) before being introduced to this lesson.

## Objective

Students will apply previous knowledge to evaluate claims made by characters in the graphic novel *Kingdom Come*.

## Procedure

Students will be asked to read the graphic novel either for homework or in class. If this is the first comic they have read, the teacher will likely need to discuss how to read the comic with them. This includes advice on moving from panel to panel, reading a narrator box before thoughts or dialogue, pausing to look for information in the drawings, and offering background information for the story as deemed necessary.

Upon completing *Kingdom Come,* students will evaluate, in writing, the following claims made by characters in the story.

1. Batman claims Gotham City is nearly utopian. In response, Superman accuses Batman of "nearly" creating a police state in Gotham (p. 74).

2. Batman describes Superman's methods as being totalitarian (p. 74).

3. Superman accuses Wonder Woman of offering suggestions that cross a "fascistic line" (p. 93).

4. Orion proclaims to Superman that liberty can be "every bit as paralyzing as fascism" (p. 104).

## Evaluation

Students will discuss each question in class, evaluating the claims made by the characters and the supporting evidence provided by their classmates. By the end of the class, students can decide by consensus the validity of each statement. The teacher will collect the students' written answers at the end of the class discussion. Students could be granted the option of rewriting their answers if the class discussion raised points they had not considered or if they want to strengthen their argument having heard counterpoints.

### Supplementary Enrichment Activities

Option I: Introduce or remind the students of the ruling principles encapsulated in enlightened despotism. Would the title "enlightened despot" be appropriate for the leadership style presented by Superman, Batman, Wonder Woman, and Orion?

Option II: Provide students an excerpt from Machiavelli's book *The Prince.* After reading it together and clarifying any questions, have the students assume Machiavelli's position and write a letter of advice to either Superman or Batman.

# Teacher Tools for Batman

## *Knightsend*

## Vocabulary List for *Knightsend*

Jasmine

Attendant

Paradox

Usurped

Perverted

Redeem

Capacity

Devise

Profound

Anxiety

Integration

Prevail

Folly

Seething

Transcends

Surveillance

Contortions

Abyss

Rogue

Wallow

Exorcise

Relevance

Knights Templar

Shrewd

Confrontation

Penance

Feint

Prowess

Heretic

Consign

Preliminaries

Mimic

Patronizing

Travesty

Loathe

Heir

Herald

Vindictive

Venerable

## Curriculum Connections

Please note the type of class in which a connection seems most natural precedes each idea.

1. **World History/U.S. History, Civics.** In the movie *Dark Knight,* a group of citizens inspired by Batman dress like him and fight crime. When Batman arrives at the scene of the crime, the "Batmen" are attempting to apprehend a group of criminals. He is prompted to subdue his "helpers" as well. As the scene ends with the "Batmen" and criminals tied up, one would-be hero asks, "What's the difference between me and you?" Batman's glib answer is that he does not wear hockey gear. What would a more complete answer be, considering that Batman is often called a vigilante? The Ku Klux Klan and lynch mobs also fall under the

umbrella of vigilantism. Batman can be used to add nuance to a discussion focused on what is a vigilante and whether there are different forms of vigilantism. Does intention matter when considering the label of vigilante? Are there times when vigilantism is necessary when other forms of justice have failed? How does John Brown fit into this discussion?

2. **World Literature.** In *Knightsend*, Lady Shiva lives for the thrill of the next adventure and the opportunity to kill or be killed. Have the students read a story about Shiva from Hindu literature and discuss the appropriateness of Lady Shiva's name.

# Lesson Plan for *Knightsend* (The 12 Labors of Batman)

This lesson is most easily incorporated into a world literature class.

## Prior Knowledge

Students should have completed a unit on the 12 Labors of Heracles before being introduced to this lesson.

## Objective

Students will apply previous knowledge to evaluate and compare the heroic quests of Batman in *Knightsend* and that of Heracles.

## Procedure

Students will be asked to read the graphic novel either for homework or in class. If this is the first comic they have read, the teacher will need to discuss how to read the comic with them. This includes advice on moving from panel to panel, reading the narrator box before thoughts or dialogue, pausing to look for information in the drawings, and offering background information for the story as deemed necessary. Teachers may want to divide the reading into sections, as appropriate.

Upon completing *Knightsend*, students will compare the heroic quest made by Batman to the 12 Labors of Heracles. The chart provided can be used to organize the students' notes for both heroes. A key component of the evaluation is not merely identifying the labors but drawing conclusions regarding what lessons each hero learned from the labor. The thrust of the lesson, therefore, is an evaluation of how the physical labors of each hero helped shape and mold their character.

## Evaluation

Students will complete the chart for homework and bring it in for discussion so they can hear the thoughts of others regarding the impact each phase of the story had on the characters. When the discussion is over, students write an essay in which they choose which three labors were most important for each character's development.

## Alternative Essay Ideas:

Option I: Which hero (Batman or Heracles) was more changed, or learned a greater lesson, from his heroic journey? Evidence from the texts must be used to support the writer's thesis.

Option II: What boon did each hero receive as a result of his heroic quest? How is each boon valuable to the recipient? As a reader, what are the most valuable lessons you could take from each story?

# 12 Labors of Batman Chart

| Batman's Challenge | Value/Lesson(s) of Challenge | Labor of Heracles | Value/Lesson(s) of Challenge |
|---|---|---|---|
| 1. Training with Shiva | | | |
| 2. Battle with first master | | | |
| 3. Battle with second master | | | |
| 4. First ascension of Gotham Tower | | | |
| 5. Battle with third master (Manimal) | | | |
| 6. Second ascension of Gotham Tower | | | |
| 7. Third ascension of Gotham Tower | | | |
| 8. Battle with fourth and fifth master | | | |
| 9. Battle with final master | | | |
| 10. Fourth ascension of Gotham Tower | | | |
| 11. Battle with Jean-Paul on the bridge | | | |
| 12. Battle with Jean-Paul in the Bat Cave | | | |

# Teacher Tools for Spider-Man

## Kraven's Last Hunt

## Vocabulary List for *Kraven's Last Hunt*

Czar
Aristocrats
Primal
Rejuvenate
Symmetry
Immersed
Essence
Recuperative
Restored
Oblivion
Metamorphosis
Blasphemous

Bequeath
Skitter
Integrity
Triumphant
Imperishable
Defiled
Mundane
Devious
Unutterably
Demented
Confession

## Curriculum Connections

Please note the type of class for which a connection seems most natural precedes each idea.

1. **World History.** In *Kraven's Last Hunt,* Kraven often bemoans the fall of aristocratic Russia; he lists individuals directly involved in its fall and others who played a part in the fall of the Soviet Union. The names include Lenin, Trotsky, Hitler, Gorbachev, and Reagan. Have students make a chart that includes the time period each individual interacted with Russia/the Soviet Union, three specific interactions, the impact each interaction had, and how they contributed to the fall of Russia/the Soviet Union.

2. **World Literature.** The subtitle of *Kraven's Last Hunt* is *Fearful Symmetry.* Throughout the story, the poetic verse "Spyder! Spyder! Burning bright / In the forests of the night, / What immortal hand or eye / Could frame thy fearful symmetry?" This line is, with the slight variation of the word Spyder, the first and last stanza of William Blake's poem "The Tyger." Students could evaluate the poem and discuss its use in *Kraven's Last Hunt.*

3. **World Literature.** Have students read *Kraven's Last Hunt* and *The Most Dangerous Game* by Richard Connell. The many parallels found in the two stories can be made into a writing assignment or a class discussion.

4. If your students have read both *Knightsend* and *Kraven's Last Hunt*, they could discuss the similarities found in the final scene as Batman rises from the Earth and Spider-Man from the sewers. A number of questions could be asked when comparing the two, including the following: What role does forgiveness play for both men? What are the symbolic elements and archetypal images present in both scenes? Which character do they think learned more from his struggle?

# Lesson Plan for *Kraven's Last Hunt*

This lesson is most easily incorporated in a world history course when the Russian Revolution is being taught.

## Prior Knowledge

Students should have learned about the fall of three civilizations.

## Objective

Students will apply previous knowledge to discuss what "Spiders" may exist throughout history that contribute to the decline and fall of civilizations.

## Procedure

Students will be asked to read the graphic novel either for homework or in class. If this is the first comic they have read, the teacher will need to discuss how to read the comic with them. This includes advice on moving from panel to panel, reading the narrator box before thoughts or dialogue, pausing to look for information in the drawings, and offering background information for the story as deemed necessary. Teachers may want to divide the reading into sections, as appropriate.

Upon completing *Kraven's Last Hunt*, the teacher will call the students' attention to Kraven's repeated comments regarding the nefarious Spider that helped bring about the fall of Aristocratic Russia. If this time period has not yet been covered in class, the presentation of a brief lesson highlighting the factors that contributed to the fall of Russia would be appropriate. These factors would be manifestations of Kraven's mythic, civilization-crushing Spider. Do the same factors present themselves during the fall of other civilizations? A three-set Venn diagram could be used to compare the fall of three civilizations.

## Evaluation

Students will have the diagrams to discuss and submit for evaluation and will answer a number of questions regarding the fall of civilizations:

1. What factors are consistent during the fall of civilizations?

2. What factors were unique to specific situations?

3. Which of these factors seem to be the most serious threat currently facing the United States?

4.  Kraven has a very organic worldview. How can civilizations be seen as organic, living entities?

5.  What role does a character like Spider-Man play in the health of a civilization?

# Teacher Tools for Green Lantern and Captain Marvel

## *Justice*

## Vocabulary List for *Justice*

Conspiracy
Confirmation
Benevolence
Lament
Profound
Inevitable
Unforeseen
Replicated
Probability
Incapacitate
Rendezvous
Extraordinary
Transformative
Physiology
Regenerate
Formidable
Armageddon
Privilege
Reckoning
Retaliation
Cohorts
Ensnare
Alliance
Microscopic
Contamination

Organic
Sentient
Diminished
Irritant
Envied
Remnant
Ambition
Endure
Habitual
Taunt
Dismantle
Steward
Elicit
Humanitarian
Prosper
Predisposition
Justifications
Hallucinogenic
Evacuation
Infuriate
Reveal
Incapable
Incarcerated
Perspective

## Curriculum Connections

Please note the type of class in which a connection seems most natural precedes each idea.

1.  **Cross Curricular.** "The many faces of Shazam!" Captain Marvel, as noted in Chapter 7, has the attributes of five figures from Greek mythology and one patriarch from the Old Testament. Students, depending on the class, could make their own magic word granting the speaker the attributes of particular people. A world history class could require the figures are from a particular time period or region. The class could be divided into groups responsible for making a "Shazam" for each continent. A U.S. history class would focus on Americans. English classes could focus on writers or characters. Even a science class could create a "magic word" to invoke the skills and intellect of particular scientists.

2.  **Civics.** "Batman's Wish." From pages 134 to 138, Batman delivers a soliloquy in which he expresses his hope for the future now that the Justice League has not only defeated the Legion of Doom but also rid the world of nuclear missiles. Students can evaluate the probability of his hope becoming a reality.

3.  **Civics.** As a variation or addition to "Batman's Wish," the reduction and nonproliferation of nuclear weapons could be discussed. You may want to share with students this thought from Buddhist monk and teacher Thich Naht Hahn, "Even if we transport all the bombs to the moon, the roots of war and the roots of the bomb are still here, in our hearts and minds, and sooner or later we will make new bombs. To work for peace is to uproot war from ourselves and from the hearts of men and women."

# Lesson Plan for *Justice*

This lesson is easily incorporated into any history or literature course.

## Prior Knowledge

Any general experience the students have in evaluating speeches or essays.

## Objective

Students will be required to analyze the speech delivered by Lex Luther in the fourth chapter of the *Justice* series.

## Procedure

Students will be asked to read the graphic novel either for homework or in class. If this is the first comic they have read, the teacher will need to discuss how to read the comic with them. This includes advice on moving from panel to panel, reading the narrator box before thoughts or dialogue, pausing to look for information in the drawings, and offering background information for the story as deemed necessary. Teachers may want to divide the reading into sections, as appropriate.

Upon reading chapter 4 of *Justice*, the teacher will ask the students to evaluate Lex Luther's speech (it is delivered throughout the course of chapter 4). A good source of basic tips for speech analysis is http://sixminutes.dlugan.com/speech-evaluation-1-how-to-study-critique-speech. Using the Web site or your own materials to present expectations for the students, have them analyze Luther's presentation. What makes it an effective or ineffective speech?

## Evaluation

Students could be required to write an analysis in an essay or use a chart to assess Luther's speech. A class discussion of their conclusions would be helpful, particularly if they are not familiar with speech analysis.

# Teacher Tools for Thor

## *The Surtur Saga*

### Vocabulary List for *The Surtur Saga*

| | |
|---|---|
| Vortex Subtle | Millennia |
| Mead Wane | Bide |
| Godspeed Guile | Hideous |
| Visage Gird | Denizen |
| Confirmation Inviolate | Barred |
| Scarce Preamble | Wrath |
| Content Maelstrom | Irresistible |
| Tidings Deluge | Augmented |
| Accursed Prodigious | Malevolence |
| Banishment Deft | Wrought |
| Ponder Asunder | Deceive |
| Liege Gratitude | Subtle |
| Nefarious Paltry | Wane |
| Raze Solemn | Guile |
| Nigh Endeavor | Gird |
| Jape Indulge | Inviolate |
| Exalt Inconspicuous | Preamble |
| Breach Hospitality | Maelstrom |
| Regaling Desolate | Deluge |
| Muster Ordeal | Prodigious |
| Deliberations Trait | Deft |
| Impermanent Loathe | Asunder |
| Valiantly | Gratitude |
| Reckoning | Paltry |
| Indifferent | Solemn |
| Girth | Endeavor |
| Voluminous | Indulge |
| Contrivance | *Inconspicuous* |
| Simulacrum | Hospitality |
| Smite | Desolate |
| Vital | Ordeal |
| Bane | Trait |
| Unfettered | Loathe |

## Curriculum Connections

Please note the type of class for which a connection seems most natural precedes each idea.

1. **World Literature/Mythology.** "The Many Names of Thor." In *Thor #379*, world serpent Jormungand confronts Thor, who is weakened by a curse Hela placed on him. Jormungand hopes to kill Thor and break the prophecies of old, ensuring his eternal life. Before the battle, Thor announces who he is in a succinct summation of the various names he is known by. Students could take the list and find the various myths and origins of these names to gain a clearer understanding of Thor's character as well as his names.

2. **Philosophy.** The two confrontations between Thor and Mephisto in Chapters 9 and 10 include an ongoing debate between good and evil as well as the nature of life and death. Students could isolate the key points each character makes and find support and counterarguments to these positions from the works of various philosophers.

3. **Civics/Current Events, Police–Community Relations and the Media.** The Jimmy Sayers story discussed in Chapter 9 can be used to introduce a section on police–community relations. The story is particularly powerful because it challenges the reader to walk in the shoes of the policeman as well as Jimmy, his mother, and the angry members of the community. The story does not present the police or the community as one side being clearly right and the other clearly wrong. How does this portrayal differ from the media coverage of this ongoing issue?

## Lesson Plan for *The Surtur Saga*

This lesson is most easily incorporated into a philosophy, world literature, or world history course.

### Prior Knowledge

Students should have learned about various philosophic or cultural views on death and enduring suffering.

### Objective

Students will apply previous knowledge to discuss Tiwaz's reflections on death and life.

### Procedure

Students will be asked to read either the entire *Surtur Saga* or *Thor #355* with the teacher introducing the necessary background to the story. If this is the first comic they have read, the teacher will need to discuss how to read the comic with them. This includes advice on moving from panel to panel, reading the narrator box before thoughts or dialogue, pausing to look for information in the drawings, and offering background information for the story as deemed necessary. Teachers may want to divide the reading into sections, as appropriate.

Upon completing their reading, the teacher will ask students to categorize Tiwaz's advice and reflections. They should be able to articulate the themes important to Tiwaz's philosophy. Looking at other philosophies or cultural interpretations they have learned, they will write an essay evaluating Tiwaz's key points through a particular lens. The writing could be approached in an academic or creative manner. An example of a creative approach would be the construction of a fictional conversation between Tiwaz, Albert Camus, and a Buddhist monk. The conversation, although fictional, would require the students to present each speaker's position accurately.

## Evaluation

Students will submit essays on the assigned due date. Teachers could lead a class discussion focused on the themes students wrote about on the due date.

### Alternative Essay Idea

Option I: In a world or American literature class, the fictional conversation could be written between Tiwaz and literary characters the students have already encountered.

# Teacher Tools for Charles Xavier and Magneto

## *Mutant Genesis* and *Fatal Attractions*

### Vocabulary List for *Mutant Genesis*

Fugitive
Charitable
Protocol
Banter
Indisputable
Hospitality
Subvert
Asphyxiation
Misanthrope
Myriad
Integration
Debilitate
Discorporate
Obligation
Despoil
Abandon
Fortification
Doppelganger
Fervently
Sanctuary

Vernacular
Abstract
Retribution
Droll
Diminish
Surreptitious
Animus
Penchant
Synchronous
Validity
Precedent
Comity
Primal
Prudent
Indomitable
Sovereign
Anomaly
Hippocratic Oath
Pretense
Sustain

## Vocabulary List for *Fatal Attractions*

| | |
|---|---|
| Subterfuge | Penance |
| Legacy | Inherent |
| Scoff | Epitaph |
| Deliberate | Swath |
| Arbitrary | Exertion |
| Unattainable | Abhorrent |
| Falter | Subservient |
| Scion | Clarion |
| Apologist | Ascension |
| Conviction | Transcend |
| Resolve | Atrocity |
| Refuge | Plaintive |
| Irrevocably | Paramount |
| Futile | Masochistic |
| Audacity | Genocide |
| Bailiwick | Wallow |
| Ambition | Archaic |
| Solace | Disillusionment |
| Benefactor | Figurehead |
| Dignity | Devastate |
| Entity | Infiltrate |
| Vague | Eradicate |
| Fortuitous | Denouement |
| Heinous | Degradation |

## Curriculum Connections

Please note the type of class for which a connection seems most natural precedes each idea.

1. **World History: Hitler and Magneto.** Have students evaluate the often-made comparison of Magneto to Hitler. What similarities and differences can they find between the two? What conclusions can they make by pinpointing Magneto's disposition at different times in his fictional life and development?

2. **U.S. History/World History: "Letter from a Westminster School."** Once the students complete *Mutant Genesis* and *Fatal Attraction,* have them consider the difficult decision Xavier made to erase Magneto's mind. Use his action to lead a discussion about difficult decisions leaders make in times of crisis.

3. **World Literature.** In *Fatal Attractions,* Magneto's orbiting fortress is called Avalon. His second in command is named Exodus. He accuses his son, Quicksilver, of being a Judas to his cause. Have students evaluate the significance of these words in the story. How does an increased understanding of them enhance the story? What is the significance of the fact that Magneto is the character who introduces all three words in the story (he names Avalon and Exodus)?

4. **U.S. History/World History.** Introduce students to Tagore's thought, "Perhaps he [Gandhi] will not succeed. Perhaps he will fail as the Buddha failed, as Christ failed and as Lord Mahavira failed to wean men from their inequities, but he will be remembered as one who made his life an example for all ages to come." How does Charles Xavier fit into this thought? Is Tagore's observation legitimate or merely a product of wishful thinking?

## Lesson Plan for *Mutant Genesis* or *Fatal Attractions* (Letter from a Westminster School)

This lesson is most easily incorporated into a civics or U.S. history course.

### Prior Knowledge

Students should have some knowledge of the American Civil Rights movement and may have read "Letter from a Birmingham Jail."

### Objective

Students will write a letter summarizing the philosophic position and mission of Charles Xavier.

### Procedure

Students will be asked to read *Mutant Genesis* or *Fatal Attractions*. If this is the first comic they have read, the teacher will need to discuss how to read the comic with them. This includes advice on moving from panel to panel, reading the narrator box before thoughts or dialogue, pausing to look for information in the drawings, and offering background information for the story as deemed necessary. Teachers may want to divide the reading into sections.

Have students read, or reread, Martin Luther King Jr.'s "Letter from a Birmingham Jail." The teacher will then lead a discussion evaluating how the essay is a clearly stated summation of King's philosophy and mission. Once the students complete *Mutant Genesis* or *Fatal Attractions,* the teacher has them assume the role of Charles Xavier and write his philosophy in the form of a letter. Students should, as King did, use outside sources and allusions to support Xavier's position.

### Evaluation

Students will submit their letters on an assigned due date. Teachers could lead a class discussion focused on the themes students wrote about during this class.

# Teacher Tools for The X-Men

## God Loves, Man Kills

**Vocabulary List for God Loves, Man Kills**

Atrocity
Evangelical
Exclusivity
Founder
Comprise
Tolerant
Surveillance
Ad Hoc
Irreparable
Insufficient
Sophisticated
Evade
Juggernaut
Martyrdom
Imminent
Sheathe
Commotion
Eradication
Genocide
Golgotha
Crucify
Miasma

Enshroud
Abyss
Affront
Amass
Temporal
Wrath
Subconscious
Liberation
Utopia
Betoken
Deviation
Template
Adversary
Mentor
Diversion
Inevitable
Arbitrary
Blasphemous
Vindication
Pyrrhic Victory
Intent
Negate

## Curriculum Connections

Please note the type of class for which a connection seems most natural precedes each idea.

1. **U.S. History/World History.** *God Loves, Man Kills* opens with the scene of two terrified youngsters fleeing the Purifiers. They are eventually caught and killed. The Purifiers are the militant arms of Stryker's crusade. Have the students list three examples of current organizations around the world that perpetrate, or at least sanction, such action. Are these organizations part of the mainstream or on the fringes of society? Students could also list examples of government-sanctioned acts of violence and acts taken by individuals not directly associated with or representing a group. Is violence coming from one of these categories more disturbing than others, or are they equal in their capacity to revolt?

2. **Civics/U.S. History/World History.** Chapter 20 of John Welwood's book *Toward a Psychology of Awakening* addresses the difference between authentic spiritual guidance and the guidance offered by cults. Using this reading or one like it, have students decide whether Reverend Stryker is an authentic spiritual leader or a cult leader.

3. **Civics.** During *God Loves, Man Kills,* Magneto uses his power to extract information form a Purifier. Nightcrawler protests that the X-Men should not use their enemies' methods because it makes them no better than Magneto. Later in the story, Nightcrawler uses his frightening appearance, his fangs, and his tail to create the perception that he is going to kill a member of Stryker's inner circle if the person does not talk. Is Nightcrawler a hypocrite for employing such a deception? The two scenes can also be used to introduce a discussion about torture and interrogation methods.

4. **Psychology.** Use James Fowler's theory of faith development to decide from which level of faith Reverend Stryker operates. Students should offer evidence from the story to support any conclusions. Students could also discuss the appeal of this stage of development and what its limitations are.

## Lesson Plan for *God Loves, Man Kills*

This lesson is applicable to a variety of classes.

### Prior Knowledge

No specific prior knowledge is necessary.

### Objective

Students will evaluate the tendency to label people and things.

## Procedure

Students will be asked to read *God Loves, Man Kills*. If this is the first comic they have read, the teacher will likely need to discuss how to read the comic with them. This includes advice on moving from panel to panel, reading the narrator box before thoughts or dialogue, pausing to look for information in the drawings, and offering background information for the story as deemed necessary. Teachers may want to divide the reading into sections, as appropriate.

Upon completing the reading, ask students to focus on Cyclops' words at Madison Square Garden and in the X-Mansion after the climactic confrontation. In both instances, he presents his view on the lack of importance of labels, even seemingly benign uses of "teacher" and "student." Lead a discussion focused on the theme of labeling. The discussion questions at the end of this plan may help.

## Evaluation

This could be a graded discussion if you have such a policy, or it can be looked on as a discussion that different students will consider and incorporate on an individual basis.

### Possible Discussion Questions

1.  Why is Cyclops so dismissive of the use of labels? What point is he ultimately trying to make?

2.  Is labeling, in and of itself, a negative thing? What important function does labeling fulfill?

3.  What are some negative aspects of labeling? Is there a relationship among stereotyping, social power, political power, and labeling?

4.  What negative aspects of labeling does Cyclops target?

# Teacher Tools for Wolverine

## *Wolverine*

## Vocabulary List for *Wolverine*

| | |
|---|---|
| Stark | Bridle |
| Elemental | Renegade |
| Rogue | Disobedience |
| August | Indulge |
| Obligation | Tentative |
| Essential | Transcend |
| Subtle | Tranquility |
| Chastise | Stagnation |
| Aspire | Brethren |
| Precept | Irreparable |
| Ephemeral | Immaculate |
| Belie | Paramour |
| Semblance | Exemplifies |
| Abide | Unpardonable |
| Demise | Mete |
| Revere | Formidable |

## Curriculum Connections

Please note the type of class in which a connection seems most natural precedes each idea.

1. **World Literature.** Have students read *The 47 Ronin* and then *Wolverine*. Challenge them to draw as many parallels between the stories as they can.

2. **Psychology.** Part of Wolverine's quest includes the ongoing struggle for self-improvement. After students have learned about various theories of human motivation and improvement (Frankl, Maslow, Rogers, and Welwood, for example), have them evaluate, through various psychological lenses, Wolverine's struggles with self-improvement.

3. **U.S. History.** Wolverine acts as a mentor to a number of X-Men. These relationships seem to evolve intact for a number of years, without any profound event that breaks the friendship. How do mentor–mentee relationships unfold in life? Consider the relationship between William Lloyd Garrison and Frederick Douglass or Sigmund Freud and Carl Jung as possible comparisons.

4. **Cross-Curricular.** Martial valor, the concept of surrendering to one's intensity, is presented in *Hagakure*. What does the fact that Wolverine is ashamed of his most intense expression of himself communicate about the relationship with martial valor? As a society in general, does the United States value or distrust intensity? Is intensity honored at your school or frowned upon? When it comes to intensity, do we teach suppression or channeling? Is intensity only valued in certain areas when exhibited by certain people, or is it widely accepted regardless of venue? How do the answers to these questions affect someone of great intensity?

# Lesson Plan for *Wolverine*

This lesson is most easily incorporated into a world history or world literature course.

## Prior Knowledge

It will help students to have some background in the samurai lifestyle and the Bushido code.

## Objective

Students will compare passages from *Hagukure* to scenes in *Wolverine*.

## Procedure

Students will be asked to read *Wolverine*. If this is the first comic they have read, the teacher will need to discuss how to read the comic with them. This includes advice on moving from panel to panel, reading the narrator box before thoughts or dialogue, pausing to look for information in the drawings, and offering background information for the story as deemed necessary. Teachers may want to divide the reading into sections, as appropriate.

Upon completing the *Wolverine* graphic novel, refresh students' memories regarding their prior learning about the samurai. Introduce the book *Hagakure* to them, emphasizing that it was written by the samurai Yamamoto Tsunetom (1659–1719). Provide the students the handout "Wolverine and the Samurai" from this plan and read the passages from *Hagakure* in the first column, clarifying them for the students. Instruct the students to fill in the second column with scenes from *Wolverine* that coincide with the passages. The last two columns are to be used to record the students' reasoning for their choice.

## Evaluation

The charts will be submitted for a grade. The charts could be discussed prior to or following collection.

# Wolverine and the Samurai

| Passage from *Hagakure* | Coinciding Scene from *Wolverine* | Reason(s) for Correspondence |
|---|---|---|
| 1. Being a retainer is nothing other than being a supporter of one's lord, entrusting matters of good and evil to him, and renouncing self-interest. | | |
| 2. There is nothing felt quite so deeply as giri. There are times when someone like a cousin dies and it is not a matter of shedding tears. But we may hear of someone who lived fifty or a hundred years ago, of whom we know nothing and who has no family ties whatsoever, and yet from a sense of giri, shed tears. | | |
| 3. And if a warrior does not manifest courage on the outside and hold enough compassion within his heart to burst his chest, he cannot become a retainer.... Examples of the ruin of merciless warriors who were brave alone are conspicuous in both past and present. | | |
| 4. Furthermore, scholars and their like are men who with wit and speech hide their own true cowardice and greed. People often misjudge this. | | |
| 5. It is spiritless to think that you cannot attain to that which you have seen and heard the masters attain. The masters are men. You are also a man. If you think that you will be inferior in doing something, you will be on that road very soon. | | |
| 6. It is unthinkable to be disturbed at something like being ordered to be a ronin. People at the time of Lord Katsushige used to say, "If one has not been a ronin at least seven times, he will not be a true retainer. Seven times down, eight times up." | | |

# Teacher Tools for Captain America

## *Civil War*

## Vocabulary List for *Civil War*

Legitimate
Paranoid
Upheaval
Figurehead
Apocalypse
Reciprocated
Genocide
Principles

Detached
Resolve
Hallucinogen
Irony
Litigious
Fray
Dilemma
Utopia

## Curriculum Connections

Please note the type of class for which a connection seems most natural precedes each idea.

1. **Civics.** "The media and freedom of speech." In Chapter 17, a quote from Jacob Needleman laments the degradation of freedom of speech into the sanctification of superficial opinion. In the same chapter, Captain America's spirit tells Thor he is tired of hearing how much the media gets wrong. Provide students a chart and assign them three news programs to watch over the course of a week and a half. Have the three programs be from three different networks. Make sure they can identify the political position of the host, the tenor of their show, their attitude toward different opinions, their receptiveness to alternative positions, and the political position of their guests. After their "field research," have them discuss the quality of these programs in light of Needleman's views of freedom of speech.

2. **Cross-Curricular.** Captain America and Iron Man are the leaders of the two factions in *Civil War*. Discuss with students the reality of symbolic gestures and symbolic leadership. How does each man's character influence the perception of his movement? Why was it symbolically important that Iron Man convinced Spider-Man to unmask? Ask the students to evaluate which symbols represent your school. Which symbols represent them as individuals?

3. **Civics.** Travis Langley, Ph.D., a psychology professor at Henderson State University, wrote a scholarly analysis of the *Civil War* story line. It is available at http://fac.hsu.edu/langlet/comics_psy/Fromm_Marvel_Travis_Langley.htm. The title of his presentation is "Freedom versus Security: The Basic Human Dilemma from 9/11 to Marvel's *Civil War.*" Preview his article and, provided it is accessible to your students, have them read it as well. You may need to summarize the article in class and accentuate your points with excerpts. Use the article and the comic to discuss the tension between freedom and security.

4. **U.S. History/World History.** In Chapter 17, we see that Captain America was disappointed in the turnout for his presentation on superhuman ethics. Throughout history we have seen various countries achieve "superpower" status. Should a world superpower be concerned that it is ethical, or should its hegemony trump ethics? How should the world interact with and approach superpowers?

## Lesson Plan for Captain America

This lesson is most easily incorporated into a civics or U.S. history course.

### Prior Knowledge

This assignment can be given as a culminating activity at the end of a quarter or semester.

### Objective

Students will consider the lives of various Americans through the lens of Jacob Needleman's American virtues.

### Procedure

To introduce students to Jacob Needleman's American virtues, assign them to read Chapter 17 of this book. Explain to them that the comic book character Captain America is used in the reading as an exemplar of American virtues. Upon completing the reading, make sure all students have a complete list and understanding of the virtues used in the chapter. Their assignment, as they will have at least a quarter's worth of learning behind them, will be to write mini-paper (3–5 pages) using their previous notes, readings, assignments, and so forth, as sources. In the paper, they will use their previous learning to provide a variety of historic examples for the virtues. The exact requirements and guidelines are subject to individual classrooms, styles, and needs. Give the students an amount of time you deem appropriate for completion.

### Evaluation

The final paper will be submitted for a grade.

## Alternative Assignment

Have the students read Chapter 17 at the beginning of a quarter or semester and clarify the American Virtues. Inform students that, as an ongoing assignment in your course, they should take information over the duration of a quarter or semester and slowly synthesize a portfolio linking the course materials to American virtues.

# Teacher Tools for *Uncle Sam*

## Vocabulary List for *Uncle Sam*

Charisma

Profound

Despair

Cynical

Contempt

Platitude

Quagmire

Undimmed

Virtue

Affluent

Apathetic

Vanity

Lynching

Malaise

## Historic People Mentioned in *Uncle Sam*

Calvin Coolidge

Mark Twain

Amede Ardoin

Bartolomeo Vanzetti

Abraham Lincoln

Douglas MacArthur

Daniel Shays

Herbert Hoover

John Brown

Ferdinando Sacco

Buffalo Bill

George Washington

Smedley Butler

Samuel Adams

## Historic Events, Locales, and Concepts Mentioned in *Uncle Sam*

Indian Removal Bill

Ford Theater

Pearl Harbor

Johnny Reb

*Common Sense*

Scottsboro Nine

Middle Passage

Shays' Rebellion

Kent State

Blackhawk Indian Massacre of 1832

Alamo

Andersonville

Damn Yankee

Dust Bowl

Labor Riots in Dearborn, Michigan

Hessians

Haymarket Square Riot

Columbian Exposition

# Curriculum Connections

Please note the type of class for which a connection seems most natural precedes each idea.

1.  **U.S. History.** Uncle Sam visits numerous historic events in the course of the story. Give students the option of picking one of these events and writing a brief, informative summary that they can share with the class either before reading the story or as events occur throughout. Why would each of these events cause Uncle Sam such shame?

2.  **Civics.** On four occasions in the story, Uncle Sam is bombarded with images of the struggles of modern Americans. Although the images run the gamut from depressing to disturbing to vile, how prevalent are these events in America? Have students research the themes in these images and decide their frequency in the United States as well as their impact.

3.  **U.S History/American Literature.** Have the students read Longfellow's poem "O Ship of State." Upon completion of the evaluation of the poem, discuss Columbia's last conversation with Sam as the ship she steered fought through the stormy seas and brought them to the Russian Bear. Britannia's final thoughts as she led Marianne away can also be included in the discussion. The use of these national symbols, their appearance, and the lines they speak may also be a valuable lesson to pursue.

4.  **Civics.** Is there a political agenda in *Uncle Sam*? Does it promote either a liberal or conservative agenda? If students deem it promotes one ideology over another, what could be added to bring greater balance to the story? Should it have greater balance, or would altering the approach diminish the story?

# Lesson Plan for *Uncle Sam*

This lesson is most easily incorporated into a civics or U.S. history course.

## Prior Knowledge

The operative time to give this assignment is at the end of the year or course.

## Objective

Students will consider possible bias in *Uncle Sam*.

## Procedure

Students will be asked to read *Uncle Sam*. If this is the first comic they have read, the teacher will need to discuss how to read the comic with them. This includes advice on moving from panel to panel, reading the narrator box before thoughts or dialogue, pausing to look for information in the drawings, and offering background information for the story as deemed necessary. Teachers may want to divide the reading into sections, as appropriate.

Once the reading and any necessary discussion is complete, ask students to consider the following questions: is there a political agenda in *Uncle Sam*? Is it written from a noticeable liberal or conservative perspective? With these thoughts in mind, ask them to write a book review in which they must recommend or not recommend the use of *Uncle Sam* in schools.

## Evaluation

A final paper will be submitted for a grade.

# Comic Bibliography

## Introduction

Miller, Frank, Klaus Johnson, and Lynn Varley, *The Dark Knight Returns* (New York: DC Comics, 1997).

## Chapter 2

Ross, Alex, and Mark Waid, *Kingdom Come* (New York: DC Comics, 1997).

## Chapter 3

Dixon, Chuck, Alan Grant, Jo Duffy, Doug Moench, and Dennis O'Neil, *Batman: Knightfall Part Three: Knightsend* (New York: DC Comics, 1995).

Dixon, Chuck, and Grahm Nolan, *Batman: Vengeance of Bane* (New York: DC Comics, 1993).

Krueger, Jim, Alex Ross, and Doug Broithwaite, *Justice Volume 2* (New York: DC Comics, 2008).

Miller, Frank, Klaus Johnson, and Lynn Varley, *The Dark Knight Returns* (New York: DC Comics, 1997).

## Chapter 4

Dixon, Chuck, Alan Grant, Jo Duffy, Doug Moench, and Dennis O'Neil, *Batman: Knightfall Part Three: Knightsend* (New York: DC Comics, 1995).

## Chapter 5

Lee, Stan, Steve Ditko, and Jack Kirby, *Essential Amazing Spider-Man, Volume 1* (New York: Marvel Comics, 2006).

## Chapter 6

DeMatteis, J. M., Mike Zeck, and Bob McLeod, *Spider-Man: Kraven's Last Hunt (Fearful Symmetry)* (New York: Marvel Comics, 1990).

## Chapter 8

Krueger, Jim, Alex Ross, and Doug Broithwaite, *Justice, Volume 1* (New York: DC Comics, 2006).

Krueger, Jim, Alex Ross, and Doug Broithwaite, *Justice, Volume 2* (New York: DC Comics, 2008).

Krueger, Jim, Alex Ross and Doug Broithwaite, *Justice, Volume 3—Hardcover* (New York: DC Comics, 2007).

## Chapter 9

Greenwald, Mark, Ralph Macchio, Keith Pollard, and Chic Stone, *Thor #299–301* (New York: Marvel Comics, 1980).

Moench, Doug, Keith Pollard, and Gene Day, *Thor #310* (New York: Marvel Comics, 1981).

Moench, Doug, Keith Pollard, and Gene Day, *Thor #311* (New York: Marvel Comics, 1981).

Simonson, Walter, *Thor Visionaries: Walter Simonson, Volume 2* (New York: Marvel Comics, 2009).

Thomas, Roy, John Buscema, and Chic Stone, *Thor #278* (New York: Marvel Comics, 1978).

## Chapter 10

Simonson, Walter, *Thor Visionaries: Walter Simonson, Volume 2* (New York: Marvel Comics, 2009).

Zelenetz, Alan, and John Buscema, *Thor Annual #13* (New York: Marvel Comics, 1985).

## Chapter 11

Claremont, Chris, and Dave Cockrum, *Essential X-Men, Volume 3* (New York: Marvel Comics, 2001).

Claremont, Chris, Barry Windsor-Smith, Louise Simonson, and Walter Simonson, *Essential X-Men, Volume 6* (New York: Marvel Comics, 2005).

Lee, Stan, and Jack Kirby, *Marvel Masterworks, The X-Men, Volume 1* (New York: Marvel Comics, 2009).

## Chapter 12

Claremont, Chris, and Jim Lee, *X-Men #1-3* (New York: Marvel Comics, 1991).

Lobdell, Scott, John Romita Jr., Jae Lee, Chris Sprouse, Brandon Peterson, and Paul Smith, *The Uncanny X-Men #304* (New York: Marvel Comics, 1993).

Nicieza, Fabian, and Andy Kubert, *X-Men #25* (New York: Marvel Comics, 1993).

## Chapter 13

Claremont, Chris, John Bryne, George Perez, John Romita Jr., Terry Austin, and Brent Anderson, *Essential X-Men, Volume 2* (New York: Marvel Comics, 2005).

Claremont, Chris, Dave Cockrum, and John Byrne, *Essential X-Men, Volume 1* (New York: Marvel Comics, 2002).

Lee, Stan, and Jack Kirby, *Marvel Masterworks, The X-Men, Volume 1* (New York: Marvel Comics, 2009).

## Chapter 14

Claremont, Chris, and Brent Eric Anderson, *God Loves, Man Kills* (New York: Marvel Comics, 1982).

Claremont, Chris, and Bill Sienkiewicz, *Uncanny X-Men #159* (New York: Marvel Comics, 1982).

## Chapter 15

Claremont, Chris, John Bryne, George Perez, John Romita Jr., Terry Austin, and Brent Anderson, *Essential X-Men, Volume 2* (New York: Marvel Comics, 2005).

Claremont, Chris, and Allen Milgrom, *Kitty Pryde and Wolverine #1–6* (New York: Marvel Comics, 1984-1985).

Hama, Larry, and Adam Kubert, *Wolverine #75* (New York: Marvel Comics, 1993).

## Chapter 16

Claremont, Chris, and Frank Miller, *Wolverine* (New York: Marvel Comics, 1987).

## Chapter 17

DeFalco, Tom, and Ron Frenz, *The Mighty Thor #390* (New York: Marvel Comics, 1988).

Gruenwald, Mark, and Rik Levins, *Captain America #400–401* (New York: Marvel Comics, 1992).

Gruenwald, Mark, and Tom Morgan, *Captain America #232–233* (New York: Marvel Comics, 1987).

Harras, Bob, and Tom Palmer, *The Avengers #347* (New York: Marvel Comics, 1992).

Harras, Bob, and Tom Palmer, *The Avengers #368* (New York: Marvel Comics, 1993).

McKenzie, Robert, Carmine Infantino, and Joe Rubinstein, *Captain America #245* (New York: Marvel Comics, 1980).

McKenzie, Roger, Sal Buscema, and Don Perlin, *Captain America #231–237* (New York: Marvel Comics, 1978–1979).

Stern, Roger, and Tom Palmer, *The Avengers #276–277* (New York: Marvel Comics, 1987).

Stracynski, J. Michael, and Oliver Coipel, *Thor #11* (New York: Marvel Comics, 2008).

### Chapter 18

Millar, Mark, Steve McNiven, Dexter Vines, and Morry Hollwell, *Civil War #1–7* (New York: Marvel Comics, 2006–2007).

### Chapter 19

Darnell, Steve, and Alex Ross, *Uncle Sam* (New York: DC Comics, 1998).

# Notes

## Chapter 1

1. S. E. Frost, Jr., *Basic Teachings of the Great Philosophers* (New York, Doubleday, 1942), p. 84.

2. Huston Smith, *The World's Religions* (San Francisco, HarperCollins, 1991), p. 25. In this passage, Dr. Smith discusses a continuum of maturity that begins with children and ends with inspirational figures such as Francis of Assisi.

3. Tom and Matt Morris (editors), *Superheroes and Philosophy: Truth Justice and the Socratic Way* (Chicago, Open Court, 2005), p. 8.

4. Ibid., pp. 8–9.

5. Ibid., p. 10.

6. Abraham Maslow, *Towards a Psychology of Being* (2nd ed.) (New York, Van Nostrand Reinhold Company, 1968), p. 105.

## Chapter 2

7. David Hinton (translator), *Confucius: The Analects* (New York, Counterpoint, 1998), p. 164. Chapter 14, verse 38.

8. Ibid., 67. Chapter 7, verse 3.

9. Joseph Campbell, *The Hero with a Thousand Faces* (New York, Bollingen Foundation, 1949), p. 98.

10. Thomas Byrom (translator), *Dhammapada: The Sayings of the Buddha* (Boston, Shambhala, 1993), p. 23.

11. Abraham Maslow, *Towards a Psychology of Being* (2nd ed.) (New York, Van Nostrand Reinhold, 1968), p. 196.

12. Superman, thanks to his rediscovered compassion, has become the archetypal world redeemer. As such, he is in a position to bring the ultimate boon to others. For details about these concepts, see Joseph Campbell, *The Hero with a Thousand Faces* (New York, Bollingen Foundation, 1949), pp. 158–192.

## Chapter 3

13. Any references to Kohlberg's theory is based on James Fowler's presentation in *Stages of Faith: The Psychology of Human Development and the Quest for Meaning* (New York, Harper One, 1981), pp. 37–86.

14. The phrase "ultimate concern" comes from James Fowler's *Stages of Faith: The Psychology of Human Development and the Quest for Meaning*, p. 4. "Our real worship, our true devotion directs itself toward the objects of our ultimate concern.... Our ultimate concern may be invested in family, university, nation, or church.... Ultimate concern is a much more powerful matter than claimed belief in a creed or a set of doctrinal propositions." For Batman, this ultimate concern is justice.

## Chapter 4

15. Viktor Frankl, *Man's Search for Meaning* (New York, Simon & Schuster, 1984), p. 116.

16. Man-Ho Kwok, Martin Palmer, and Jay Ramsay (translators), *Tao Te Ching* (London, Vega, 2002). In Chapter 22 of the *Tao Te Ching* by Lao-Tzu, we see a list of paradoxes one must endure to become a more complete person. For example, "If you want to become whole, let yourself be partial. If you want to become straight, let yourself be crooked." Bruce Wayne, therefore, standing in front of the yin-yang symbol, is also living the words of Lao-Tzu.

17. Eknath Easwaran (translator), *Bhagavad Gita* (Nilgiri Press, Tomales, CA, 1985). The passage is found in chapter 4, verse 42.

18. An example of such a reaction is again found in *Bhagavad Gita* (ibid.). In chapter 2, Krishna attempts to incite Arjuna and help him transcend his despair. Krishna knows that Arjuna is trapped in a cycle of doubt and self-pity and, although acknowledging this, does not lose sight that there is more to Arjuna than these lowly traits. "This despair and weakness in a time of crisis are mean and unworthy of you, Arjuna. How have you fallen into a state so far from the path of liberation? It does not become you to yield to this weakness. Arise with a brave heart and destroy the enemy." Literally, the enemy Arjuna faces is an opposing army made up of former allies, but the inner enemy is fear and doubt. This mirrors the struggle Bruce is engaged in as the ninjas assault his body and fears assault his mind. Therefore, "God hates a coward" can be seen as using symbolic or metaphoric language to rouse someone from inaction and fear, not literally to label him or her a coward.

19. This again brings us to chapter 22 of the *Tao Te Ching*, where Lao-Tzu states, "If you want to become full, let yourself become empty." In Lao-Tzu's writing, one would become full of the inexhaustible energy provided by the Tao. Other traditions have other names for this "filling up," but it is a worldview that Bruce has not embraced because he has always kept that place filled by the power of his nearly indomitable will.

20. Viktor Frankl, *Man's Search for Meaning* (New York, Simon & Schuster, 1984), p. 147.

## Chapter 5

21. Nelson Mandela, *Long Walk to Freedom* (New York, Holt, Rinehart and Winston, 2000), p. 458.

22. Erik H. Erikson, *Insight and Responsibility: Lectures on the Ethical Implications of Psychoanalytic Insight* (New York, W. W. Norton & Company, 1964. On p. 131, he defines generativity as the instinctual power behind various forms of selfless "caring."

## Chapter 7

23. The version of *The Republic* cited here was found at http://classics.mit.edu/Plato/republic.html. The passage is found in book II.

24. Ibid. The passage is found in book IV. The individual Socrates describes is one who will "be at peace with themselves" and, therefore, much more capable of being at peace with and bringing peace to societal matters. Paradoxically, the person could win praise for their involvement even as they have reached a point where such praise is secondary to the sensibility to do and honor the good and the just regardless of praise or acclaim.

25. This concept is given a more thorough examination by Michael Thou in *Superheroes and Philosophy: Truth, Justice, and the Socratic Way*, pp. 130–143.

26. Harvey C. Mansfield, Jr. (translator), Niccolo Machiavelli, *The Prince* (Chicago, University of Chicago Press, 1985), p. 70.

## Chapter 8

27. The term "shadow" is drawn from Jungian psychology. Carl Jung used the word shadow to represent the "negative" side of one's personality—weaknesses, hidden or unconscious desires, repressed aspects of an individual's personality, and unpleasant qualities people generally like to hide. It is important to note that struggling with one's shadow can lead to discovering strengths hidden within the darkness of the shadow, diamonds found in the depths of the earth. Therefore, by confronting their shadows, Marvel and particularly Green Lantern are doing "shadow-work," finding the diamonds in the darkness. A full treatment of the shadow can be found in the book *Meeting the Shadow: The Hidden Power of the Dark Side of Human Nature* (New York, Jeremy P. Thatcher/Penguin, 1991), edited by Connie Zweig and Jeremiah Abrams.

28. Frodo's exact words are, "I wish he had never found it, and that I had not got it! Why did you let me keep it? Why didn't you make me throw it away, or destroy it?" As his conversation with Gandalf continues, his self-pity deepens as he asks, "Why did it come to me? Why was I chosen?" J. R. R. Tolkien, *The Fellowship of the Ring* (New York, Houghton Mifflin, 1993), pp. 58–60.

29. The thoughts presented on the ego and "I" self in this paragraph come from the work of John Welwood, *Toward a Psychology of Awakening: Buddhism, Psychotherapy, and the Path of Personal and Spiritual Transformation* (Boston, Shambhala, 2002), pp. 35–47.

30. The concepts of "freedom from" and "freedom to," although not used by Tom Morris, are inspired by his discussion about "fear of" and "fear that," found in *Superheroes and Philosophy: Truth, Justice, and the Socratic Way* (Chicago, Open Court, 2005), pp. 49–55.

31. The use of the terms "realization," "actualization," and "being" are concepts discussed in detail and depth by John Welwood, *Toward a Psychology of Awakening: Buddhism, Psychotherapy, and the Path of Personal and Spiritual Transformation.*

## Chapter 9

32. H. A. Guerber, *Myths of the Norseman from the Eddas and Sagas* (New York, Dover Publications, 1992), p. 82.

33. Passages that explicitly mention Thor and Odin's preferences for different social classes are found in Kenin Crossley Holland, *The Norse Myths* (New York, Pantheon Books, 1980), pp. xxvi and 218. This tension between Thor and Odin is evident in a number of Norse myths. Page 218 of Holland's book directs you to one such myth.

34. Edith Hamilton, *Mythology: Timeless Tales of Gods and Heroes* (New York, Penguin Books, 1940), pp. 314–315.

35. Ibid., pp. 314–315.

36. Ibid., p. 314.

37. Ibid., p. 308.

38. The Norse Myths, p. 176.

39. *Myths of the Norseman from the Eddas and Sagas,* p. 216.

## Chapter 10

40. Elisabeth Kubler-Ross, *Death: The Final Stage of Growth* (Englewood Cliffs, NJ, Prentice-Hall, 1975), p. x.

41. Elisabeth Kubler-Ross, *On Death and Dying: What the Dying Have to Teach Doctors, Nurses, Clergy and Their Own Families* (New York, Macmillan, 1969), pp. 38–137.

42. Viktor Frankl, *Man's Search for Meaning* (New York, Simon & Schuster, 1984), pp. 49–50.

43. In Norse mythology, Odin sacrifices his eye in an effort to gain knowledge of Ragnarok. He is depicted, in both mythology and the Marvel universe, with a single eye.

44. The image of Thor wrestling and being defeated by the elderly Tiwaz has a parallel in Norse mythology. The story involves Thor's journey into the realm of Utgard. Thor and his companions face a number of challenges presented by the giant mage Utgard-Loki. One challenge is for Thor to wrestle Elli, Utgard-Loki's old foster mother. Elli embarrassed Thor by defeating him with casual ease. It is later discovered that Elli is the personification of old age, a force that eventually overwhelms everyone. Thor's struggles with Tiwaz can be seen as Thor wrestling with wisdom, especially because each match is followed by more detailed conversation.

45. Marcus Borg, *Reading the Bible again for the First Time: Taking the Bible Seriously but Not Literally* (New York, Harper Collins, 2001), pp. 167–168.

46. Ibid., p. 167.

47. It could be said that the goal of Ecclesiastes is to follow Aristotle's doctrine of the mean. Harris Rackham (translator), *Aristotle: The Nicomachean Ethics* (Ware, Hertfordshire, United Kingdom, Wordsworth Editions, 1996), pp. 39–47.

48. The essay is found in Elisabeth Kubler-Ross, *Death: The Final Stage of Growth*, pp. 87–96.

49. Elisabeth Kubler-Ross, *On Death and Dying: What the Dying Have to Teach Doctors, Nurses, Clergy and Their Own Families*, p. 138.

## Chapter 11

50. When stating that the X-Men may address social issues unintentionally, I mean the comic book series and the characters have been allowed to evolve to reflect the times and therefore address issues that the series was not originally written to confront. The comic, with its origin being 1963 and the main characters being victims of prejudice, makes for a natural connection to the Civil Rights movement that was well underway by the time *X-Men #1* was published. Since then, issues including diversity, religion, and gay rights have all been addressed in this comic and the movies inspired by it. For example, in the movie *X2: X-Men United*, a teenage boy admits to his parents than he is a mutant. This "coming-out" scene can easily be viewed through the lens of a gay teen coming out to his family. The fact that Bryan Singer, the director of *X2*, is openly gay communicates that the scene is intentionally set up this way. This does not change the fact that the original comic was not written to address this specific issue. Therefore, the comic itself, because of its original theme, has evolved to address specific issues it was not originally intended to confront. This malleability is one of the strengths of the X-Men franchise.

51. A third option is presented by a group of mutants known as the Morlocks. Living in the sewers beneath New York City, the Morlocks have given up on positive relations with humans but are equally unwilling to risk their lives seeking dominion over humans. They are resigned to dropping out of society and avoiding all contact with human beings. Their surrounding, the damp and dirty sewers, reflects their psychology and self-worth. It can also be seen as a commentary on the pitiful attempt to follow a "separate but equal" approach to mutant–human relations. Magneto will, on occasion, seek isolated segregation as well, but his venue and surroundings when doing so are far different from that of the Morlocks.

52. Genosha first appeared in the X-Men comics in 1988. The fictional island is located near South Africa, creating a viable comparison of Genosha's mutant slave society and South African apartheid.

53. Alan Bullock, *Hitler and Stalin: Parallel Lives* (New York, Vintage Books, 1993), p. 143.

54. Ibid., p. 143.

55. Ibid., p. 144.

56. Ibid., p. 886.

57. An excerpt of Malcolm X at the Audobon is found in Joanne Grant (editor), *Black Protest: History, Documents, and Analyses 1619 to the Present* (New York, Ballantine Books, 1968), p. 449.

58. Ossie Davis in Joanne Grant (editor), *Black Protest: History, Documents, and Analyses 1619 to the Present* (New York, Ballantine Books, 1968), p. 458.

59. Ibid., p. 457. It is worth noting that Davis's observation that Malcolm X challenged blacks to acknowledge and abandon the submissive posture they took around whites is also a necessary step Martin Luther King Jr. believed had to be made. Consider this thought found in King's "Letter from a Birmingham Jail": "One [force in the black community] is a complacency, made up in part of Negroes who, as a result of long years of oppression, are so drained of self-respect and 'somebodiness' that they have adjusted to segregation." Throughout "Letter from a Birmingham Jail," King passionately repudiates white moderates who prefer the façade of peace, sustained the drained self-respect of blacks, to King's direct interventions. Students I have encountered rarely consider King as someone who challenged the conventions of people, often viewing him in an overly sterile light, lacking a clear sense of the intensity he possessed. Conversely, they are sometimes surprised by the thoughtfulness of Malcolm X, seemingly convinced that his raging intensity had no intelligent supports.

60. Ibid., p. 458. It is difficult to imagine someone ever describing Magneto as having "completely abandoned" his hatred of humankind. This is an important distinction when trying to pinpoint Magneto's character. Malcolm X

loses his hatred but not his intensity, whereas the best we can say about Magneto is he tempers his hatred and opens up to specific humans.

61. The story containing the first meeting of Magneto and Charles Xavier was published in 1982. The date 1962 is when the story is set, not when it was released.

62. For more details regarding precritical naïveté, critical thinking, and postcritical naïveté, see Marcus Borg and N. T. Wright, *The Meaning of Jesus: Two Visions* (New York, HarperCollins, 1999), pp. 247–248, and Marcus Borg, *Reading the Bible Again for the First Time: Taking the Bible Seriously but Not Literally* (New York, HarperCollins, 2001), pp. 49–51.

63. The strength and appeal of this critical thinking phase also plays a part in, and is elaborated on, in James Fowler, *Stages of Faith: The Psychology of Human Development and the Quest for Meaning* (New York, Harper One, 1981). The fourth stage of Fowler's theory is called Individuative-Reflective Faith. At this point, people begin to reflect critically on the tacit acceptance of their value system. It is a phase during which our conscious mind is king and the driving force of our lives. It can, but does not have to, give way to Stage Five, Conjunctive Faith. Guy Claxton, *Hare Brain, Tortoise Mind: How Intelligence Increases When You Think Less* (New York, HarperCollins, 1997), also emphasizes the need to reevaluate the primary position Western culture gives to critical analysis (what he calls the "d-mode of the mind") and rediscover the benefits of the mind's slower processes (coined the "undermind"). Such a shift is similar to the transition from Fowler's Stage 4 to Stage 5 and the transition from critical thinking to postcritical naïveté.

64. Marcus Borg, *Reading the Bible Again for the First Time*, pp. 159–179, has an extended evaluation of conventional wisdom and subversive wisdom. The phrase "domesticate reality" is found on p. 168.

65. Ping Ho Wong, "A Conceptual Investigation into the Possibility of Spiritual Education," *International Journal of Children's Spirituality* 11, no. 1 (April 2006), pp. 73–85). The concepts of "Spiritual Geniuses," a "spectrum of transcendence," and "degrees of mystical experiences" are presented in this article.

66. This excerpt from Martin Luther King Jr.'s "Letter from a Birmingham Jail" is found in Robert Diyanni (editor), *One Hundred Great Essays* (New York, Pearson Education, 2005), pp. 428–429.

67. Nelson Mandela, *Long Walk to Freedom* (New York, Holt, Rinehart and Winston, 2000), p. 459.

68. Ibid., 459. Mandela pinpoints stages of his "hunger for freedom" as wanting simple, transitory freedoms only for himself, honorable freedoms for himself, freedom for other blacks in South Africa, and freedom for the oppressor as well as the oppressed. In *The Analects*, Confucius discusses such development as well, succinctly summarizing his disposition at age fifteen, thirty, forty, fifty, sixty, and seventy.

69.  Abraham Maslow, *Maslow on Management* (New York, John Wiley & Sons, 1998). Maslow stresses that the most effective method of motivating individuals is to challenge them with the realities of the next step in their development from where they currently are. Xavier can be seen as making one of two possible errors, overestimating Magneto's readiness or rushing his development. Xavier also sets Magneto in a situation in which he will lack support. The longtime enemy of the X-Men, now becoming headmaster of the school, will, because of his long-standing animosity with the group, create intense tension.

70.  Joanne Grant (editor), *Black Protest: History, Documents, and Analyses 1619 to the Present*, p. 458.

## Chapter 12

71.  NBC News for History (Producer), *King* (Documentary, United States: A&E Televisions Networks, 2008). King's anxiety is a trait mentioned by a number of interviewees in this documentary.

72.  Mario M. Cuomo and Harold Holzer (editors), *Lincoln on Democracy: His Own Words, with Essays by America's Foremost Civil War Historians* (New York, HarperCollins, 1990), p. 79, and Jacob Needleman, *The American Soul: Rediscovering the Wisdom of the Founders* (New York, Penguin Group, 2002), pp. 241–267.

73.  Alan Bullock, *Hitler and Stalin: Parallel Lives* (New York, Vintage Books, 1993), p. 142.

74.  Perry M. Rogers (editor), *Aspects of World Civilizations: Volume II* (Upper Saddle River, NJ, Prentice Hall, 2003), pp. 72–73.

75.  Alan Bullock, *Hitler and Stalin: Parallel Lives* (New York, Vintage Books, 1993), pp. 338–339.

76.  Rabindranath Tagore's quotation was found at www.gandhiserve.org.

77.  Mario M. Cuomo and Harold Holzer (editors), *Lincoln on Democracy*, pp. 253–254. These pages include Lincoln's response to Horace Greeley, which includes his definition of official duty (saving the Union) and personal wish (that all men everywhere could be free).

78.  http://www.americanrhetoric.com/speeches/gwbush911jointsessionspeech.htm

79.  Mario M. Cuomo and Harold Holzer (editors), *Lincoln on Democracy*, p. 91.

80.  Parker J. Palmer, *A Hidden Wholeness: The Journey Toward an Undivided Life* (San Francisco, Jossey-Bass, 2004), pp. 4–5.

81. Stephan B. Oates, *Abraham Lincoln: The Man Behind the Myths* (New York, Penguin Books, 1984), p. 112. "What is more, the Proclamation did something for Lincoln personally that has never been stressed enough. In truth, the story of emancipation could well be called the liberation of Abraham Lincoln. For in the process of granting freedom to the slaves, Lincoln also emancipated himself from his old dilemma. His proclamation now brought the private and the public Lincoln together: now the public statesman could obliterate a wicked thing the private citizen had always hated."

## Chapter 14

82. William Stryker may be familiar to students because it is the name of the primary antagonist in the film *X2: X-Men United*. In the film, Stryker is a military operative working for the U.S. government rather than the leader of an Evangelical church.

83. A moving account of Elizabeth Eckford's ordeal can be found in Joanne Grant (editor), *Black Protest: History, Documents, and Analyses 1619 to the Present* (New York, Ballantine Books, 1968), pp. 272–276.

84. Alfred Church and William Brodribb (translators), *The Complete Works of Tacitus* (New York, Random House, 1942), pp. 380–381.

85. A full treatment of these concepts is found in Marcus Borg, *Reading the Bible Again for the First Time: Taking the Bible Seriously but Not Literally* (New York, HarperCollins, 2001), pp. 3–51.

86. Huston Smith, *The World's Religions* (San Francisco, HarperCollins, 1991), p. 327.

87. John Welwood, *Toward a Psychology of Awakening: Buddhism, Psychotherapy, and the Path of Personal and Spiritual Transformation* (Boston, Shambhala, 2002). The concept of spiritual bypassing is discussed on pp. 11–14 and 207–213. Chapter 20 includes an evaluation of how cult leaders misuse spiritual principles.

## Chapter 15

88. The Immanuel Kant passage is found in Perry M. Rogers (editor), *Aspects of World Civilizations: Volume II* (Upper Saddle River, NJ, Prentice Hall, 2003), pp. 46–47.

## Chapter 16

89. William Scott Wilson (translator), Yamamoto Tsunetomo, *Hagakure* (New York, Kodansha International, 1979), p. 26.

90. Ibid., pp. 27–28. The passage on p. 27 can be read as a direct repudiation of the tendency to mask rudeness in the disguise of "telling it like it is."

91. Theses thoughts regarding the development of Bushido are found in Kultur (Producer), *Samurai Japan: A Journey Back in Time* (Documentary, Eagle Rock Entertainment, 2008).

92. Thomas Cleary, *Soul of the Samurai: Modern Translations of Three Classic Works of Zen & Bushido* (Tuttle Publishing, North Claredon, VT, 2005), p. 104.

93. William Scott Wilson (translator), Yamamoto Tsunetomo, *Hagakure*, p. 95.

94. Ibid., pp. 100–101.

95. Thomas Cleary, *Soul of the Samurai*, p. 83.

96. William Scott Wilson (translator), Yamamoto Tsunetomo, *Hagakure*, p. 50.

97. Eknath Easwaran (translator), *The Dhammapada* (Nilgiri Press, Tomales, CA, 1985). The passage is found in chapter 9, verse 119. The inverse is also presented in verse 120, "The good man may suffer as long as he does not reap what he has sown."

98. William Scott Wilson (translator), Yamamoto Tsunetomo, *Hagakure*, p. 51.

99. Eknath Easwaran (translator), *The Dhammapada*. The passage is found in chapter 12, verse 159.

100. Thomas Cleary, *Soul of the Samurai*, p. 89.

101. Ibid., p. 90.

102. William Scott Wilson (translator), Yamamoto Tsunetomo, *Hagakure*, p. 54. The necessity of following the path of the ronin to truly become a samurai is communicated in the passage, "If one has not been a ronin at least seven times, he will not be a true retainer. Seven times down, eight times up."

## Chapter 17

103. Jacob Needleman, *The American Soul: Rediscovering the Wisdom of the Founders* (New York, Penguin Group, 2002), pp. 19–25.

104. Ibid., p. 20.

105. Ibid., p. 21. An egoistic idiosyncrasy is any trait individuals have that they deem essential to their character, even if its removal does not truly change the person's inner world. The argument that dress codes violate people's ability to express themselves falls into this category. Creative people can find a variety of manners to express their creativity and are comfortable doing so, regardless of the clothes they wear. The attachment to a particular clothing style as an, if not the, essential form of expression is therefore an example of egocentric idiosyncrasy.

106.   Ibid., p. 21.

107.   Larzer Ziff (editor), *Ralph Waldo Emerson: Selected Essays* (New York, Penguin Books, 1982), p. 192.

108.   Jacob Needleman, *The American Soul*, p. 25.

## Chapter 18

109.   Guy Claxton, *Hare Brain, Tortoise Mind: How Intelligence Increases When You Think Less* (New York, Harper Collins, 1997), p. 79.

110.   Ibid., p. 79.

111.   Excerpt from Karl Pearson's *National Life from the Standpoint of Science*, found in Perry M. Rogers (editor), *Aspects of World Civilizations: Volume II* (Upper Saddle River, NJ, Prentice Hall, 2003), pp. 138–139.

112.   The racial component is given a more pertinent treatment in Reginald Hudlin, *Black Panther: Civil War* (New York, Marvel Publishing, 2006). In this graphic novel, the reader witnesses the Black Panther make his decision to join Captain America as well as his efforts at global politics as he discusses the Registration Act with other Marvel characters who can be considered heads of state. This graphic novel acts as a companion to *Civil War*.

## Chapter 19

113.   The inspiration for the "America is a crack baby" metaphor is Collin Raye's song *What If Jesus Comes Back Like That?* In the song Raye asks, in lyrical form, "If Jesus returned as a crack baby, how would he be treated?" My good friend Jay Apicelli introduced me to this song.

114.   http://classics.mit.edu/Plato/republic.html. The metaphor of the ship of state is found in book VI. Henry Wadsworth Longfellow also wrote a poem, *O Ship of State* available at http://worldbooklibrary.com/eBooks/Poetry_Collection/longf05.html.

# Index

# About the Author

JAMES ROURKE is a history teacher at the Norwich Free Academy in Norwich, CT. He is the author of *From My Classroom to Yours*.